Dionysian Art and Populist Politics in Austria

Dionysian Art and Populist Politics in Austria

William J. McGrath

New Haven and London, Yale University Press

1974

Library of Congress catalog card number: 73-86908
International standard book number: 0-300-01656-5

Designed by John O. C. McCrillis
and set in Baskerville type.
Printed in the United States of America by
The Murray Printing Co., Forge Village, Mass.

Published in Great Britain, Europe, and Africa by
Yale University Press, Ltd., London.
Distributed in Latin America by Kaiman & Polon,
Inc., New York City; in Australasia and Southeast
Asia by John Wiley & Sons Australasia Pty. Ltd.,
Sydney; in India by UBS Publishers' Distributors Pvt.,
Ltd., Delhi; in Japan by John Weatherhill, Inc., Tokyo.

To Carl E. Schorske

Contents

Preface

All translations from the German in this book are my own unless otherwise indicated. In the case of the musical texts I have provided both the German and an English translation to facilitate an understanding of the close relationship between words and music while also allowing the reader who does not understand German to follow the ideas.

In writing this book I have accumulated many debts of gratitude. The basic research was made possible by a Fulbright-Hays Fellowship, and my stay in Vienna was made both more enjoyable and fruitful by the helpfulness of Dr. Anton Porhansl and the other members of the Fulbright Commission in Vienna. Important additional research was made possible by a grant from the Leo Baeck Institute in New York.

I would like to thank Dr. Wanda Lanzer of the Adler Archive in Vienna for locating and helping me use the manuscripts dealing with the Telyn Society and Adler's youth. The staff of the Goethe-Schiller Archive in Weimar was also extremely helpful in providing the materials from the Nietzsche Nachlass needed to trace the relationship between the philosopher and the Pernerstorfer circle. I would also like to thank the personnel of the Austrian State Archives, the Austrian National Library, and the Vienna City Library for their assistance with the manuscript materials.

In the course of my research and writing I have received valuable advice and criticism from Norman Rabkin, Hanna Gray, William H. McNeill, Hans Mommsen, Klemens von Klemperer, and Leonard Krieger. I am most deeply indebted to Carl Schorske for the training, criticism, advice, and friendship which have given invaluable support to this study from its inception to its completion. I would also like to thank my wife Juliet, whose patience, interest, and critical ability have been so important to me in our many discussions of this project. Of those who have helped in the preparation and typing of the manuscript I am most grateful to Judy Shattuck and Kathy Nagy-Farkas.

W. J. McG.

Introduction

In essence, this book attempts to trace the intellectual biography of a group: its origins, the principal influences in the development of its collective outlook, and its subsequent impact on the political and cultural history of Vienna during the late nineteenth and early twentieth centuries. This group, the "Pernerstorfer circle," was made up of men who as high school and university students had been forced to confront the political and social crises of nineteenth-century Austrian liberalism; facing these crises together, they developed a group response which conditioned their efforts to create an alternative culture in a wide variety of fields. Some members of the circle such as Gustav Mahler and Victor Adler have become famous for their contributions to twentieth-century culture, but others have sunk into oblivion, including those who were most important in formulating the group outlook: Engelbert Pernerstorfer, the man who gave his name to the circle, and Sigfried Lipiner, the boy genius who excited the admiration of Friedrich Nietzsche and Richard Wagner. Even in the case of Mahler and Adler, both of whom have been carefully studied as individuals, the importance of their shared intellectual development has been largely overlooked.

The natural compartmentalization of academic disciplines has made the musical scholar reluctant to pursue deeply the social and philosophical ingredients in Mahler's music just as it has led the political scholar to ignore the psychological and aesthetic dimensions of Adler's politics. The widely disparate nature of the fields into which the members of the circle channeled their talents—music, politics, literature, history—has led scholars to neglect the highly significant intellectual bonds which continued to exist across the boundaries of these fields. Probably the two most important of these bonds were a shared psychological framework and a sophisticated use of theatrical symbolism, and, in tracing these common intellectual characteristics from their historical point of origin to their expression in the mature works of the circle's members, it becomes clear that at least in Austria there was a significant intellectual relationship in the development of symbolist art and populist politics.

In response to the political and cultural crises of the brief liberal era, the members of the circle were drawn with increasing force to the ideas of three great thinkers whose works expressed profound alienation from liberal ideals: Schopenhauer, Wagner, and Nietzsche. Although it has frequently been argued that Nietzsche's influence began to be felt significantly only in the 1890s, the history of the circle shows that as early as the 1870s this philosopher attracted an intensely loyal following among the student population of Vienna. The members of the circle read Nietzsche's earliest works shortly after they were published, and from them they developed an understanding of his philosophy which differs markedly from that widely held today. Taken together, his work and that of his mentors Wagner and Schopenhauer provided the ingredients for a coherent all-encompassing philosophy which the members of the circle synthesized and then gradually transformed through application in areas that were often remote from the primary interests of these thinkers. In studying this group as a group I have thus found it necessary to deal with materials ordinarily assigned to several different disciplines in order to follow historically the natural unfolding of its Wagnerian—Nietzschean ideology. Since this ideology proclaimed the unity of the arts and the coherence of social and cultural development, I have examined it within an equally comprehensive field of social and cultural analysis in order to explore fully its origins, aims, and accomplishments.

Just as this kind of group history suggests hitherto unexplored interdisciplinary relationships, so too does it impose limitations on the comprehensiveness with which any individual member of the group is examined. Except for some of the minor figures in the circle, each of its members fused the collective outlook of the circle with other ideas and objectives of a more particular nature; and while I have attempted to indicate the existence and importance of these individual involvements, I have not attempted to explore them systematically. In no case is there a comprehensive analysis of any one character's thoughts and deeds, but rather, each figure is examined from a point of view intended to reveal the nature, extent, and significance of his involvement in the group outlook. Even though Victor Adler's Marxism ultimately proved to be of greater substantive importance to his politics than his interest in Nietzsche and Wagner, I have not dealt with the Marxist component of his development since it did not figure significantly in his relationship to the circle as a whole. Nor, on the other hand, has there been any attempt to deal comprehensively with the full range of influences which Nietzsche and Wagner exerted on Austrian intellectual history during this period. Although the Pernerstorfer circle may well have been the most important single agency in the dissemination of such influences, they were also spread by other individuals and groups; and where, as in the case of the urban theorist Camillo Sitte or of the *Academic Wagner Society*, these individuals and groups were relevant to the central theme of the circle's history, I have attempted to indicate that relevance without examining their activities in detail.

If the method and scope of this study have been determined in large part by the collective, interdisciplinary nature of its subject, it is also true that this subject was chosen in the hope of developing an approach that could deal historically with the simultaneous appearance of similar intellectual phenomena in widely disparate fields without invoking the vague notions of a "spirit of the time" or of ideas that were "in the air." Believing rather that ideas inhabit specific minds and books in specific times and places, I have sought to find documented connections that could explain such parallel developments. In tracing the bonds of personal friendship, common background, shared experience, and acknowledged intellectual exchange, I have attempted to construct what might best be called a *Bildungsgeschichte*. The nearest English equivalent—educational history—does scant justice to the German word *Bildung*, with its implicit concepts of formation and cultural achievement, both of which are central to my aim of showing the successive metamorphoses of the group outlook from its rebellious inception, through various tentative formulations, to its final expression in artistic and political form.

In surveying the mature achievements of the circle's members it is impossible to ignore the relationship between these achievements and the crusade for radical political and cultural change which preoccupied them during their adolescence and early manhood when generational conflict tended to give their intellectual development a revolutionary impetus. One of the circle's members, Victor Adler, actually did go on to preside over the successful revolution which brought the Austrian Republic into being amidst the ruins of the Habsburg Empire in 1918. Another, Heinrich Friedjung, who has often been described as Austria's greatest historian, devoted himself to this profession only after the apparent failure of the political hopes he had earlier shared with Adler. His finest work, *The Struggle for Supremacy in Germany*, was a direct outgrowth of the frustrated political ambitions of his youth. While Engelbert Pernerstorfer and Max Gruber did not earn lasting renown, they too were able to translate their youthful revolutionary aspirations into accomplishments which earned them international prominence during their lifetimes. Pernerstorfer's political activities—first as one of the founders of the pan German (*deutschnational*) movement, and later as the leader of the socialist delegation in the lower house of parliament (*Reichsrath*)—never took him far from the path of his lifelong friend Adler. In Gruber's case the political drives of his student days were redirected toward the application of medical science to social problems, and it was in this field that he gained the distinguished reputation which ultimately brought his elevation to the nobility. Even in the realm of art the circle was able eventually to find a spokesman of genius who could give expression to its radical cultural and social ideals. Although Gustav Mahler joined the group ten years after formation of the original society, the cultural mission which still informed its members affected him deeply and shaped the creation of some of his most profound and beautiful music.[1]

Even a cursory appraisal of the circle's accomplishments suggests their extraordinary range as well as their innovative quality, and in attempting to account historically for this burst of creative energy

1. For Victor Adler (1852–1918) see Julius Braunthal, *Victor und Friedrich Adler* (Vienna, 1965). This excellent study makes use of the documents concerning Adler's youth recently made available in the Adler Archiv. In most respects it supplants Max Ermer's *Victor Adler* (Vienna, 1932), but the latter work retains some value in placing Adler's career in the context of the labor movement as a whole. The career of Heinrich Friedjung (1851–1920) is traced by Robert A. Kann in *Neue deutsche Biographie* (Berlin, 1961), vol. 5, and by H. von Srbik in *Deutsches biographisches Jahrbuch* (Berlin and Leipzig, 1928), vol. 2; A. J. P. Taylor offers a good summary of his career in the introduction to his translation of Friedjung's *The Struggle for Supremacy in Germany 1859–1866* (New York, 1966). The career of Engelbert Pernerstorfer (1850–1918) is traced by his adopted son, Robert Arthaber, in *Neue oesterreichische Biographie* (Vienna 1952), vol. 2. For Max Gruber (1853–1927) see Otto Frank, *Max von Gruber* (Munich, 1928). For Mahler's association with the circle see Eduard Castle's *Geschichte der deutschen Literatur in Oesterreich-Ungarn im Zeitalter Franz Josefs I* (Vienna, n.d.), vol. 2, pp. 1560–70. While brief, Castle's discussion of the circle in its later years is quite perceptive.

it is essential to begin with an understanding of how the young men of this society oriented themselves toward the regnant liberal culture that provided the early environment for their thoughts and actions. The growth of their dissatisfaction with liberalism and their success in nurturing their discontent, first at the *Gymnasium* (secondary school) and later at the university, were intimately bound up with the nature of Austrian liberalism and the tribulations which beset it during the first years of its brief span of power. In their feeling of isolation from the values of their liberal elders, the young men of this circle drew on the ideas of thinkers such as Nietzsche to evolve a set of ideals which they regarded as far more relevant to the problems and conditions of their time; and in this they saw themselves as pioneers for a whole generation of students estranged from the values of an embattled liberal culture.

From the vantage point of subsequent history, the outlook of the circle can also be seen to prefigure many of the attitudes which came to fruition in the new conservatism that emerges as such a powerful force in twentieth-century German thought. Klemens von Klemperer has carefully delineated the complex nature of this intellectual movement in his *Germany's New Conservatism* and, as he shows, Nietzsche's ideas had an important influence on most German thinkers within this movement.[2] Fritz Stern has explored further the anti-modernist *völkisch* (populist) characteristics of this cultural reaction in his *Politics of Cultural Despair* where he examines the ideas of such men as Paul de Lagarde, Julius Langbehn, and Moeller van den Bruck.[3] It is important to note, however, that the völkisch reaction was a European phenomenon which also involved well-balanced, intelligent, and creative individuals as well as the eccentrics Stern describes. George Mosse observed that all over Europe the younger generation felt the urge to break with the bourgeois world and, to resuscitate a culture that had lost its vitality. In Germany this movement "sought to express its freedom through contact with nature, defined as the landscape of the *Volk*," and, as Mosse emphasizes, it gained strength from the reaction against the new urban industrial order: "Youth was seeking an end to the alienation produced by

2. Klemens von Klemperer, *Germany's New Conservatism: Its History and Dilemma in the Twentieth Century* (Princeton, 1968), pp. 36–40.
3. Fritz Stern, *The Politics of Cultural Despair* (Garden City, N. Y., 1965).

industrial society . . . In short, the revolt against society, parents and school swelled into a revolt against the bourgeois age."[4]

Because of the close association between the völkisch movement and the resurgence of anti-Semitism at the turn of the century, the importance of Jews within this movement has often been neglected but, as Mosse stresses, many young Jews were attracted to the völkisch ideal and many even accepted the negative stereotype of the Jew fostered by the movement in which "the Jew was presented as the antithesis of that genuineness which Germans longed for. Jews were described as intellectual and therefore artificial. They lacked roots and thus rejected nature. They were urban people possessed of special aptitudes for expanding even more the hated capitalist society."[5]

In Austria the beginnings of the völkisch movement substantially preceded the development of virulent anti-Semitism as a significant part of the völkisch outlook, and during this early phase Jews were strongly attracted to the movement. The members of the Pernerstorfer circle, most of whom were Jewish, were typical of many others in this respect. The close ties between Jews and Austrian liberalism seems to have had the effect of making Jews of the younger generation during the 1870s particularly sensitive to the failures of liberalism. Having imbibed the assimilationist drives of their parents, they espoused völkisch ideas with a fervor which went far beyond that of the older generation, and when liberalism seemed to turn its back on völkisch concerns they were quick to criticize it for doing so. Whether or not they were in some sense trying to prove the authenticity of their own Germanness in this way remains difficult to say, but certainly many of their criticisms of liberal failures seem to reflect the longing for community and acceptance appropriate to their Jewish assimilationist background.

Since the political, social, and economic crises of Austrian liberalism did much to force forward the development of the circle's political and cultural critique, the history of their generational reaction must be examined within the context of the period's changing sociopolitical reality. For the members of the circle, the external logic of events interacted dialectically with the internal

4. George Mosse, "The Influence of the *Völkisch* Idea on German Jewry," *Studies of the Leo Baeck Institute* (New York, 1967), pp. 84–86.

5. Ibid., p. 87.

logic of the philosophy they espoused to teach them how to exert a dynamic and powerful force for change within the decaying Habsburg Empire.

To understand this external logic of events one must turn first to the highly complex phenomenon that was Austrian liberalism. One important characteristic that distinguished the liberal movement in Austria from liberalism in England, France, or even Germany was its relative weakness vis à vis the traditional power centers of monarchy, aristocracy, and church—a weakness which reflected the political conditions that shaped the early history of liberalism in Austria. As in Germany and France, the liberal tradition in Austria had its immediate origins in the eighteenth-century Enlightenment when the various reforms of Maria Theresa and her son Joseph II set in motion a tradition of reform which came to be known as Josephinism. Although it can in no sense be simply equated with the liberal tradition, Josephinism helped prepare the way for liberalism and merged with it in the second half of the nineteenth century. The central thrust of Josephin political reform lay in the attempt to reduce the prerogatives and influences exercised by the aristocracy through their estates, and to replace them in their former administrative and judicial functions with a bureaucracy loyal to the central monarchy. In support of this policy German was introduced as the official administrative language throughout most of the Habsburg dominions in 1784, and although this step was not accompanied by a policy of Germanization in non-German areas, it did give the German language a position of unique importance as a binding force within the Empire's cultural and linguistic diversity.[6]

The centralization of political authority was also accompanied by important legal reforms which tended to strengthen the position of the middle class vis à vis the aristocracy. As Valjavec notes, the feeling for equality under the law (*Rechtsgleichheit*) which characterized Josephinism from the outset "favored the development of certain anti-feudal tendencies, an antipathy to privileges, and the endeavor to introduce as balanced as possible a division of all obligations and rights from an economic point of view." Valjavec sees this principle as one of the most fundamental and durable elements of the Josephin tradition: "The state under law [*Rechtsstaat*] is an ideal of Josephinism

6. Eduard Winter, *Der Josephinismus* (Berlin, 1962), p. 187.

which regardless of all ideological setbacks after 1789 nonetheless proceeded toward realization step by step . . . . In the civil law code of the year 1811 it was specifically laid down that natural law prevailed as basic and subsidiary law, which brought with it a corresponding emphasis on individuality."[7] The ideal of the Rechtsstaat had found elaboration and justification in the writings of Immanuel Kant whose ideas strongly influenced this legal codification. Georg Franz, referring to the author of the code, notes that "Zeiller, basing himself on Kantian philosophy, placed the capstone on the natural law edifice of the German Enlightenment with his law code."[8]

The increased emphasis on individuality which Valjavec mentions as an element of legal reform was, of course, a fundamental aspect of Enlightenment thought in general as well as of both the Josephin and liberal traditions; and here too the philosophy of Kant was extremely influential. Drawing on the ideas of Rousseau, Kant elaborated the concept of the autonomy of the individual as the basis for his moral philosophy, and in this concept he found justification for his deep faith in the freedom and dignity of man. In the economic sphere the analogue to this faith in the individual was a belief in competitive free enterprise which also became firmly rooted in liberal culture during the nineteenth century.

Within the Josephin tradition, however, economic individualism was muted and counterbalanced by a strong social concern, a concern for the good of society as a whole. In describing the Josephin state as a welfare state, Valjavec argues: "Particularly during Joseph's decade social thought comes strongly to the fore. The pursuit of social aims occupied not only a broad but also an extraordinarily important position in the Josephin world view." In the following decades this social concern gradually declined in the face of the conservative reaction to the French Revolution and Napoleon, as well as in recognition of the fact that the Josephin state had "no proper instrument for the energetic pursuit of these problems."[9] Only after the 1848 revolution did these social interests revive somewhat to play a role in the last stages of the Josephin tradition.

7. Fritz Valjavec, *Der Josephinismus, zur geistigen Entwicklung Oesterreichs im 18. und 19. Jahrhundert* (Brno, 1944), pp. 84–85.

8. Georg Franz, *Liberalismus, Die deutschliberale Bewegung in der habsburgischen Monarchie* (Munich, 1955), p. 14.

9. Valjavec, pp. 86–87.

For the most part, the tradition of reform associated with Maria Theresa and Joseph became moribund during the long Metternichian era following the Napoleonic wars, and it is at this point that the early history of Austrian liberalism diverged most markedly from that of liberal movements in France and Germany. Throughout Europe Metternich used his considerable influence not only to suppress any new revolutionary activity but also to combat the spread of liberal ideas and institutions in any form, and although this policy met with varying degrees of failure in western Europe, it was largely successful within the Habsburg Empire. Not only did Josephin reform from above come to a halt, but also censorship and strict control of travel served to isolate Austria from contact with the surviving liberal movements of the West. Moreover, the economic development on which liberalism depended for its growth was also retarded within Austria on the grounds of its potential political danger. Only within the state bureaucracy and the families associated with it did the tradition of Josephin reform manage to perpetuate itself to any significant degree, and here its influence was felt primarily in the humanizing of administrative procedures rather than in any continued reform activity.

In the course of the first half of the nineteenth century while Metternichian reaction held sway in Austria, the outlook of the various western European liberal movements underwent a marked development reflecting the deeper changes going on in the social and economic life of Europe. Georg Franz notes in his history of Austrian liberalism: "From Goethe's death (1832) to that of Metternich (1859) there occurred the decisive change in German and European life from spirit to matter . . . from the whole to the individual. The modern individualistic and atheistic outlook which determined the life of the coming generations was theoretically elaborated during this period" (p. 395). This new world view was associated with a more radical liberalism which tended to emphasize revolutionary change rather than the absolutist reforms from above characteristic of Josephinism and enlightened despotism generally.

In 1848 this newer revolutionary liberalism triumphed momentarily in Vienna, but the effectiveness of Metternich's earlier policies can be seen in its subsequent history. Because the Vienna revolution was more an imitation of foreign examples than the expression of a deeply based revolutionary movement within Austria, it failed to develop an adequate base of support, and within the year conservative forces had regained control of the situation. From this point on, liberals of the more militant stamp had to reckon with the fact that they had revealed their weakness in the crucial power struggle with the dynasty and its armies. In the light of this failure they found it necessary during the subsequent neoabsolutist period from 1850 to 1859 to accommodate their outlook and activity to the older tradition of Josephin reform.

The coming together of these two traditions of militant liberalism and Josephinism yielded an outlook usually described as *alt-liberal* (old liberal) to distinguish it from the more doctrinaire "high liberalism" of the period after 1867, and this outlook found expression in the career of Anton von Schmerling (1806–93), one of the most prominent old liberal personalities of the day. In 1848 Schmerling had played an important role in the political activity generated by the revolutions in Germany and Austria, most importantly in the deliberations of the Frankfurt Assembly where he represented the position of the Great Germany (*grossdeutsch*) constitutional liberals. Afterward he had served briefly as justice minister in the government of Felix Schwarzenberg from which he resigned when it abandoned constitutional government in 1851. Schmerling's political activities made him the foremost figure of the liberal movement in Austria during the neoabsolutist period, and in 1859 when military defeat at the hands of the French and the Italian armies discredited the neoabsolutist regime it was to Schmerling that Franz Joseph ultimately turned to form a liberal, constitutional government. As Franz notes (p. 264), "Schmerling was accepted as the undisputed leader of the liberal movement, as the man of the Josephinists as well as of the upper bourgeoisie. An old liberal in his political views, he represented a moderate constitutionalism which would assure the centralized unity of the Empire." Pursuing the Josephin ideal of a strongly unified state, Schmerling also sought to assure that Germans would exercise leadership within the state, and in foreign affairs this approach was paralleled by a vigorous grossdeutsch policy aimed at preserving and strengthening Austria's position in Germany.

On the question of strengthening constitutional reforms and individual rights, Schmerling again assumed a Josephin position in supporting the Emperor's decision to withhold further concessions. On such issues Schmerling regarded himself as a loyal servant of the crown. "His liberalism was 'of the old-bureaucratic-estate oriented sort,' and this bureaucratic strain remained dominant in his political activity" (p. 264). Eventually, Schmerling's reluctance to push further reforms produced a division within liberal ranks which grew deeper as his policies met with repeated reverses. These setbacks and the multiplying differences between the Josephins supporting him and the more doctrinare liberals forming the left wing of the constitutional party eventually so weakened his position that he was forced to resign in 1865 to make way for a new conservative government.

In 1867 when liberalism returned to power in the wake of yet another military defeat, this time at the hands of the Prussian army, it was a liberalism that differed markedly from that of Schmerling and the other adherents of the Josephin tradition. Within the Empire the former centralist policy was abandoned in favor of a dualism in which Austria and Hungary became equal partners, and in foreign affairs Austria acknowledged Prussian supremacy within Germany while continuing to pursue an anti-Bismarck diplomatic course. Compared to Schmerling's policy with its hopes for a Great Germany led by a unified, centralized Ausria in which the German population would play the dominant role, the new middle-class ministry (*Bürgerministerium*) represented a complete about-face which shattered the aspirations of German national unity and glory fostered a few years earlier.

The new "high liberal" government also reflected a marked shift from Schmerling's old liberalism in economic and financial matters as well as in political style. As Franz notes, (p.152) "Only at the beginning of the dualistic, constitutional era did journalists as well as economic and financial tycoons come to the fore: only after 1867 did the real flood of liberalism throughout public life begin." In the 1870s this full flood of liberalism brought with it the "boundless greed for money and pursuit of profits of the 'take-off' period ['*Gründerzeit*'] with mushrooming bank failures, bankruptcies and collapses." Franz stresses the departure this represented from the old liberalism: "Next to the bureaucratic servant of the state appears the parliamentary business politician who for good pay represents the interests of his estate, of a class, and not last of all of his own well-being." Franz also sees a significant sociological change occurring in the leadership of the liberal constitutional party at this time: "The professor of law and the lawyer, the expert and the legal specialist took the place within the party of the noble and bureaucratic servant of the crown. A lower-middle class quality characterized the new men and their politics; lawyerish sophistry and professorial pedantry dominated the political process" (pp. 317–18).

The year that the high liberal Bürgerministerium came to power, 1867, was also the year that the Pernerstorfer circle was formed, and it was against this newer, more doctrinaire liberalism that the members of the circle reacted during their Gymnasium and university years. They came to see in it an expression of individualism which eschewed concern for the social question, an emphasis on cosmopolitanism which neglected the issue of German nationalism, and a preference for a scholarly intellectual style which ignored the passions of the heart. Moreover, the subsequent crises that beset the liberal governments of the 1870s—the Franco-Prussian War, the economic collapse of 1873, the Ofenheim scandal—all served to deepen their disillusionment. Increasingly they, and students like them, felt impelled to count themselves among the opponents rather than the supporters of the liberal movement.

Toward the older Josephin liberalism, the members of the circle had a somewhat more ambiguous relationship. Although they broke sharply with this tradition in their revolutionary enthusiasm and their faith in democracy, still in many ways they can be seen to have carried on and radicalized elements of the Josephin outlook. The social concern that marked the reign of Joseph II was one such element, and the strong emphasis on German language and culture beginning under Joseph and reaching its fruition under Schmerling was another. By the time the members of the circle were receiving their education, Josephinism had largely lost its identity as a coherent outlook distinct from liberalism but, as Valjavec notes, one of the exceptions to this situation was where education remained in the hands of the Benedictines.[10] Since the members of the circle were educated by this order it seems possible that certain of the affinities of their outlook with Josephinism may have grown out of their educational background.

In a certain sense, then, the "antiliberal" reaction of the circle was as much a rebellion within liberalism as an external attack on

10. Valjavec, p. 89.

it. The members of the circle certainly saw themselves as antiliberal in most of their political activity, but, viewed from the historical perspective of the converging Josephin and liberal traditions, the activities of the circle's members can be seen as placing them in an extremely fruitful position on the volatile margin of a rapidly changing liberal culture. Responsive to the criticisms of the new liberalism from without and sensitive to the merits of the old liberalism from within, they reacted to the various crises of their formative years by synthesizing ,from these diverse influences, ideas and cultural values of great richness and power.

Part I: The Discontents of Youth

Ah, then, in very truth I've had you taught to reason down all justice, if you think you can prove this, that it is just and right that fathers should be beaten by their sons!

ARISTOPHANES

1. The Telyn Society

In the bardic festivals of medieval Wales, when the poets gathered to compete in evoking the muse, their words were accompanied by the sound of the telyn, a harp which custom invested with profound significance for the national identity and creativity of the Welsh people.[1] In conjuring up the image of this ancient culture, the small group of Viennese Gymnasium students who met in March 1867 to form the Telyn Society chose a symbol which was remote indeed from the comfortable middle-class setting of their deliberations. But incongrous as such a symbol may have been, it suggested a range of aspirations that were to exercise an enduring influence on the future development of the circle's members. In part the name expressed their respect for the Celtic traditions of their monastic school, the *Schottengymnasium,* which traced its history and name back to the middle ages when most of the Benedictine monks of the Schotten monastery were of Irish, Welsh, or Scottish origins.[2] By the late nineteenth century little more than the name of the order remained to testify to its Celtic roots, but to the members of the Telyn Society this was enough to inspire them to look back to the richly artistic Celtic folk culture to find the model for their own artistic and cultural activities. In addition to this tribute to the tradition of their school, however, a more contemporary political motive in their choice of the name Telyn can also be discerned, for just as the middle years of the nineteenth century had seen a rebirth of Celtic cultural nationalism in the form of efforts to reestablish bardic festivals such as the Eisteddfodd, so too in Germany the movement toward national unification was accompanied by a resurgence of interest in Germanic folk culture. To young German-speaking Austrians, who in 1866 had seen their homeland excluded from the process of political reunification, the example of the Celtic peoples—who like the Germans had maintained their national identity

1. Eugene O'Curry, *On the Manners and Customs of the Ancient Irish,* ed. W. K. Sullivan (New York, 1873), vol. 3, pp. 351–55.

2. Albert Hübl, *Geschichte des Unterrichtes im Stifte Schotten in Wien* (Vienna, 1907), p. 4.

through artistic and cultural rather than political ties—must have been particularly relevant. This faith in the capacity of an artistic folk culture to fulfill essentially political aims was later to become a central element in the circle's outlook.

With one important exception, the young men of the Telyn Society all came from prosperous middle-class families, and the physical surroundings in which they held their meetings at Victor Adler's house suggested anything but folk consciousness. Located in the fashionable Viennese suburb of Ober-Döbling, the Adler home was modest but pleasantly set in a small garden. Victor's father Salomon, a well-to-do Jewish merchant recently arrived from Prague, looked with favor on the meetings of the group and regularly provided high tea (*Jause*) and dinner for them all.[3] Max Gruber's family came from an even higher stratum of Viennese society; his father was a well-known physician and his uncle was one of Vienna's most fashionable architects. Gruber recalled years later that the "dark spaces of his parental home in the most thickly built section of the old city were flooded by the sunlight of music and poetry."[4] Although life was considerably less comfortable for Heinrich Friedjung's family, in this instance too his childhood environment was solidly middle class.[5]

The one member of the circle who came from a markedly different social background was its acknowledged leader, Engelbert Pernerstorfer whose parents were artisans. His father, who had died when Pernerstorfer was only three, had been a tailor, and after his death the mother, grandmother, and an assistant carried on the business in their tiny apartment. Years later Pernerstorfer still retained a vivid picture of the squalor of his childhood home.[6]

> From the narrow entry hall one entered the small kitchen through a single, poorly fitting door—from there into the room, which was scarcely five meters square. This room received its light from a single window which opened onto the

3. Engelbert Pernerstorfer, "Aus jungen Tagen," *Der Strom* 2 (July 1912): 98.

4. Max von Gruber, "Kleine Mitteilungen," *Münchener medizinische Wochenschrift* 70 Jg. (3 Aug. 1923): 1038. This article will henceforth be cited as "Mitteilungen."

5. Jonny Moser, *Von der Emanzipation zur antisemitischen Bewegung* (Ph.D. dissertation, University of Vienna, 1962), p. 73. Robert A. Kann, *Neue deutsche Biographie*, vol. 5, p. 451.

6. Engelbert Pernerstorfer, "Aus Meiner Kinderzeit," *Oesterreichischer Arbeiter-Kalender für das Jahr 1911*, pp. 67–68.

> courtyard and faced a wall some four steps distant, so that it was impossible for a direct ray of sunlight to enter it. There was always water standing on the floor at the base of the walls. And in this room four people worked and slept.

This atmosphere was remote indeed from the sunlight of music and poetry which his friend Gruber enjoyed.

Pernerstorfer's family background also differed from that of his friends in providing a direct link to a revolutionary past. His father had taken part in the revolution of 1848, participating in the fighting at the Nussdorfer line during the October Days. Moreover, after the revolution had been suppressed, he carefully packed away his uniform and weapons in the assumption that they would soon be needed again. Since it was usually Pernerstorfer who assumed the most radical stance in the various discussions and activities of the society, it seems probable that one factor in the development of the circle's radical outlook was his continuation of a family political tradition.

For the other members of the society, familial tradition could offer nothing more radical than the usual middle-class (*bürgerlich*) conviction that science, learning, and art would eventually overcome existing political and social problems. For these young men the primary impetus toward radicalism appears to be tied to a powerful generational reaction. Erik Erikson has noted that in German middle-class families of this period the rebelliousness characteristic of adolescents of any time and place often assumed an extreme form due to the particular nature of the German family structure. He argues that typically a young man would "extend his idealistic or cynical hostility over the whole sphere of *Bürgerlichkeit*," and as Erikson indicates, the term *Bürger* was used quite broadly to mean "a kind of adult who has betrayed youth and idealism and has sought refuge in a petty and servile kind of conservatism." He notes that adolescents often "would form small bands of intellectual cynics" and other associations in which the common feature was "the exclusion of the individual fathers as an influence and the adherence to some mystic-romantic entity: Nature, Fatherland, Art."[7]

The pattern which Erikson discerns fits the outlook and the psychological situation of the Pernerstorfer circle quite closely, and

7. Erik H. Erikson, *Childhood and Society* (New York, 1963), pp. 334–35.

one of the circle's members, Max Gruber, has left a vivid picture of the iconoclasm and mental anguish involved in this adolescent revolt. Looking back to his youth from late in his life, Gruber described the complex psychological factors at work in his rejection of paternal ideals. He recalled how his elder brother, "under the seal of strict silence with respect to our highly conservative father," taught him that religion was nothing but deception and illusion. In addition, "he inflamed my national feeling: his glowing hatred of the Habsburg-Lothringens overflowed into me, hatred of this dynasty which was Germany's misfortune, hatred of their state which had to be shattered if the nation were to be united, if a new strong German empire under Prussia's leadership were to come into being." He went on to relate that by the time he was sixteen, his reading of Saint-Simon, Proudhon, Marx, Engels, and other socialists had led him to the conclusion that "the existing economic order, loaded with incurable faults, deserved to be completely destroyed." Even late in life, Gruber recalled vividly the psychological effects of this youthful rebellion:[8]

> Torn loose from everything existing around me, separated from my beloved father in all these things, robbed of any support, I stood on a surface which shook volcanically. With a passionate longing for order and law I was confronted only by the chaos of a world of presumptions and realities collapsing into ruins, ordained for destruction. . . . Years passed in which I had the feeling of being a lost swimmer struggling against the waves of the ocean. Thus I had to experience passionately within myself the entire inner dismemberment, the monstrous spiritual and moral distress and struggle of an individualistic time.

It should be noted that in this description Gruber felt that he spoke not only for himself but also for the circle as a whole. As he observes in concluding, "That is what I and the circle of my like-minded [*gleichstrebenden*] childhood friends experienced—actually a piece of the cultural history of our time." However ambitious the latter claim may be, the circle's subsequent history shows that the intense adolescent discontent which the circle experienced was shared by

8. Gruber, "Mitteilungen," p. 1038.

many Viennese students during this period, and that the particular historical situation in which these students found themselves intensified and focused their discontent in such a way as to magnify greatly its force and historical significance

Another member of the circle, Heinrich Friedjung, has provided a vivid description of that historical situation in his *Struggle for Supremacy in Germany*, and while the conclusions of this work have been subject to certain revisions concerning the events and personalities involved, it nonetheless offers a valuable insight into the way Friedjung and his circle interpreted the events surrounding the conflict between Austria and Prussia. Austria had been defeated in 1866, a few months before the Telynen formed their club, and Friedjung made clear the profound implications of this loss in the eyes of young German-speaking Austrians. He wrote: "The verdict of history had been delivered and Austria had been defeated in the struggle with Prussia for supremacy in Germany. Austria had had to pay for the suppression of all independence of thought ever since the Counter-Reformation." For Friedjung, Metternich was but one of a long series of Habsburg ministers whose suppression of freedom had paved the way for Austria's exclusion from the national culture of which she had been the acknowledged leader for over six hundred years. Nor in his view did the tragedy end with the defeat of 1866; bitterness kindled a desire for revenge: "Austria did not at first abandon her claims in Germany and undoubtedly the main reason for the appointment of Beust to the supreme direction of Austrian policy was the expectation that he would be able to organize a powerful opposition to Prussia in Germany." Prior to the Austro-Prussian war, Beust—then the chief minister of Saxony—had been one of those who argued most forcefully for Austria to undertake the disastrous conflict with Prussia, and following 1866 he continued to follow the same ill-fated path. "The Austrian government determined also to appeal to its own peoples, especially the Germans and the Magyars, for the war of revenge against Prussia. This was the reason for the most far-reaching event in the domestic policy of Francis Joseph—the Austrian provinces were granted the Constitution of December 21, 1867, and Hungary received a measure of self-government such as it had never enjoyed since the Imperial armies freed the land from the Turk."[9]

9. Heinrich Friedjung, *The Struggle for Supremacy in Germany 1859–1866*, trnas. A. J. P. Taylor and W. L. McElwee (New York, 1966), pp. 302, 307.

According to Friedjung, this policy of revenge had also led to the negotiations for an alliance with Napoleon III against the Prussians, a development with important domestic repercussions within Austria. Friedjung argued that Francis Joseph and Napoleon had met at Salzburg and they had agreed it was necessary to introduce liberal institutions in Austria in order to satisfy public opinion in Europe. Thus, in Friedjung's eyes, liberalism's accession to power in Austria was but a by-product of Austria's need to gain the assistance of Napoleon III, the occupant of what Victor Adler described as "the worm-eaten throne of despotism."[10] When this was done for the purpose of attacking the cultural fatherland of German Austrians—for that was how the Telynen viewed the matter—the intensity of their distaste for the new liberal government becomes comprehensible. As Friedjung concluded, "someone had to pay the price, and the real sufferers by the defeat of 1866 were the Germans of Austria; they lost their political center of gravity and have never recovered it."[11]

Friedjung's history does much to illuminate the historical basis for the two highly emotional reactions which Gruber says that he and his fellow Telynen experienced during their high school years. Not only the hatred for the Habsburgs and their state but also the insecurity generated by the rejection of accepted social values were rooted in those events which, in the brief span from 1866 to 1870, had shattered the previously stable world of German Austrians. In the eyes of the Telynen the liberal ideals that formed the substance of their parents' world had been turned against the interests of Austria's German population and were being used to further the disastrous conflict with the united German homeland that Bismarck was bringing into being.

Disillusioning as was the association of Austria's new liberal government with the loss of the Germanic homeland, this was but one dimension of the disenchantment which the Telynen suffered at the hands of the Bürgerministerium. As Max Gruber testified, the collapse of faith in paternal values which he and his friends experienced extended to the belief that "the existing economic order,

10. Adler to Pernerstorfer, 21 Aug. 1870, Victor Adler Archiv, Vienna.

11. Friedjung, *Struggle for Supremacy,* p. 310.

loaded with incurable faults, deserved to be completely destroyed." As was the case with their passionate German nationalism, the radicalism of the group's economic and social outlook reflected their frustration over specific government poliices. In this instance their dissatisfaction centered on the hostile reaction of the Bürgerministerium to the appearance of a working-class movement after 1867. Taking advantage of a relaxation of restrictions on nonpolitical organizations, the workers' leaders used worker educational societies as the basis for the development of a political program and an extensive following. On 11 May 1868, the leaders of the movement presented their demands to Dr. Carl Giskra, the liberal Minister of the Interior. To their proposal for universal suffrage he responded that this would be inappropriate for Austria now or later; when they raised the "social question" he declared that the social question ceased to exist at the Austrian border. However adamant Giskra's opposition, the movement continued to gain strength. Increasingly the government attempted to prohibit all large gatherings of workers while the leaders of the movement continued to schedule such meetings in spite of the prohibitions.[12] In this burgeoning conflict the Telynen once again found their sympathies to be with the government's enemies. As Pernerstorfer later recalled,[13]

> In 1868 and 1869 we were still *Gymnasiasten,* and because of the heavy demands of the school were not able to take part in any meetings. Nonetheless, we did indeed follow with the greatest interest what we could learn from the newspapers. In addition we held subscriptions to socialist periodicals in common. I remember the *Felleisen,* the *Proletarier* and the Leipzig *Volksstaat.* Since the various parents of the members belonged to bourgeois circles, all of these publications went to my address.

The climax of the conflict between the Bürgerministerium and the workers occurred on 13 December 1869, when between 20,000 and 30,000 workers assembled at their factories and marched in well-organized ranks to the Parliament Building where the government was presented with various demands. Although the government did

12. Ermers, *Victor Adler*, pp. 39–46.

13. Engelbert Pernerstorfer, "Kleine Erinnerungen," *Der Kampf* 3 (1909–10): 377. This article will henceforth be cited as "Erinnerungen."

grant certain concessions to the workers, Interior Minister Giskra moved swiftly to arrest and try the leaders of the demonstration on charges of treason.[14]

The massive workers' demonstration made a deep impression on the young Pernerstorfer, who witnessed it on his way home from school, and a short time later both he and Victor Adler contributed to a fund to help the families of the imprisoned leaders.[15] In the socialist *Volkswille,* (16 April 1870) their two-gulden contribution was cited under a motto taken from Freiligrath's poem "Bread": "You despots, you cannot smother the angry cry of the hungry people."[16] Pernerstorfer went on to establish a close working relationship with this newspaper as a reporter covering judicial proceedings.

In July 1870, after the socialist leaders were convicted of treason and sentenced to between five and six years of hard labor, the government moved to dissolve various workers' organizations in the hope of destroying the movement's organizational structure.[17] Among others, the Vienna Workers' Educational Society fell victim to this action, and once again the young men of the Pernerstorfer circle reacted with outrage. Victor Adler, vacationing with his family in Baden, the fashionable resort near Vienna, wrote to Pernerstorfer that his earlier carefree mood had vanished "as soon as I heard that the Society had actually been dissolved. And we must remain calm, we cannot smash the cowardly scoundrels; but the day will come! Now we must once again begin anew. The worker's Educational Society is dead! Long live the Society for all!"[18] Almost immediately on Adler's return from his vacation, he, Pernerstorfer, and the other members of the Telyn Society set about to realize the new beginning envisioned in the letter.

Early in August 1870 they established a new Socio-Political Society, the purpose of which, in the words of its architects, was "the clarification and establishment of our views on the social question." While the membership of the new society differed little from that of

14. Ermers, p. 46.
15. Pernerstorfer, "Erinnerungen," p. 377.
16. Ludwig Brügel, *Geschichte der oesterreichischen Sozialdemokratie* (Vienna, 1922), vol. 3, p. 374.
17. Ermers, p. 50.
18. Adler to Pernerstorfer, 21 Aug. 1870, Adler Archiv.

the previous literary club, the tone of its meetings was distinctly more radical. The charter called for the reading and discussion of social democratic literature, and the minutes of the club reveal that in the course of their discussions the circle's members eventually reached agreement on the principle that the liberal policy of economic noninterference would have to be abandoned in favor of vigorous action by the state. In particular, they found the ideas of the German socialist, Ferdinand Lassalle, to their liking.[19]

In the circle's movement toward social radicalism, the impulse provided by anger over the government's repression of the workers' organizations was powerfully reinforced by the generational tensions described by Gruber. One of Victor Adler's letters provides a vivid picture of this process. Although Adler's father was unusually generous toward his son's circle of friends, he by no means sympathized with their socialist inclinations, for he was himself a highly successful capitalist and indeed a member of the Vienna stock exchange's board of arbitration.[20] This created a domestic political polarization which sometimes surfaced at the family dinner table, and in a letter to Pernerstorfer of April 1871, Adler recounted such an occasion: "The [Paris] Commune was the topic of conversation. Now I am in no case in agreement with this movement, but naturally I must defend it against the objections and characterizations used by my father, such as: murderers, thieves, tramps." Noting wryly that it was a matter of course that in such debates "the paternal authority must win" Victor Adler told how he was forced to swallow his anger and lapse into defiant silence in the face of a rising tide of insults. "Finally it is regretted that I have lost all feeling for morality and justice and that the difference between mine and thine is unclear to me, and all of a sudden just such a tramp and thief sits there at the table." Meanwhile, according to Adler, his mother had become convinced that his stubbornness reflected an oath of secrecy he had taken as a member of an underground organization. The dispute ended unresolved when his parents retired for the night.[21]

However intense the circle's sympathy for socialism and the plight of the workers, this concern in no way replaced or diminished its

19. The records of this club were kept in a *Vereinsbuch* which is now in the Adler Archiv; for the club's aims, see p. 1; see also pp. 38–42.

20. Braunthal, *Victor und Friedrich Adler*, p. 14.

21. Adler to Pernerstorfer, 4 April 1871, Adler Archiv.

commitment to radical German nationalism. Indeed, the events of 1870 seem to have had the effect of firmly binding these two causes together as a logical and natural alternative for young men who found the status quo repugnant. During the early months of 1870 when the government was acting within Austria to destroy the labor movement as a political force, its foreign policy aimed at securing an alliance with France against Prussia in order to recoup the losses of 1866. On the outbreak of the Franco-Prussian War in July 1870, the Austrian government found itself in a position of awkward neutrality, and once again the members of the Pernerstorfer circle reacted strongly. In their eyes, the government's opposition to German unification went hand in hand with domestic reaction. Pernerstorfer later recalled, "If possible, this Germanic state of mind with us was strengthened still more by the fact that certain factions regarded as belonging to a reactionary and anti-German *camarilla* wanted to make common cause with France."[22] The combination of German nationalism and socialism thus afforded the circle an opportunity to express its vehement opposition to both the government's domestic and foreign policies. This attitude is strikingly illustrated in the August 1870 letter that Adler wrote to Pernerstorfer expressing his outrage at the dissolution of the Vienna Workers' Educational Society. After discussing this problem, he went on to allude to the atmosphere of the fashionable middle-class resort his family was visiting: "Forgive me, but I can endure it no longer! All around me there are friends of France—out of opportunism, out of loyalty to Austria, or much more, to imperial banknotes. I must be black-red-gold. Surely the red, the one red—with the blood of my heart I would like to color all flags red."[23] For Adler, red, the color of international socialism, was also the one color needed to transform the black and gold of imperial Austria into the black-gold-red which had traditionally symbolized German unity.

When the history of the years from 1866 to 1871 is viewed through the eyes of these young men who experienced it so passionately, it becomes possible to understand the depth of their political and psychological reactions. The deep insecurity generated by their rejection of the political and social world of their parents and govern-

22. Pernerstorfer, "Erinnerungen," p. 377.
23. Adler to Pernerstorfer, 21 Aug. 1870, Adler Archiv.

ment drove them to seek revolutionary alternatives to the ideals of that world. In Max Gruber's eyes he had experienced a generational fall from innocence, a fall from the unified and secure world of his parents to one in which the ideals and values he had been taught to esteem were seen as irreconcilably opposed to one another. As he later wrote, "I had eaten of the tree of knowledge. There was no return."[24] Yet it was precisely the desire to return to the garden of these lost unities—political, social, psychological, and artistic—and to regain this lost sense of wholeness which was to inspire the members of the Telyn Society in so many of their later interests and activities.

However sharply the Telynen rejected parental values and government policy, their discontent clearly did not extend to the institution primarily responsible for their early education, the Schottengymnasium. Indeed this Benedictine monastic school seems to have provided a favorable environment for their efforts to find an alternative to the outlook which events had discredited in their eyes. Many years after he had left the school and at a time when the Gymnasium education in general was under heavy attack, Pernerstorfer testified to the deep affection which he and so many others still felt for their school. "How is it that so many of the older generation have never looked back with fright on their Gymnasium days? How is it that even now, after so many years, many of them look back on their school days much rather with joy and pensive melancholy?" In light of the critical attitude which Pernerstorfer continued to maintain toward the other experiences of his childhood, there is no reason to doubt his assertion that this was not just the usual nostalgia for lost youth: "On the contrary, there are quite positive concrete facts which rise up in our memories and make that period seem so lovely and glorious. Above all it is the picture of our teachers which we recall and which fills our hearts with respect and gratitude."[25]

Alfred von Berger, a fellow student who shared Pernerstorfer's affection for the Schottengymnasium, has provided a highly subjective but nonetheless revealing description of these Benedictine

24. Gruber, "Mitteilungen," p. 1038.

25. Engelbert Pernerstorfer, "Ein Blatt Dankbarer Erinnerung," *Festgabe zum 100 jahrigen Jubilaum des Schottengymnasiums,* ed. Heinrich Ritter von Wittek (Vienna, 1907), p. 222. This collection of essays by alumni of the Schottengymnasium offers an invaluable insight into the character of the school and the nature of its educational ideals. It will henceforth be cited as *Festgabe.*

monks. Berger recalled that when one spoke with teachers such as Pater Hugo Mareta or Pater Sigismund Gschwandner one felt "pleasantly touched by the fresh, wholesome breath of Lower Austrian nature and countryside, by the fragrance of grain and the smell of pine needles, by the aroma of vine blossoms and the coolness of the beech trees in the Vienna woods." To Berger the personalities of his teachers were peculiarly expressive of all that was unique to the local Viennese temperament, "for it was always characteristic of the Benedictines not to cut themselves off from the countryside and its population, but rather to coalesce intimately with the land and its people."[26]

In his memories of the Schottengymnasium Berger saw the school not as a world unto itself but as an integral part of the larger community of city and province, and in this Berger's testimony agrees fully with that of another alumnus of the school, the outstanding literary historian Jacob Zeidler. Zeidler, who also attributed great importance to this sense of community, saw it as the natural product of the monastery's history: "Within the jurisdiction of the city of Vienna—whose history it shared through centuries and from whose inner and outer districts it received the basic stock for its future growth—the once rural order gradually absorbed more and more urban—indeed metropolitan—characteristics into its essence." According to Zeidler, the monastery and its school were open to all the powerful influences exercised by the social and cultural life of Vienna, and as a result the necessity of constantly comparing the eternal verities of their education with the rapidly changing conditions of city life produced in the school's students a strong sense for the integration of ideality and reality. "The powerful force of external city life that here sounded the bass in the school harmony of the good, the true and the beautiful, did allow a youth to play and dream but also prevented life from becoming only a dream by directing his attention through a hundred gaps in the school hedge to the hustle and bustle of real life." It was for this reason, Zeidler felt, that every well-educated student came to think of himself

26. Alfred Freiherr von Berger, "Aus der Jugendzeit," *Festgabe*, p. 22. Berger graduated in 1871, the year after Adler, so his description applies to essentially the same period the members of the circle spent at the school. Lists of the school's graduates by year are printed in Hübl, *Geschichte des Unterrichtes*. For Adler and Berger, see p. 298.

as a "Zoon politikon"—a member of the communal body politic.[27]

Although one factor in the enthusiasm of the Telynen for their school may well have been the favorable contrast between the monastery's tradition of community involvement and the liberal tradition of autonomous individualism, another dimension of their education appears to have been much more important in arousing their sympathies. Here too Alfred von Berger's memories of his school provide a valuable insight. He writes, "In my boyhood fantasies I always saw the monastery church as a building carried in the left hand of an old Babenberg duke . . . and transferred in enlarged scale from the strong man's palm to the earth." In Berger's vivid imagination church and monastery were part of a medieval tableau honoring the Babenberg duke responsible for their foundation, and in his view the order's medieval Germanic associations continued to shape the nature of its education even in his own time. "Indeed when I heard Father Hugo Mareta's inspired lectures on the *Nibelungenlied* . . . I often had the feeling that the mysterious poet of the German national epic . . . might long ago have been a guest in the wine cellar of the Schotten monastery and that inspired by a sample of the best Aventuren he might have given his best for his joyous companions." Berger's daydreams suggest how deeply the educational traditions of the monastery were rooted in the medieval era in which the German *Volk* had achieved cultural and political greatness. As Berger noted, "From ancient times the Benedictines were teachers, educators and bringers of culture from whom the ignorant and crude inhabitants in whose midst they built their houses not only learned gardening, viticulture, and other peaceful arts, but also received the ennobling sparks of classical learning and culture."[28]

While Berger evokes a vivid image of the medieval Germanic Volk which Father Hugo Mareta's lessons on middle-high German conjured up in the minds of his students, the somewhat less impressionistic descriptions of this teacher provided by Jacob Zeidler and Friedrich von Wieser, the economic theorist, reveal more clearly why this image proved so attractive to students, and how this Germanic national consciousness was related to the strong feeling of member-

27. Jakob Zeidler, "Aus dem schottischen Literaturwinkel (Literarisch-pädagogische Jubiläums-Arabesken)," *Festgabe*, pp. 256–57. Zeidler graduated in 1875 (Hübl, p. 303).

28. Berger, *Festgabe*, pp. 21–22.

ship in the local community of city and province discussed earlier. Wieser, a classmate of Heinrich Friedjung, recalled, "How profoundly we were moved by the *Nibelungenlied* when we studied it in the original text! For us South Germans, for us Austrians, middle-high German has not only the magic of a mother tongue but also that of our particular dialect."[29] The similarity of middle-high German to Austrian German and even more specifically to the local Viennese dialect, not only infused the heroes of the *Nibelungenlied* with vitality, but conversely allowed the dialect itself to be used as a source for investigating linguistic history. Zeidler recalled how, in the case of his Viennese students, "Mareta was able with a minimum of grammatical instruction to make middle-high German grow directly out of the native dialect . . . so that the treasure which every Viennese possesses in the knowledge of his native idiom, became vital and effective." By means of this approach Mareta was able to employ linguistic analysis to achieve a rare degree of aesthetic participation on the part of his students. As Zeidler observed, "Suddenly we were in the midst of 'Ez troumde Kriemhilte,' ('Kriemhild was dreaming') the sound of the foreign-familiar tones rustled pleasantly in our ears—all at once our entire relationship to our beloved mother tongue was different."[30] Wieser's reaction was similar: "Created by an Austrian poet, the figures of the *Nibelungenlied* approached our inner feelings more closely than any we had experienced in classical poetry, and in our youthful exuberance we could feel ourselves to be the heroes who met at Bechelären [Pöchlarn]."[31] The identification of Mareta's students with the heroes of this German national epic, facilitated by the similarity of its language to the Viennese dialect, thus served to reinforce the sense of attachment to local traditions and customs. Conversely their pride of membership in the local community was elevated beyond mere parochialism by their feeling that the community's cultural origins were rooted in the era of German national greatness. As Zeidler observed of Mareta, "Just because he was able to arouse our poetic sense first with a local work of art such as the *Nibelungenlied*—a glittering gem of pan-German poetry—he preserved us permanently from all particularism and

29. Friedrich Freiherr von Wieser, "Arma virumque cano," *Festgabe,* p. 323. Wieser graduated in 1868 (Hübl, p. 297).

30. Zeidler, *Festgabe,* p. 359.

31. Wieser, *Festgabe,* p. 323.

narrow-minded regionalism while cherishing and protecting a love for German-Austrian literature."[32]

The attraction which this image of the ancient Germanic Volk exerted on Berger, Zeidler, and Wieser was felt by members of the Pernerstorfer circle as well. One indication of how deep an impact the Gymnasium lessons in middle-high German made on Pernerstorfer is seen in the fact that this interest dominated his subsequent academic career at the university where he took various courses in Gothic, old German, middle-high German and historical philology.[33] At a point much later in his career he continued to regard the initial Gymnasium lessons on this subject as one of the most significant aspects of the school's educational program. In 1911 he wrote, "Here in Austria . . . the German Gymnasium is the one school which conveys to students that knowledge of the middle-high German language which enables them to become acquainted with the literary, spiritual life of the German people in ancient times."[34] In spite of his Jewish background—or perhaps because of its assimilationist character—Victor Adler seems to have shared his friend's enthusiasm. After the conclusion of his sixth year at the Schottengymnasium, the year in which students learned middle-high German, Adler set out for Munich on a summer excursion, and in writing back to Pernerstorfer and the other Telynen he devoted most of his letter to describing in loving detail the various heroes of the *Nibelungenlied* depicted in a set of murals he had seen.[35] Clearly, Adler had also been impressed by Father Hugo Mareta's lessons.

In examining the various influences that shaped the revolutionary mission of Pernerstorfer and his friends, it becomes clear that the education they received at the Schottengymnasium did much to lend positive direction to the energies generated by their dissatisfaction with the outlook of their parents and the policies of their government. While any explicit discussion of politics was obviously out of the question inside the classroom, the traditions of the monastery and its school inculcated values rooted more in the outlook of an earlier era of Austrian culture than in its liberal present. During the

32. Zeidler, *Festgabe,* p. 360.

33. Pernerstorfer's courses at the university are listed in his *Index lectionum,* now in the Adler Archiv.

34. Pernerstorfer, "Der Wert der antiken Bildung," *Zeitfragen* (Vienna, 1918), p. 94.

35. Adler to Pernerstorfer, 19 Aug. 1868, Adler Archiv.

years from 1866 to 1871 when Bismarck was reestablishing a unified German Empire, the figures of the *Nibelungenlied* inevitably took on a certain political significance, and the close attention with which these heroes were studied in Mareta's classes could only intensify the discontent his students felt toward the liberal government's opposition to German unification. Similarly, the strong sense of community which both Berger and Zeidler attributed to the school must have been particularly appealing to students who felt the kind of shattering insecurity that Max Gruber described as typical of his generation. This sense of community was a composite of many elements—the Benedictine order's tradition of community involvement, the perpetuation of Josephin social concern,[36] the fanciful association of the order with the heroes of the *Nibelungenlied* as symbols of a powerful Germanic community—and perhaps most immediately, the feeling evoked by the community of the monastic brotherhood itself. In student eyes these various elements merged in the history of the monastery; and as partakers of its ancient store of wisdom they could feel themselves part of a community embracing monastic brotherhood, city, province, and nation. At a time when the liberal faith in individualism seemed to suggest indifference to social misery, the community of the Benedictine fathers introduced students such as Adler or Gruber to alternative values which seemed in certain respects more relevant to modern problems and more consistent with traditional beliefs. Small wonder that they should prefer them to the liberal values of their natural fathers.

With their graduation from Gymnasium and entry into university life, the Telynen opened an important new phase in the development of their outlook. Their elite cloister school on the edge of Vienna's inner city had offered them intellectual refuge from the conflicts besetting the liberal order, and by the time they left the school in 1870 the broad outlines of a social and political alternative to that order had begun to take shape in their minds. From their monastic retreat they moved to the university quarter, located near the center of the inner city, where they became members of an intellectual community which was not only much larger and much

36. Pernerstorfer contrasts the relatively broad social spectrum represented in the Austrian Gymnasium with the more restricted middle- and upper-class character of the north German Gymnasium. See Pernerstorfer, "Der Wert der antiken Bildung," p. 79.

more complex but also much more deeply involved in political activity. This new environment proved highly congenial to the radical outlook the members of the circle had begun to develop, for here at the University of Vienna they were able to give their ideas philosophical substance and consistency while at the same time developing the means for translating these ideas into political reality.

The Socio-Political Society continued to be the principal forum for the circle's discussions during the first year at the university, but the particular purpose of this club—the establishment of a position on the social question—had apparently been accomplished to its members' satisfaction by the summer of 1871 when they abandoned it in favor of a "reawakening of the Telyn spirit." As Adler explained in a letter to Pernerstorfer, "No formal society was established, but every Sunday we will spend a certain amount of time discussing literature, aesthetics, philosophy and science."[37] In shifting the focus of their discussions from specific political and social problems to the larger concerns of art, philosophy, and science the Telynen began to prepare themselves, however unconsciously, for what was soon to become a systematic search for philosophical alternatives to the ideals of liberal culture.

In addition to these informal meetings which were to continue for over a decade, the members of the circle also became involved during their second year at the university in a much larger and much more specifically political organization, the *Leseverein der deutschen Studenten Wiens* (Reading Society of Viennese German Students). In the course of its seven-year history this society was to develop an extremely powerful influence on Vienna's student population, and by virtue of the positions they secured within the society, the members of the Pernerstorfer circle were to have a strong voice in determining how that influence was used. The history of this student organization thus provides a crucial element for understanding how and why the outlook of the Pernerstorfer circle came to play such a significant role in the political and cultural life of fin de siècle Vienna.

The formal establishment of the Leseverein occurred on 2 December 1871, when some four hundred students from both the university and the technical college assembled to create an organization intended "to adhere to and represent the German character

37. Adler to Pernerstorfer, 9 June 1871, Adler Archiv.

of the University of Vienna at every opportunity." The desire to include this statement in the by-laws of the society produced an immediate conflict with the government, which charged that this would violate the rule requiring that such university organizations be nonpolitical. When the society's leadership yielded on this issue at an organizational meeting in January 1872, the more militant nationalists—primarily members of the fraternities (*Burschenshaften*) —walked out as a block leaving only the Burschenshaft "Arminia" (to which both Adler and Pernerstorfer belonged) as a supporter of the society.[38] This rather inauspicious beginning left the organization with serious financial problems due to the loss of membership.

Although the members of the Pernerstorfer circle apparently played no significant role in founding the Leseverein, even at its inception a number of factors augured well for their future involvement in the society. Not only did the circle and the Leseverein have similar views on the crucial issue of German nationalism, they were also united in common admiration of Vienna's revolutionary past. However innocuous the term reading society might sound in English, no Austrian student could have forgotten the crucial role played by the Legal-Political Reading Society in the revolution of 1848, and thus the name of the society itself served to recall the heroic revolutionary tradition of Vienna's academic community. In such an organization Pernerstorfer might well expect to fulfill the hopes which had moved his deceased father to preserve his revolutionary uniform and weapons. In addition to these factors, however, the nature of the Leseverein's leadership also offered members of the circle the prospect of an early entrée into positions of influence, for a remarkably large proportion of the society's officers were graduates of the Schottengymnasium. Of the initial slate of officers, this school contributed not only the librarian (Anton Haider) and the finance chairman, both of whom had graduated in 1870 with Adler, but also the president Franz von Liszt, who had graduated the year before, and the vice president who had graduated with Friedjung the year before that.[39] In addition to the tie of being

38. Paul Molisch, *Politische Geschichte der deutschen Hochschulen in Oesterreich von 1848 bis 1918* (Vienna, 1939), p. 83. Albert Hiller, "Der Leseverein der deutschen Studenten," *Die Lesevereine der deutschen Hochschuler an der wiener Universität,* ed. Lese- u. Redevereine der deutschen Hochschuler in Wien-Germania (Vienna, 1912), p. 11.

39. Hübl, *Geschichte des Unterrichtes,* pp. 296–98 and *Erster Jahresbericht des Lesevereines*

former schoolmates of the Telynen, these officers had also been exposed to the same educational influences that had helped to shape the circle's outlook, and under those circumstances it is not surprising that the circle's members should eventually be drawn into the inner councils of the Leseverein.

However favorable the Pernerstorfer circle's long-range prospects for advancement within the Leseverein, it also seems clear that on certain political issues the initial outlook of the reading society was much less radical than that of the circle. While these two groups were fully united in their enthusiasm for the German nationalist cause, the members of the Leseverein seem to have been generally much less alienated from the political and social values of the liberal order, and specifically much less concerned about the social question. Although it was eventually to assume a more militant stance, the society's initial political position was much closer to that of the progressive wing of the liberal movement than to the protosocialism of the Pernerstorfer circle.[40]

Unfortunately, the kind of detailed analysis of the Leseverein's political position essential to understanding how this process of radicalization occurred has been made difficult by the official ban on student political activities. While this ban apparently did nothing to reduce such activities, it did inhibit the society from expressing any official political position. Thus to a certain extent the picture of the society's social and political convictions must be reconstructed indirectly by examining the ideas of those public figures whom the Leseverein chose to honor, those who were frequently invited to address the society, and those who aided the organization financially by becoming supporting members. Without arguing that the society would have accepted fully the ideas of these men, it does seem probable that repeated contacts indicate a community of interest with respect to their primary concerns.

For example, the society's political outlook obviously had much to do with the strong support it received from members of the

---

der deutschen Studenten Wiens, über das Vereinsjahr 1871–72 (Vienna, 1872), p. 7. This series will henceforth be cited as *Jahresbericht* followed by the academic year covered in the report.

40. For the outlook of the society at the time of its establishment see Karl Beurle, *Beiträge zur Geschichte der deutschen Studentenschaft Wiens* (Vienna, 1893), pp. 31–32, and Albert Hiller, *Der Leseverein*, pp. 10–15.

Deutscher Verein, for in addition to the president Dr. Josef Kopp and the vice president Max Menger, at least three other leading members of this influential society became supporting members of the Leseverein during the first year of its existence.[41] Kopp had created the Deutsche Verein in 1867 to provide a forum for those progressive liberals who favored a more militant defense of German interests in both domestic and foreign policy.[42] In 1870 this question became a key political issue when the liberals divided into rival "Old" and "Young" factions to contest election to the new Reichsrath. According to Richard Charmatz, "He who put his Austrianism over his Germanism was 'old'; he who felt that he had come into the world as a German, but whose patriotism included Austria, was 'young.' "[43] Although the Old Liberals won the great majority of the contests, those Young Ones (*Jungen*) who were elected formed the Progressive Club within the Reichsrath, while Kopp's Deutscher Verein became their extraparliamentary center of activity. The political program put forward by the society hailed both the Prussian victory over France and the reconstitution of the German Empire, and went on to call for the creation of a close political and economic alliance between Germany and Austria-Hungary. It also denounced the influence exercised by the Polish aristocrats in the politics of the Austrian half of the Empire. Max Menger specifically called for making Galicia autonomous, a move which would have so reduced the Slavic population of the Austrian section as to leave the German Austrians in a dominant position. On other domestic issues Kopp's society favored an expansion of the franchise and further guarantees for civil liberties, while displaying little concern for the social question.[44] It seems apparent that a common enthusiasm for the German nationalist cause constituted the primary factor in the association of the Deutscher Verein leaders with the Leseverein.

An indication of the Leseverein's outlook on social problems can be seen in its close association with Professor Lorenz von Stein.

41. As supporting members of the Leseverein, the three, Nicolaus Dumba, Dr. V. von Capesius, and Dr. Heinrich Jacques, all contributed to its financial support. For their activities in the Deutsche Verein see the *Neue Freie Presse,* 21 July 1870, p. 8. This newspaper will henceforth be cited as *N.F.P.*

42. F. F. Masaidek, *Georg Schönerer und die duetschnationale Bewegung* (Vienna, 1898), p. 9. Eduard Pichl, *Georg Schönerer* (Oldenburg, n.d.), vol. 1, p. 12.

43. Richard Charmatz, *Deutsch-oesterreichische Politik* (Leipzig, 1907), p. 72.

44. Ibid., p. 162. *N.F.P.* (24 May 1870), p. 3; N.F.P. (27 Feb. 1871), pp. 3–4.

Stein was among the small number of professors on whom the Leseverein bestowed honorary membership during its first year, and he reciprocated by participating in each of the annual lecture cycles held by the society during its first four years.[45] Since the admission fees to these lectures provided the organization with one of its most important sources of income, this represented a substantial gesture of support. Stein was also the only faculty member willing to risk official displeasure by openly participating in the activities of the Leseverein after 1877 when the government began actively opposing the society.[46]

One of the most popular and effective lecturers at the university, Stein had also written over thirty books and articles on social, political, and economic subjects by 1870. His most popular and important works included *Der Sozialismus und Kommunismus des heutigen Frankreichs (Socialism and Communism in France Today)*, *Die Gesellschaftslehre (Social Theory)*, and smaller studies of socialism and social movements in Germany and Britain. Although Stein later went on to concentrate on economic and political subjects, his social thought served as the foundation for all of his later works (including his *Lehrbuch der National-Ökonomie* [*Textbook on the National Economy*]).[47] While sensitive to the depressed living conditions of the proletariat, Stein argued that the kind of class conflict espoused by socialism and communism would destroy the possibility of a viable social order, and as an alternative he put forth the ideal of an organic society in which motivation would be determined by the common good rather than by the selfish desires of an individual or a class. This ideal organic society bore a marked resemblance to the existing social order in that it postulated the necessary division of society into upper, middle, and lower classes, but Stein also demanded an amelioration of the living conditions of the workers and a higher degree of social mobility.[48] Although far from the socialism of the Pernerstorfer circle, Stein's ideas did depart from the accepted liberal faith in the greatest possible freedom of the individual and in a laissez-faire economic and social policy.[49] Considering the unusual closeness of

45. *Jahresbericht* 1871–72, p. 6; 1873–74, p. 7; 1874–75, p. 11. For the 1872–73 period, *Deutsche Zeitung* (22 Feb. 1873), p. 7. This newspaper will henceforth be cited as *D.Z.*

46. Beurle, *Beiträge*, p. 40.

47. Heinz Nitschke, *Die Geschichtsphilosophie Lorenz von Steins* (Munich, 1932), p. 136.

48. Ernst Grünfeld, *Die Gesellschaftslehre von Lorenz von Stein* (Halle, 1908), pp. 68–71.

49. Charmatz, *Deutsch-oesterreichische Politik*, pp. 34, 166, 316.

Stein's relationship to the Leseverein it seems not unlikely that the Society's views on the social question were influenced by his ideal of an integrated, organic society, cognizant of its obligation to raise the living and educational standards of the working class.

While there is no evidence of radicalism in the Leseverein's outlook on the social question, the issue of German nationalism aroused in the society's leadership much the same strong sense of discontent with government policy felt by the Telynen. As a Reichsrath deputy some fifteen years later (1888), Pernerstorfer recounted an incident which illustrates clearly the emotions generated by the government's attitude. He began by recalling that at that time the "reconstitution of the German Empire had been greeted with the most intense jubilation by the entire German academic youth of Austria, even though it was . . . repugnant to the ruling circles". As an expression of their feelings, members of the Leseverein had planned to celebrate the anniversary of the Frankfurt peace ending the Franco-Prussian War, but when they attempted to do so the police forbade the meeting. In addition to preventing the celebration, the government exerted pressure on the university faculty and administration to restrain other political activities of the students. As a result, the officers of the Leseverein were called before the Rector of the university to account for their actions, and according to Pernerstorfer this elicited from them such a bitter outburst of feeling that in his view at least half of his colleagues might have "experienced a bitter fate" had it not been for the sympathetic and understanding attitude of the Rector.[50]

During these early years of the Leseverein's existence, it is clear that most of its youthful passion was focused on the conviction that the government was not responding to the German nation's call to greatness, and even though the society as a whole was not yet so deeply dissatisfied as the Telynen, the issue of frustrated German nationalism aroused a degree of bitterness that provided fertile ground for more generalized discontent. In this context the influence which the Telynen came to exert within the Leseverein, as well as their continuing search for intellectual alternatives to liberal values, became factors of crucial importance in determining the course that the reading society would follow.

50. *Stenographische Protokolle über die Sitzungen des Hauses der Abgeordneten des oesterreichischen Reichsrathes in den Jahren 1887 und 1888,* X session, vol. 6 (Vienna, 1888), p. 6992.

By the time the confrontation with the Rector occurred (1872 or 1873), both Pernerstorfer and Adler had been drawn into the leadership of the Leseverein, where they joined the relatively small group which was to control the organization during its remaining five years. One of Adler's letters describing an unsuccessful challenge to the position of this clique reveals that he soon came to play a central role in the political life of the society. In this particular incident it was Adler who led the battle to discredit the charges of financial mismanagement which constituted the basis of the challenge, and his allies in the struggle included no fewer than four past, present, or future presidents of the Leseverein (three of whom were alumni of the Schottengymnasium).[51]

When this internal challenge took place (May 1874) Adler was librarian of the society and Pernerstorfer was its secretary, but even though Pernerstorfer, Adler, and Max Gruber all occupied important offices within the society at various times, the primary interest of the Telynen lay less in high office than in positions that would give them a strong voice in directing the society's intellectual activities. For example, during the Leseverein's second year Pernerstorfer and Adler joined with Alexius Meinong to set up and direct a project for holding regular scholarly discussions on various topics, and during the first semester of the following year (1873–74), Pernerstorfer and Adler served as first and second librarians of the Leseverein. Since the library maintained reading rooms and subscribed to various newspapers and periodicals, these positions were of great importance in setting the intellectual tone of the society.[52] Having made themselves the intellectual arbiters of the Leseverein, the Telynen managed to retain this position during most of the remaining four years of the society's existence.

At the same time the members of the Pernerstorfer circle were advancing within the Leseverein to positions that would assure their

51. Adler to Pernerstorfer, 26 May 1874, Adler Archiv. The presidents were Franz von Liszt, Julius Delena, Anton Haider, and Rudolph Maresch, all of whom except Maresch had graduated from the Schottengymnasium. *Jahresberichte*, 1871–78; Hübl, pp. 297–98.

52. Karl Beurle provides the following description of the society's activities: "Der Verein fasste das studentische Vereinsleben im grossen Style auf. Es wurde eine Bibliothek gegründet, welche auf allen Gebieten des Wissens das Neueste und Beste bot und von den Mitgliedern auch rege benützt wurde. Studien- Sprech- und Schachzimmer vervollständigten die Vereinsräume." Beiträge, p. 32.

ideas a wide student audience, the substance of those ideas was undergoing significant development. The decision of the group in June 1871 to "reawaken the Telyn spirit" by shifting from sociopolitical subjects to those of literature, aesthetics, philosophy, and science led them to investigate and then direct student attention to a number of thinkers whose ideas challenged the most basic philosophical and cultural assumptions of the liberal order. The interest of the Telynen in these thinkers began when Adler, like so many other intellectuals disillusioned with liberalism, found his way to Schopenhauer. Pernerstorfer later described Adler's study of Schopenhauer as having "the greatest influence on his development and his philosophical thought,"[53] and this strong impact is also clear in Adler's letter to Pernerstorfer describing his first encounter with the philosopher. This was the same letter of 9 June 1871 which announced the resurrection of the Telyn spirit, and in it Adler declared, "As for myself, I am being rather industrious—(100 pages at a sitting!) and the work is by Schopenhauer. . . . Schopenhauer is absolutely first rate.—I brought another of his works home with me today." Adler promised to send the books to Pernerstorfer as soon as he finished explaining the main ideas to the other members of the group.

After discussing his latest intellectual discovery, Adler wrote in the same letter that he had decided to pursue a career in medicine, a field to which his newfound interest in Schopenhauer proved surprisingly relevant. Quoting the philosopher's remark that "these men who concern themselves with crucibles and retorts must be taught that simple chemistry does indeed qualify one to be a druggist, but not to be a philosopher," Adler declared he would not have that said of him; and in pursuing this resolve to place his study of science in a larger philosophical framework, he met with considerable encouragement from some of Vienna's foremost medical scientists. In a letter of 5 in August 1872 to Pernerstorfer, Adler referred briefly to an essay by Rokitansky "which has had a very exciting impact, at least on me." This was almost certainly Karl Rokitansky's *The Solidarity of all Animal Life* (*Die Solidarität alles Thierlebens*), for an entry in Adler's diary a month later reveals the unmistakable influence of this rather strange paper by one of the most distinguished

53. Pernerstorfer, "Aus jungen Tagen," p. 101.

members of the Vienna medical school. The essay was unusual in that it attempted to synthesize the ideas of Darwin and Schopenhauer into what Erna Lesky has described as a "grandiose biosociological tableau." In essence Rokitansky argued that the only ethical solution to the struggle for survival envisioned by Darwin and Schopenhauer was a kind of community of sympathy (*Solidarität des Mitleids*) that would help man overcome his naturally aggressive individual nature. With respect to the rather negative view of individualism implicit in this Schopenhauerian position, Erna Lesky observed of Rokitansky, "The resolute fighter for progress and freedom was not spared seeing individualism of the liberal stamp degenerate into ruthless egotism."[54]

Considering his disillusionment with liberal laissez-faire social policy and his enthusiasm for Schopenhauer, it is not surprising that Adler should find Rokitansky's essay exciting, and the passage from his diary reveals that he also found in this philosophical position at least a partial answer to his own inner uncertainties. Dated mid-September 1872, the entry is written in stream-of-consciousness fashion: "I seek to find a mode which justifies my existence or makes it possible—my situation within myself: confusion, chaos . . . my ego like everyone's is subject to egotism—sympathy [*Mitleid*] expanded by reflection to world suffering [*Weltleid*]—world pain [*Weltschmerz*]—A concept so abstract that it becomes ludicrous since it rejects, or rather ignores, the individual—And yet, I believe that is my outlook."[55] However disconnected the formulation, this passage offers a rare insight into the workings of Adler's mind as he attempted to bring together his new scientific and philosophical concepts to order the confusion of values and principles he felt within himself. Rokitansky's ideas, colored by a growing disillusionment with the liberal credo he had once so fervently espoused, allowed Adler to connect his highly disparate interests in science, philosophy, and politics in such a way as to suggest at least the possibility of a coherent alternative to current values. Rokitansky's "biosociological" adaption of Schopenhauer pointed to the egoism of the individual as society's central problem, and proclaimed the collective power of sympathy as the way to overcome that egoism.

54. Erna Lesky, *Die Wiener medezinische Schule im 19. Jahrhundert* (Graz-Cologne, 1965), pp. 138–39.

55. The pages containing this entry are all that remain of the diary (Adler Archiv).

In espousing this ethical collectivism which "ignored the individual," Adler once again revealed his deeply felt need for a return to that sense of community which he had been taught to value in the Schottengymnasium, and which seemed to have vanished in the competitive world of liberal economics.

The Schopenhauerian approach to science which Adler admired in Rokitansky's essay was also shared by one of Rokitansky's most prominent students and colleagues, Theodor Meynert. A professor of psychiatry, Meynert played an extremely prominent role in the intellectual life of Vienna's students during this period, and his association with the Leseverein was particularly close. Like Lorenz von Stein, Meynert was one of those professors elected to honorary membership in the Leseverein during its first year, and he frequently participated in the lecture cycles which provided financial support to the organization. In 1876 and 1877 he served as one of the professorial members of the society's executive committee.[56] In addition to the association with Meynert within the Leseverein, Adler later worked closely with him as a medical student, and Pernerstorfer eventually became the private tutor of Meynert's children.[57] Although Meynert's academic specialty was physiological psychiatry—which might seem remote indeed from the general political and cultural concerns of these student groups—a consideration of his particular approach to this subject reveals a number of points that suggest the intellectual basis of these close relationships.

Although the actual lectures which Meynert delivered to the Leseverein have not been preserved, their titles concerned essentially the same topics discussed in other lectures which were later brought together in his *Collection of Popular Scientific Lectures on the Structure and Functions of the Brain* (*Sammlung von Populär-wissenschaftlichen Vorträgen über den Bau und die Leistungen des Gehirns,* Vienna, 1892). These lectures show that Meynert's scientific theories were set in a context which made them relevant to popular student interests in a number of ways. In an address on the functioning of the brain, given in 1872, (p. 23), he began by observing, "The sum of functions attributed to the brain in the following discussion allows the brain not just to receive the image of reality [*Weltbild*] but actually to create it." He

56. *Jahresbericht,* 1871–72, pp. 6, 11; 1873–74, p. 7; *N.F.P.* (24 Feb. 1876), p. 7; *Jahresbericht* 1876–77, pp. 29, 16–17.

57. Dora Stockert-Meynert, *Theodor Meynert und seine Zeit* (Vienna, 1930), pp. 78–79.

went on to say that this view was held not only by abstract thinkers of the Kantian school, but also by some of the most prominent natural scientists of the day—citing Rokitansky's view that the further physics and physiology progressed, the more support they would provide for the idealist world view.[58]

Meynert seems to have acquired most of his knowledge of Kant's ideas through Schopenhauer, whose work, according to Meynert, had greatly clarified the relationship of Kant's thought to the natural sciences.[59] Although Meynert did not accept some of Schopenhauer's most fundamental doctrines, such as his pessimism, he does seem to have translated other important elements of Schopenhauer's theory into physiological terms. For example, Meynert's psychology postulated the existence of a primary and secondary ego (*Ich*). The childish primary ego, motivated by concerns of bodily pain and pleasure, existed in a state of constant interaction with a secondary ego, motivated by abstract concepts—a distinction similar to Schopenhauer's dichotomy between will and intellect.[60] Using this idea as the basis for discussing the freedom of the will, Meynert observed that the closest one could come to freedom in the world of thought was "the conviction (which has completely freed itself from the primary ego) of the illusory nature of the world of appearance, and with it of one's own self."[61] This theory reflected Schopenhauer's concept of rising above the principle of individuation to the realization that the separate existence of the individual self was an illusion.[62] Meynert also followed Schopenhauer in the belief that sympathy (Mitleid) played a crucial role in causing the individual to move beyond the illusion of individuation to a realization of his essential oneness with all other persons—a realization which Meynert called the idea of mutualism.[63]

The concept of mutualism (or human brotherhood) gave a certain degree of political orientation to Meynert's thought. Since mutualism was one of the highest products of the secondary ego, its effectiveness

58. The address was delivered before the Vienna Anthropological Society. This work will henceforth be cited as *Sammlung*.

59. *Sammlung*, p. 77 (from an 1878 lecture).

60. *Sammlung*, pp. 34–36 (from an 1872 lecture).

61. *Sammlung*, p. 66 (from an 1880 lecture).

62. Arthur Schopenhauer, *Schopenhauer Selections*, ed. De Witt H. Parker (New York, 1956), pp. 269–71. This work will henceforth be cited as *Selections*.

63. Meynert, *Sammlung*, pp. 171–72 (from an 1888 lecture).

depended upon the degree to which it overcame the mind's more primitive urgings; and Meynert thought that one of these elementary demands was the desire for money. He believed that this desire would disappear "as soon as personal property ceases to exist, which can happen without particular damage to the development of our species to a noble humanity."[64] The socialistic tone of this statement was no accident, for according to Meynert's daughter Dora her father later expressed the greatest admiration for the selfless character of his former student Victor Adler and maintained that the ideals for which the socialist leader worked were not far from his own. She also indicated that her father followed Pernerstorfer's later political career with great sympathy.[65]

Meynert's feeling for the political outlook of the Telynen as well as the nature of his psychological theories suggest a number of significant points about the outlook that was evolving within the Pernerstorfer circle and the Leseverein at this time. Meynert's remarkable fusion of philosophy and physiology brought him to an a affirmation of the social element of man's nature. In contrast to the Darwinian morality proclaimed by certain liberal thinkers, he asserted that the degree to which humanity alleviated the struggle for survival was the measure of its civilization. To such students as Pernerstorfer and Adler, who strongly felt the need for restoring the sense of community their society had lost, Meynert's conception of "mutualism" was highly relevant. Where Lorenz von Stein offered a social and economic rationale for reemphasizing social coherence and responsibility, Meynert's work developed the psychological and philosophical foundations of a more communitarian outlook. Taken together they suggest that during the first three years of the Leseverein's existence, when the Telynen were establishing themselves as its intellectual leaders, the society was developing particularly close relationships with professors whose ideas supported the need for much greater community responsibility. With the Telynen in the vanguard, the Leseverein was to go much farther in this direction during the next few years.

64. Quoted by Ledwig Freyberger, "Zur Erinnerung an Theodor Meynert: Gedenkenblätter eines Schülers," *Deutsche Worte* 12 (1892) : 725. The date of the statement is not given.

65. Dora Stockert-Meynert, pp. 79–80. According to her, Meynert's revolutionary inclinations first manifested themselves in his youth and remained with him throughout his life.

From 1874 on both the influence and the political radicalism of the Leseverein increased steadily in response to a deepening sense of public scandal over the corruption apparent in Austria's political and economic life. Outraged at what they saw as the moral bankruptcy of capitalist materialism as a whole, the society's intellectual leaders reacted by looking back to the German idealist tradition to find the firm moral standards on which a new socioeconomic system could be based. In this way they also began to lay the foundations for a future order which they perceived only in its dimmest outlines. In its fourth year (1874–75) the presidency passed to Anton Haider, under whose able leadership the society solved some of its most troublesome organizational and financial problems. In their previous yearly report, the officers had lamented their inability to create a firm financial basis for the society due to the continuing boycott by members of the Burschenschaften; but Haider managed to end the boycott and bring these fraternities into association with the society. With this development the paid membership jumped to 414 for the winter semester, compared with 275 for the preceding year,—thus eliminating the organization's financial problems. At this point its membership constituted somewhat less than 10 percent of the university's total student population.[66]

With its numbers augmented and its finances in order, the Leseverein was in a strong position to respond to the spectacular developments which occurred in the political and economic life of Austria during this year. By the late 1860s Austrian industrialization and capitalization had gathered enough momentum to convince even the most timid and inept that the path to fame and fortune led through the offices of a stock company. From 1867 to 1874, over a thousand licenses were issued for the formation of joint stock companies, and during this period no fewer than twenty-nine different railroad companies came into being. Although many of these undertakings were built on the most insubstantial foundations, all went well for a time, and profits reached astronomical proportions. In the years 1870–72 the *Vienna Bank Society* paid annual dividends of 27, 40, and 80 percent; the average clear profit for capital investment for the take-off period (*Gründerepoche*) was 14 to 22 percent. Then,

66. *Jahresbericht* 1873–74, p. 3; 1874–75, pp. 3–6. The percentage is based on information in the student newspaper, which indicates that the student body numbered about 5,000. *Alma Mater Organ für Hochschulen,* ed. Max Breitenstein, Jg. 2, p. 309.

in May of 1873, the inevitable crash occurred. On May 8th alone, one hundred firms declared themselves insolvent, initiating a financial crisis of the first order.[67]

The cry of official corruption had been raised by the *Wiener Tagblatt* in 1870, long before the crash, but with the financial collapse public outrage reached the point where even the Austrian Parliament was forced to act. Its investigation disclosed the insubstantial basis of the previous boom and also led eventually to legal action against one of the more successful entrepreneurs, the Ritter von Ofenheim. Ofenheim had made his fortune as the general director of the shoddily built Lemberg-Czernowitz Railroad, and when his criminal trial finally began on 4 January 1875, it assumed profound symbolic significance as a trial of the social, economic, and moral system which had produced him.[68] In his final summation and address to the jury, the state prosecutor Graf Lamezan drew attention to this larger significance. He declared, "Today the gentlemen of the jury must decide between two extremes, between the . . . people on the one side, and the defenders of material interests on the other. . . . It must be decided whether it is possible that, in the sphere of material transactions, of trade and commerce, certain basic principles of ethics and morality are valid."[69] Ofenheim replied to the argument that his actions were immoral with the contemptuous remark that "one cannot build railroads with moral aphorisms."[70]

On 27 February 1875 the jury found him innocent, and the following morning the *Neue Freie Presse,* the voice of Austrian liberalism, expressed its delight at this outcome: "The people's court has spoken, spoken as was to be expected by impartial men. . . . They have given back to his family, back to his enterprises, a bold, important, intellectually well-endowed entrepreneur, who was led from a glittering position in life into prison, into the prisoner's dock." After noting that Ofenheim's conviction would have implicated every government from that of Schmerling to the current one—the entire governmental history of Austrian liberalism—the

67. Richard Charmatz, *Oesterreichs innere Geschichte von 1848 bis 1907* (Leipzig, 1909), vol. 1, p. 118.

68. Ibid., pp. 118–19.

69. *N.F.P.* (17 Feb. 1875), p. 8.

70. Charmatz, *Innere Geschichte,* p. 119.

Presse commended the jury for its "rare political tact" (28 February 1875). Two days later (2 March) the paper condemned those who failed to accept the jury's conclusion by appealing to a higher morality: "Was this trial initiated because of a crime against the moral law? Does this 'higher morality,' then, belong to the competence of law and justice? So far as we know there is no earthly tribunal for crimes against the moral law."

Nonetheless, many felt that if indeed Ofenheim were innocent of any formal crime, this cast discredit not on the men who had falsely accused him but on the legal system which found it impossible to condemn activities that seemed so flagrantly immoral. The clear involvement of ministers and parliamentary deputies in the Ofenheim affair only made the situation more scandalous. One of the most prominent liberal personalities of the day, the former Interior Minister Dr. Karl Giskra, was compromised seriously enough to incur banishment from the imperial court, and several months after the conclusion of the trial the Minister of Trade, Dr. Anton Banhans, found it necessary to resign.[71]

These events had an immediate impact on members of the Leseverein. From its establishment the society had existed in an uneasy relationship with the ideals and practices of Austrian liberalism. The dedication of its members to German nationalism in particular, and to a certain extent their interest in the social question, represented political tendencies which alarmed many liberals, and in the dispute concerning the celebration of the German victory over France their nationalism had led to a direct conflict with the government. In spite of these points of friction, however, it is also clear that until the Ofenheim scandal the Leseverein continued to seek support from the same social and financial system on which their liberal elders relied. During the first year of its existence the largest benefactor of the society was Victor Adler's father, who, during the years when the Telynen were meeting in his house to discuss socialism, was busy amassing a substantial fortune in real estate and the stock market.[72] Another much less scrupulous member of liberalism's monied elite who found his way into the society's membership lists by means of a substantial contribution was none other than Victor

71. Ibid., p. 119.
72. Braunthal, *Victor und Friedrich Adler*, p. 14.

Ritter von Ofenheim.[73] In the Society's fourth yearly report this name, along with another which represented similar interests, S. M. von Rothschild, disappeared from the membership rolls, and the report declared, "Hopefully, those days in which our society had to seek its support in distant circles are forever past."[74] The society's horror at having enjoyed the benefits of this tainted money served to encourage an increased militancy in its opposition to liberalism from this time forward.

The full depth of moral indignation aroused in members of the Leseverein by the Ofenheim affair can be seen in an address delivered to the society by Dr. Johannes Volkelt, a young philosophy professor who had recently become closely associated with the Pernerstorfer circle.[75] Volkelt, who by 1875 had already published works on Hegel, Schopenhauer, and Eduard von Hartmann, gave his lecture on "Kant's Categorical Imperative and the Present" less than two weeks after Ofenheim's acquittal, and it began with a straightforward presentation of Kant's basic position. In discussing Kant's theory of knowledge, however, Volkelt gave heavy emphasis to the idea that because the mind of the perceiving individual shapes all perception, it is impossible to know the true nature of the thing-in-itself. Because Kant set limits on what was accessible to understanding, Volkelt concluded that the knowing subject was nowhere on firm ground, either in observing the outer material world or the inner subjective world.[76] Volkelt then drew attention to the profound contrast which he felt existed between this subjective, uncertain knowledge and the feeling of solidity conveyed by Kant's moral code. Above all Volkelt stressed the strict demands which Kantian ethics made upon the individual (pp. 7–11): "You see, then, that Kant does not make the following of the moral law easy for men. He is of the sternest severity in the separation of moral action from all motives of desire and

73. *Jahresbericht* 1873–74, p. 15.

74. Ibid., 1874–75, p. 4.

75. See *N.F.P.* (3 Jan. 1926), p. 21. This relationship seems to have been quite close, for even though Volkelt left Vienna for Jena before the fall of 1875, contacts were maintained through visits and correspondence. For example, when Adler learned in 1881 that his friend Karl Kautsky was planning to go to Jena to complete work on his doctorate, he wrote to Volkelt requesting that he do whatever he could to help Kautsky. (Victor Adler, *Briefwechsel mit August Bebel und Karl Kautsky,* ed. Friedrich Adler, Vienna 1954, p. 5.)

76. Johannes Volkelt, *Kants kategorischer Imperativ und die Gegenwart* (Vienna, 1875), pp. 5–7. This work will henceforth be cited as *Kategorischer Imperativ.*

dislike." Kant's idea of virtue did not involve calm, cheerful development, but a constant struggle against desire and inclination; and the reward for the successful pursuit of such a struggle was the autonomy of the individual: "Thus once again: duty for the sake of duty! Insofar as man has the capability for this, he is absolute, and can be compared with nothing in the world of appearances" (pp. 13–14).

Having emphasized the stringent nature of Kantian ethics, Volkelt went on to contrast this upright integrity with the attitude of contemporary society, which centered its interests around the word *bequem* (comfortable). He felt that the progress of science and technology had made man soft and dependent: "You see, we live in a time of generalized upholsterization [*Auspolsterung*]." Volkelt then traced the consequences of this comfortable ethical code in private and public life. He contrasted the idea that monetary reward should stand in direct relation to work accomplished, with the attitude of Dr. Karl Giskra, "the defender of the frivolous 'theory of tipping' " (p. 16). The former Interior Minister, who a few years earlier had been regarded as one of liberalism's brightest hopes, had casually admitted accepting an enormous gratuity from Ofenheim with the explanation that in Austria it was customary to accept tips,[77] and by mentioning his name in this context Volkelt not only transformed his philosophical discussion into direct political commentary but also focused the immense moral indignation aroused by the Ofenheim scandal on the liberal order which allowed men like Ofenheim and Giskra to thrive.

Arguing that the frivolous, comfortable spirit conveyed by the German word for tip—*Trinkgeld* (literally drinking money) dominated all phases of contemporary culture, Volkelt directed the remainder of his address to a corrosive analysis of the various facets of that culture. The same kind of superficial mind that busied itself with brochures and elegant feuilletons also supported a theater life dominated by the light and inconsequential. "What are pieces of the Offenbach genre but tedious nonsensical giddy nothingness which has put on a glittering, dancing seductively charming mask?" After dealing with popular religion in a similar vein, and noting that the journalistic world could well afford to pay more attention to the Kantian principle that a man has no price, Volkelt turned his

77. Richard Charmatz, *Lebensbilder aus der Geschichte Oesterreichs* (Vienna, 1947), p. 93.

attention to the realm of business and finance. In tone and substance Volkelt's lecture had begun as a dispassionate scholarly treatise, but as its analysis of contemporary society unfolded, it developed an increasing polemical force which now reached its climax in a scathing denunciation of the business world's ethical standards. Referring to the *Börsenhelden*—those heroes of the stock exchange whose highest aim in life was the enjoyment of the greatest possible sensual pleasure—he declared, "In the eyes of these men of paper and gold, who have lost their souls in the rising and falling tides of the money market, ideality has long since been discarded from the order of the day; morality is regarded as something purely conventional, something manufactured from social considerations." How could one expect men of this stamp to understand when people took offense at the outrageously disproportionate relationship of profit to actual work? Observing that Ofenheim's acquittal was a victory for the "corruption party," Volkelt concluded,

> In the Ofenheim trial two moral worlds have collided with sharp clarity. The one is the moral viewpoint of the money crowd, the other is the newly developing morality of a future social order. The followers of this morality are united in the feeling that things cannot continue with the former motives, that something more solid, more genuine, must fill the place of that windy morality and substitute for the filthy mutual exploitation of pure egoism, something which finds its own satisfaction in labor for the common good, for an ideal beneficial to the people, to the state.

Volkelt then closed his lecture by hailing the members of the Leseverein as the bearers of this new idealistic social spirit.[78]

Two resolutions passed by the Leseverein's executive committee in the period immediately following the lecture reveal how fully the society's leadership shared Volkelt's views. First, at a special meeting on 19 March the committee decided to help pay the costs of printing the speeches delivered by Graf Lamezan, the state prosecutor in the Ofenheim trial. A week later they decided unanimously to have 1,500 copies of Volkelt's lecture printed and distributed at the society's expense.[79] Never before in its four-year history had the

78. *Kategorischer Imperativ*, pp. 17, 18, 20.
79. *Jahresbericht* 1874–75, pp. 11, 7.

Leseverein accorded anyone such an honor, and it marked the occasion by printing the lecture with an endorsement: "Since the executive committee can only accord its complete agreement to the views expressed therein, and feel that a dissemination of the lecture is desirable, it unanimously decided in its meeting of March 24 to publish this address."[80]

Volkelt's address and the Leseverein's reaction to it suggest not only the profound dissatisfaction of the society's members with the practices of the existing liberal order but also the direction in which this dissatisfaction pointed them. As Volkelt himself later described it in tracing his own political development, "From Hegel, moving through Lassalle, I had become involved in radical socialism; in addition, however, as a result of the prevailing political conditions in Austria a deutschnational tendency in my thought and feeling asserted itself more and more."[81] In his talk Volkelt had criticized the technological, ethical, philosophical, cultural, religious, political, economic, and social outlook of high capitalism, and to this all-inclusive list of denunciations the Leseverein had enthusiastically affixed its seal of approval. But Volkelt also went on to indicate, at least vaguely, possible remedies for these various cultural ills. For the economic, social, and political problems he proposed a kind of idealistic collectivism as an alternative to the materialistic individualism of the classical liberal. He assumed that wages and profits should stand in a direct relationship to work accomplished and that the individual should derive his primary satisfaction from a conviction that his work was of value to society as a whole. It should be noted that Volkelt says he arrived at this position of "radical socialism" through the works of Ferdinand Lassalle, a theorist whose ideas were particularly influential in the pre-Marxian stage of Austrian socialism. Although the Leseverein had manifested a certain concern with the social question from the time of its establishment, the enthusiasm with which it now endorsed Volkelt's full-fledged attack on capitalism indicates that the moral indictment of liberalism, represented by the Ofenheim scandal, had produced a

80. *Kategorischer Imperativ,* p. 3.

81. Johannes Volkelt, "Mein philosophischer Entwicklungsgang," *Die deutsche Philosophie der Gegenwart in Selbstdarstellung,* ed. Raymund Schmidt (Leipzig, 1921), p. 205. Volkelt indicates that his introduction to socialism occurred while he was in Vienna; he left Vienna late in 1875. This article will henceforth be cited as "Entwicklungsgang."

definite radicalization in the society's social, economic and political outlook.

While Volkelt's all-embracing critique of liberal culture explicitly drew attention to what he regarded as its unhealthy commitment to materialism, his philosophical introduction to this critique carried subtle implications of an even more basic questioning of liberal assumptions. This can be seen in a certain undertone of irrationalism which manifested itself in Volkelt's treatment of Kant's theory of knowledge. While Kant had found scientific certainty in his theory that man's knowledge of the outer world was shaped and conditioned in a predictable fashion by the forms of human perception, Volkelt emphasized that nonetheless man's knowledge of a thing did not correspond with the reality of the thing-in-itself. Where Kant found satisfaction in the theory that all perceptual distortion was predictably uniform, Volkelt stressed the fact that the distortion did exist. Volkelt did not explicitly develop this distrust of conscious perception; he merely drew attention to this degree of uncertainty as a contrast to the certainty and assurance of Kantian ethics. Nonetheless his distrust of the products of reason did find expression in his belief that scientific and technological advances were sources of moral corruption. In his autobiographical essay, Volkelt later wrote (p. 205) of his attitude during this period: "I was powerfully impressed with the right of *Phantasie* to the direction of life." While the German Phantasie means imagination, it also conveys many of the irrational connotations of the English word fantasy.

Volkelt's speech thus provides the first tentative indication that the Leseverein was beginning to question the strict rationalism so basic to the liberal outlook. By connecting scientific rationalism and technology with the moral laxity revealed in the Ofenheim scandal, Volkelt seemed to suggest that scientific rationalism itself might share in the disgrace, and the subsequent history of the Leseverein indicates that many members of the society accepted this implication. The ultimate effect of the Ofenheim scandal on the development of the Leseverein thus seems to have been to transmute its dissatisfaction with certain specific liberal policies into almost total opposition to the values of liberal culture; and during the next three years of the society's existence this opposition was to find important encouragement in the ideas of Wagner and Nietzsche.

2. Nietzsche as Educator

Although Johannes Volkelt had described the Ofenheim scandal as the collision of two moral worlds, the world of the bourgeois entrepreneur and the still undeveloped morality of a future social order, the intellectual shape of the new world view which he saw developing within the Leseverein was still unclear at the time of his speech in 1875. While such positive features as idealism and social consciousness had become visible, the negative elements contributed by the rebellion against liberal ideals still predominated. During the final three years of the Leseverein's existence, from 1875 to 1878, its new *Weltanschauung* (world view) began to take on more substance as the members of the Pernerstorfer circle first explored and then expounded the theories of Nietzsche and Wagner. As the ideas of these thinkers helped to crystallize many of the inchoate intellectual tendencies of both the circle and the Leseverein, they also increased the impetus to radical action aimed at the realization of this emerging order.

In a 1926 *Neue Freie Presse* article entitled "Einiges über Nietzsche," Volkelt told how he became acquainted with Nietzsche's work. "It was in 1875 when I first heard Nietzsche's name mentioned in a meaningful way by Victor Adler, with whom I cultivated a stimulating association in Vienna at that time. He said that I must thoroughly read Nietzsche's works; that this would be an extraordinary experience for me." Volkelt followed this advice and discovered in the *Birth of Tragedy* and *Untimely Observations* what he described as a new world "in which profundity and magnificence of spirit appeared united, and the unprecedented daring of an iconoclastic thinker struggled against the spirit of the time."[1] Both Adler's warm recommendation of Nietzsche and Volkelt's enthusiastic response reflect the extraordinary impact of the philosopher's work on the outlook of the Telynen. Of all the thinkers who attracted their interest, none exercised a more powerful influence on their development than he.

1. *N.F.P.* (3 Jan. 1926), p. 21.

The Nietzsche who so inspired the Telynen was not by and large the Nietzsche most familiar today, for the modern reader tends to think first of the late Nietzsche of *Zarathustra* or the *Genealogy of Morals*, the Nietzsche who repudiated many of the ideas he had expressed earlier in *Untimely Observations* and the *Birth of Tragedy*. While there are sparks of the late Nietzsche's antisystematic aphoristic quality in these early works, nonetheless they are still dominated by the systematic and comprehensive metaphysical structure presented in Schopenhauer's *World as Will and Idea.* In these early works Nietzsche stands in an intellectual relationship to Schopenhauer not unlike that of the early Marx to Hegel; in both cases the "disciples" revolutionized their inherited metaphysical systems by bringing them down to earth and grounding them in the experiences of real life. In Nietzsche's case, however, the real overturning of Schopenhauer's system proceeded slowly and was completed only after his break with Wagner in the late 1870s. By that time the common intellectual outlook developed by the Telynen, and more specifically their interpretation of Nietzsche, had largely been formed, and while individual members of the circle did subsequently read and appreciate certain of Nietzsche's later works, they also tended to interpret them within the more systematic framework of the early Nietzsche.[2]

In 1875, when student disgust at public corruption had been greatly intensified by the Ofenheim scandal, what the Telynen found in Nietzche was a thinker who seemed to offer not only an explanation for the debasement of contemporary culture but also an alternative set of cultural values. He echoed many of the themes which had attracted them to the teachers of the Schottengymnasium as well as to scholars such as Stein, Rokitansky, and Meynert, but he went much farther then these men in that he evoked an image of a vital and coherent culture which could provide a model for overcoming the cultural malaise confronting the circle.

In both its rebellious mood and its artistic approach, Nietzsche's first great work, *The Birth of Tragedy from the Spirit of Music*, spoke directly to the intellectual needs of the Pernerstorfer circle. The drawing which Nietzsche chose to adorn the title page of the book indicates how fully he shared the revolutionary aspirations of these

2. See chapters 4 and 5.

young men; it depicted the unbound Prometheus—his defiant gaze directed upward toward the gods who had imprisoned him, his foot resting triumphantly on the eagle which has been their instrument of torture. In his preface to Richard Wagner, Nietzsche expressed the hope that this image would convey the extreme urgency of his message and, as he went on to make clear, this message directly concerned the culture of his time: "Upon a serious perusal of the essay my readers should become aware with a sting of surprise that I have been grappling with a crucial German issue—an issue situated at the very center of German hopes and aspirations."[3] Since the subject matter of his book concerned Greek tragedy, Nietzsche expected many of his readers to be shocked that such importance should be attributed to an aesthetic topic, "especially if they are in the habit of looking at art merely as a merry diversion, a light carillon sounding on the edges of earnest pursuits." Nietzsche firmly rejected any such light view of art and maintained indeed that art was the highest human task, the true metaphysical activity, and that it played a central role in the processes of cultural growth and decay which he saw as the essence of historical development.

While both the aesthetic approach and the Promethean mood of Nietzsche's work echoed the outlook which the Telynen had begun to develop in their Gymnasium days, the substance of the philosopher's arguments went far beyond the circle's previous position in developing a coherent intellectual framework for a critique of liberal culture. Nietzsche began by raising the problem of the origins of Greek drama; and in suggesting that it had evolved from religious ritual he indicated the basis of his approach to Greek culture as a whole, including politics and philosophy as well as art. Nietzsche argued that Greek religion was dominated by two very different kinds of worship—that of the Olympian gods represented by Apollo, and that of the mystery cults centering on the figure of Dionysos. The Olympian deities embodied above all the ideal of "luxuriant, triumphant *existence*" and to Nietzsche, working within the philosophical framework established by Kant and Schopenhauer, this necessarily implied a preoccupation with concrete phenomenal

3. Friedrich Nietzsche, *The Birth of Tragedy and the Genealogy of Morals,* trans. Francis Golffing (New York, 1956), p. 16. To avoid an ambiguity I have restored the original "German" in "deutscher Hoffnungen" from Golffing's "our hopes."

reality in all its particularity. Apollo also represented the plastic arts of image and symbol, the arts which Schopenhauer believed to be closely tied to phenomenal reality (*Birth of Tragedy,* pp. 22, 26). The mystery cult of Dionysos, on the other hand, represented a foreign, Asian influence which had made itself felt in Greek life at various times in the past. In contrast to the intellectual restraint with which the Olympians were venerated, the worship of Dionysos involved an orgiastic outpouring of emotion in which the revelers lost their individual identities in a pantheistic unity of feeling (p. 23):

> Not only does the bond between man and man come to be forged once more by the magic of the Dionysiac rite, but nature itself, long alienated or subjugated, rises again to celebrate the reconciliation with her prodigal son, man. . . . Now that the gospel of universal harmony is sounded each individual becomes not only reconciled to his fellow but actually at one with him—as though the veil of Maya had been torn apart and there remained only shreds floating before the vision of mystical Oneness. Man now expresses himself through song and dance as the member of a higher community.

The unity of the religious celebrants found its primary artistic expression in music, the art which Schopenhauer distinguished from all others as a direct expression of the undifferentiated will.

Nietzsche argued that these two very different religious traditions had co-existed in varying relationships over a long period of Greek history, and that the greatest periods of Greek culture were those in which the two forces had been in dialectical balance (pp. 25–26). Thus in the greatest dramas of Aeschylus and Sophocles the essence of Dionysian wisdom concerning man's perpetual unity with, and alienation from, nature found expression in tragic Apollonian myth. Nietzsche also saw the political form of Greek life as a product of this delicate balance of Dionysian emotion and Apollonian cultural forces. While Dionysian emotion was basically alien to political instinct in that it ultimately led the individual to abandon particular worldly concerns for contemplation of the mystic Oneness, Apollo, on the other hand, was the founder of states and the genius of the principle of individuation governing earthly life. The implicit danger of the latter force lay in the threat of a completely secularized political culture, a danger which Nietzsche believed had been realized in the Roman Empire. In Greece during the great age of the Persian wars, however, the forces had been properly balanced and the mystic community of the Dionysian rite provided the spiritual center for the political community of the Greek city state. "Placed between India and Rome, and tempted to choose one solution or the other, the Greeks managed a classically pure third mode of existence" (p. 125). In its great age, then, the Greek city state had realized the ideal of community and had celebrated this delicate synthesis in the tragedies of Aeschylus and Sophocles.

To Nietzsche the breakdown of this synthesis and the accompanying "degeneration of the Greek national character" indicated "how inextricably bound up with one another are art and the people, myth and custom, tragedy and the commonwealth" (p. 138). He believed that the works of Euripides marked the point at which classic Greek culture began to decline; and in discussing this process of degeneration, he demonstrated the relevance of his theory to the problems of his own time. According to Nietzsche, Euripides intended to "eliminate from tragedy the primitive and pervasive Dionysiac element, and to rebuild the drama on a foundation of non-Dionysiac art, custom and philosophy." However, in his unsuccessful pursuit of the ideal of pure Apollonian contemplation, Euripides himself masked the "brand-new demon called Socrates" (pp. 76–77). To Nietzsche, Socrates symbolized the spirit of scientific rationalism which brought about the destruction of ancient Greek culture through its opposition to the Dionysian spirit. Nietzsche saw the pernicious influence of Socratic rationalism—the chief characteristic of what he called Alexandrian culture—extending from the time of the ancient Greeks into his own day: "our whole modern world is caught in the net of Alexandrian culture and recognizes as its ideal the man of theory equipped with the highest cognitive powers, working in the service of science, and whose archetype and progenitor is Socrates." Alexandrian culture, opposing Dionysian wisdom, sought to dissolve myth, and worshiped a "god of engines and crucibles" (pp. 108–09). Nietzsche also criticized the optimism and faith in progress which characterized the Socratic-Alexandrian culture of his time. He believed that even though an Alexandrian culture needed a slave class to exist permanently, its optimism forced it to prate about the dignity of man and the nobility of labor, thus preparing the way for its own destruction through the aroused indignation of this class (p. 110).

Nietzsche believed that Kant and Schopenhauer had taken the first steps in exposing the basic weakness of contemporary culture, for Kant had shown the limits of reason and logic while Schopenhauer had exposed the hollowness of optimism (p. 111). It was from another source, however, that he expected the regeneration of modern culture to come: "Out of the Dionysiac recesses of the German soul has sprung a power which has nothing in common with the presuppositions of Socratic culture" (p. 119), and this power, the musical tradition of Bach, Beethoven, and Wagner, would reverse the process of degeneration by awakening the Dionysian spirit in the modern world. He thought that German music could restore the forces responsible for the greatness of ancient Greek culture for "music is capable of giving birth to myth, . . . and above all, to tragic myth, which is a parable of Dionysiac knowledge" (p. 101). Myth provided the creative natural power of any healthy culture and only in tragic myth could the Dionysian and Apollonian spirits interact creatively (p. 136). "To understand tragic myth we must see it as Dionysiac wisdom made concrete through Apollonian artifice. In that myth the world of appearance is pushed to its limits, where it denies itself and seeks to escape back into the world of primordial reality" (p. 132).

In the closing portion of his study, Nietzsche turned to the work of Richard Wagner to show how music and tragic myth could combine to evoke both Dionysos and Apollo. He saw in Wagner's *Tristan und Isolde* a rhythmic movement between a Dionysian music which brought the listener close to a submergence in the universal will and an Apollonian myth which "bent upon reconstituting the nearly shattered individual, asserts itself, proffering the balm of a delightful illusion." He argued that "the parable of myth saves us from the direct intuition of the cosmic idea, as idea and word save us from the undammed pouring forth of the unconscious will" (pp. 127–28). By means of this dialectical interaction within Wagner's opera, Apollonian art was forced to transcend itself in the attainment of Dionysian wisdom: "Dionysos speaks the language of Apollo, but Apollo, finally, the language of Dionysos; thereby the highest goal of tragedy and of art in general is reached" (p. 131).

By discussing the development of Greek tragedy in terms of an interaction of all-encompassing cultural forces, and by suggesting the relevance of this cultural dialectic to the contemporary problems of the German nation, Nietzsche's work offered the Telynen powerful reinforcement in their revolt against the values of their time. It held out the prospect of a restoration of that sense of community the members of the circle had learned to value as students at the Schottengymnasium when they studied the *Nibelungenlied*, so the circle had every reason to accept Nietzsche's theory that cultural coherence depended on the vitality of the artistic-religious forces inherent in Germanic myth. Nietzsche's work thus provided a coherent philosophical framework for a cultural ideal radically opposed to that of Austrian liberalism with its faith in progress and scientific rationalism. In Nietzsche's view this faith had destroyed the mythic foundations of ancient culture and produced a contemporary civilization wracked by the division and fragmentation implicit in the nature of scientific reason. To overcome this malaise, he exhorted his readers to "hold fast to our luminous guides the Greeks. It is from them that we have borrowed, for the purification of our aesthetic notions the twin divine images, each of whom governs his own realm" (p. 138). To the Telynen, already steeped in the classical education of their Gymansium, this ideal of the pre-Socratic Greek community exercised a powerful attraction which was to shape their thoughts and actions for years to come.

In the preface to his *Birth of Tragedy,* Nietzsche paid homage to Richard Wagner as the "sublime protagonist" of his work, and this recognition of Wagner as the leader of the crusade for German cultural rebirth was widely accepted among student circles. Even though Nietzsche's writings offered a much more lucid and powerful exposition of the movement's basic tenets, the words of the Master—as expressed in essays on the widest variety of topics as well as in his ambitious operatic dramas—always carried a greater weight of authority. To cultivate a wider public appreciation of Wagner's art and to ensure a proper understanding of his theories, the Viennese followers of the composer established the Vienna Academic Wagner Society in 1873. Victor Adler joined the society the following year and took part in its first mass pilgrimage to Bayreuth in 1876.[4] Al-

4. *Zweiter Jahres-Bericht des Wiener Akademischen Wagner-Verein für das Jahr 1874* (Vienna, 1874), p. 55. These reports will henceforth be cited as *Wagner-Verein* followed by the year of the report. Adler to Pernerstorfer, 27 Aug. 1872, Adler Archiv.

though most members of the Pernerstorfer circle eventually joined the Wagner Society the organization never became the primary focus of the circle's activities—even when those activities centered around Wagnerian causes.

Nonetheless the society did much to popularize Wagner's works among the Viennese, and in lieu of an official organ for the movement (a lack filled in 1878 with the appearance of the *Bayreuther Blätter*) the yearly reports of the society helped to explain important facets of Wagnerian ideology to the faithful. In the report for 1874, the year Adler joined, the society published a study entitled "Richard Wagner and German Art," by Camillo Sitte, a well-known architect and city planner. This essay provides a good illustration of the way in which Wagnerites believed the regenerative forces Nietzsche saw at work in Wagner's operas could be used to illuminate and overcome the deficiencies of their own culture. Sitte argued that most contemporary works of art either reproduced the natural world with the greatest possible photographic accuracy or conveyed rational precepts through naked allegory. In either case they failed to stir the emotions. Sitte wrote of this kind of art:

> Gradually it has moved ever further from its home and has become a subordinate element of scholarship. It no longer mightily arouses pure feeling; it no longer fills the heart [*Gemüth*] with sweet and also powerful emotions, but rather it engages the cold, calculating and dissecting [*trennenden*] reason; it provides illustrations to the textbook of science and history.[5]

In this criticism of the disintegrated art of contemporary culture, Sitte focused his attention on its failure to engage the whole man, and in so doing he echoed the important Wagnerian doctrine of wholeness (*Ganzheit*). In "The Art Work of the Future" (1849), Wagner had declared that any attempt to express the highest and the truest would necessarily involve the man of understanding united with the man of heart and the man of body. This wholeness of human character would yield a greater unity of mankind as a species and ultimately a unity of the totality of nature. The ideal of wholeness also lay behind the Wagnerian *Gesamtkunstwerk* (the unified work of art) which would appeal to the unified man. Politically, the doctrine

5. Camillo Sitte, "Richard Wagner und die deutsche Kunst," *Wagner-Verein,* 1874, p. 15.

of wholeness expressed itself as nationalism, for Wagner believed that the nation was the natural unit within which man could find unity with his fellow man. Sitte made it clear that the new art would revolve about a national hero; "The focus of this German art work of the future cannot be Apollo, the *beautiful* man, nor Christ the *suffering* man, but only Siegfried, the *strong* man." Such a figure would be "an embodiment of the essence and aspiration of the whole nation. The whole nation would again find itself ideally embodied in this one."[6]

As expounded by Nietzsche and Sitte, the Wagnerian credo reveals itself to be a full-blown ideology with a reasonably coherent philosophic structure and a well-developed political, social, and cultural program. It drew together various ideas traditionally associated with German romanticism and incorporated them into an outlook which seemed to offer an answer to the divisions of the capitalistic industrial order accepted by most liberals. Recognizing Schopenhauer's basic truth that the essence of man's worldly existence consists in the destructive conflict of one will with another, this ideology taught that man should attempt to overcome the conflict by reconciling the opposing forces in a vital unity. From the seemingly irreconcilable dichotomy of Schopenhauer's Will and Idea it moved to the ideal of a dialectical unity of Dionysos and Apollo in which man would find wholeness on all levels of existence—psychologically in the integration of passion and intellect, aesthetically in Wagner's unity of tone and word, politically in the community of the national folk. To those who had suffered the shattering disillusionment in paternal ideals which Max Gruber described as "a piece of the cultural history" of his time, this outlook seemed to explain the inherent flaws in those ideals while holding out the emotionally satisfying prospect of a return to the community whose loss they mourned.

Thanks to the position of the Telynen within the Leseverein der deutschen Studenten, the ideas of Nietzsche and Wagner soon gained a much larger student audience than that of the Pernerstorfer circle alone. In 1875 the yearly report of the Leseverein contained a brief note thanking the Wagner Society for its support, thus indicating that contact had been established between the two groups,[7] and short-

6. Richard Wagner, *Gesammelte Schriften und Dichtungen,* ed. Wolfgang Golther (Berlin, n.d.), vol. 3, p. 66. This work will hereafter be referred to as *Schriften.* Sitte, "Richard Wagner," pp. 20, 21.

7. *Jahresbericht* 1874–75, p. 8.

ly thereafter the first formal discussion of Nietzsche's work took place in the Leseverein. The subject was the second of Nietzsche's *Untimely Observations, On the Uses and Disadvantages of History,* and the discussion leaders were Victor Adler and Joseph Paneth, a man who later formed close friendships with both Nietzsche and Sigmund Freud.[8] Unfortunately no evidence remains to indicate the actual course the discussion followed, but the nature of the subject reveals much in itself. Nietzsche's *Uses and Disadvantages of History* directed far more attention to contemporary problems than had his earlier works, but the basic outlook was close to that expressed in the *Birth of Tragedy.* Nietzsche criticized contemporary culture for an excess of scientific, scholarly reason, while ridiculing the liberal faith in history, progress, and justice. Again he advanced the theory that this culture could be regenerated only by replacing the one-sided faith in reason with a concern for both reason and feeling.[9]

This lecture on Nietzsche and the discussion which followed had important consequences for the Pernerstorfer circle. As Pernerstorfer related many years later, "In the debate a very young and unprepossessing [*unansehnlich*] young man who came forward to speak immediately arrested the entire audience with the suggestive power of his words." The young man, Siegfried Lipiner, almost immediately became an important member of the circle.[10] Since art was central to the Nietzschean outlook, and since Lipiner could claim to be both an artist and a master of Nietzsche's philosophy, he spoke with considerable authority during the next few years as the circle set out to realize the goals of that philosophy.

Although not yet twenty years old, Lipiner began his artistic career in 1876 with the publication in book form of his dramatic poem *The Unbound Prometheus,* the first of several attempts to inspire the Promethean revolt envisioned in Nietzsche's *Birth of Tragedy.* Indeed certain parts of the poem, such as Prometheus' encounter with Pure Learning (one of the characters who speake for the values Prometheus rejects), were little more than versifications of Nietzsche's

8. Engelbert Pernerstorfer "Siegfried Lipiner," *Zeitschrift des Oesterreichischen Vereines für Bibliothekswesen* (Vienna, 1912), vol. 3, p. 122. This article will henceforth be cited "Lipiner."

9. Friedrich Nietzsche, *Gesammelte Werke,* Musarionausgabe (Munich, 1922), vol. 6, pp. 239, 284–85. This edition will henceforth be cited as *Werke.*

10. "Lipiner," p. 122. For Siegfried Lipiner (1856–1911) see Hartmut von Hartungen, *Der Dichter Siegfried Lipiner 1856–1911* (Munich, 1932).

cultural critique. Where the philosopher had said of learning, "It is cold and dry, it has no love and knows nothing of a deep feeling of dissatisfaction and longing,"[11] Lipiner's Pure Learning boasts that learning "teaches *observation*. That is true life. It is healthy and cold, and it stills the hot passions of the sick heart."[12] Where Nietzsche had warned against the misuse of the historical outlook in declaring, "We require it [history] for life and action, not for comfortable withdrawal from life and action,"[13] Lipiner's Pure Learning inquires, "Sir, don't you know the viewpoint? You must observe all this *historically*. Then you will be calm and postpone action."[14] Small wonder that on reading the poem Nietzsche should say, "It is as if I met my elevated and apotheosized self in it."[15]

However slight the aesthetic merit of Lipiner's poem, its emphasis on the need to move from scholarly abstraction to a passionate activism accurately reflects the mood of the Pernerstorfer circle at this stage of its history, and it was after Lipiner's admission to the circle that its impact on the intellectual life of university students reached its height. Pernerstorfer spoke without exaggeration in claiming that "for the Viennese student body of that day, this circle was an intellectually vital center of a unique sort,"[16] and the focus of its activity in the 1876–78 period was a new *Rede Klub* (Discussion Society) formed within the Leseverein. Although it had begun to function in 1876, the club formally organized itself in March 1877 when Max Gruber and Victor Adler became its principal officers.[17] The club's

11. Nietzche, *Werke,* vol. 7, p. 99.

12. Siegfried Lipiner, *Der entfesselte Prometheus* (Leipzig, 1876), pp. 47–48. This work will henceforth be cited as *Prometheus.*

13. Nietzsche, *Werke,* vol. 6, p. 229.

14. Lipiner, *Prometheus,* p. 49.

15. *Friedrich Nietzsches Gesammelte Briefe,* ed. Elisabeth Förster-Neitzsche and Fritz Schöll (Berlin, 1902), vol. 2, p. 538. This work will henceforth be cited as *Briefe.*

16. "Lipiner," p. 122.

17. This is suggested by the list of topics and speakers provided by the yearly report on the discussion evenings. Thie first five evenings from 18 Dec. 1876, to 17 March 1877 were devoted to a wide variety of economic, educational, legal, and more general topics; and none of the speakers listed was a member of the Pernerstorfer circle (*Jahresbericht* 1876–77, p. 29). Then, on 21 March the Rede Klub elected its officers, and in the following discussion evening (7 April) Max Gruber spoke on "The Nature and Goal of the Rede Klub," and Victor Adler gave a talk entitled, "On the Newest Phenomena in the Life of our Organization" (*Jahresbericht* 1876–77, p. 29). Since it would certainly be appropriate for the officers to discuss such topics on the occasion of the club's formal establishment, it seems quite probable that Gruber and Adler were indeed the principal officers.

statement of aims and ideals was printed in the Leseverein's annual report, and it clearly shows the influence of the Wagnerian-Nietzschean attack on pure learning *(Wissenschaft)*. Noting the formation of the discussion section, the report declared, "The goal of such a body cannot be that of giving some facile learned addresses to which even more learned [*wissenschaftlichere*] discussions are appended. This will not suffice for a serious effort [*Streben*]." The report also echoed Nietzsche's plea for the reconciliation of learning with "life." "In these lectures learning will always be used with regard and reference to life." The Rede Klub delineated three areas of primary concern. The first included matters immediately affecting student life; the second embraced historical-social topics. The report declared, "We are citizens of a state, we are members of a race [*stamm*] for whose welfare we must work." The third area of concern was philosophy. "Philosophy is the common ground on which all fields of learning stand, from which they must take their limitations and certainty. It presses ever more mightily to the service of the ideal and promotes unity between knowledge and action." The aims of the Rede Klub thus suggested that the traditional concerns of the Leseverein would now be approached with a Nietzschean-Wagnerian distrust of pure learning.[18]

After completing its formal organization with a discussion of aims and ideals led by Adler and Gruber, the Rede Klub devoted three of the year's four remaining sessions to Wagnerian topics, concluding with a report by Lipiner on the third of Nietzsche's *Untimely Observations, Schopenhauer as Educator*—a work which ultimately had the effect of bringing the members of the Pernerstorfer circle into an entirely new relationship with the philosopher.[19] In this essay Nietzsche remained within the framework of cultural criticism he had developed in his *Birth of Tragedy,* but he went much farther in his criticism of contemporary institutions and in his discussion of how those who accepted the Wagnerian-Nietzschean ideology should act to realize the aim of cultural regeneration. The work thus bore directly on the Rede Klub's ideal of uniting knowledge with action.

18. Ibid., pp. 5, 6; although subsequent discussion topics indicate that student affairs were discussed, the nature of the questions involved is not revealed.

19. Ibid., p. 29; the other Wagnerian lectures involved two talks by Guido Adler entitled "Bayreuth 1876."

In *Schopenhauer as Educator,* Nietzsche placed somewhat greater emphasis than before on the economic weaknesses of the existing order, but as before, he saw this as part of a larger cultural development. "The waters of religion are receding, leaving behind swamps and stagnant pools. . . . The sciences, pursued without measure and in a blind laissez-faire spirit, are disrupting and dissolving all firm beliefs; states and the educated classes are carried along by a contemptible economic system."[20] He argued, "Nowadays almost everything is determined by the crudest and the worst forces, by the egotism of the money-makers and the military despots. The state, in the hands of the latter, makes the attempt, as does the egotism of the money makers, to organize everything anew from itself outward." Nietzsche foresaw a destructive but inevitable "atomistic revolution," the expectation of which, along with "the greedy exploitation of the moment, bring out every form of cowardice and selfish drive of the soul." In substance, tone, and language Nietzsche's analysis closely resembled that embodied in Volkelt's speech to the Leseverein at the height of the Ofenheim scandal, but Nietzsche was far more specific than Volkelt in suggesting a means for combating the evils of his time. He spoke of the need for inspiring "images of man" which would move the individual to transcend his base motivations for a more noble ideal, and he held up Schopenhauer's life as an example of such a noble image (pp. 39–40). The importance of these noble images to Nietzsche's outlook is seen in his assertion: "Only he who has given his heart to some great man receives the *first consecration of culture.* The sign of this is shame without self-loathing, hatred of one's own narrow and shriveled nature, sympathy with the genius who tears himself away from our dullness and dryness" (p. 61).

Both the word "consecration" and the description of the "sign" betray the spiritual nature of the individual's devotion to such a noble image, and this religious dimension was deeply rooted in Nietzsche's idea of the cultural community. In the *Birth of Tragedy,* he had explored the religious-artistic bases of the ancient Greek cultural community, and in his *Schopenhauer as Educator* he attempted to draw the consequences of this example for the contemporary individual (p. 56):

20. Friedrich Nietzsche, *Schopenhauer as Educator,* trans. James W. Hillesheim and Malcolm R. Simpson (Chicago, 1965), p. 37.

> Here I have come to the point of answering the question of whether it is possible to reach the great ideal of Schopenhauerian man through one's own regular activity. Above all, it is certain that these new duties are not the duties of the isolated individual; rather one belongs to a mighty community which is held together not by external forms and laws but by a fundamental idea. This is the fundamental idea of *culture*.

The essentially spiritual nature of Nietzsche's conception of culture can be seen not only in this capacity of drawing men together, but also in what he referred to as the "metaphysical meaning of culture" (p. 79). He argued, "Just as nature needs the philosopher, so she also needs the artist for a metaphysical purpose, namely, for her own self-enlightenment so that she may at last see as a clear and distinct image what she never sees in the flux of becoming—and thus reach self-knowledge" (p. 56). Thus, through his participation in the cultural community, man would learn to serve nature's deepest purposes.

On the individual level the cultural community would imbue its members with the desire and the strength for self-transcendence: "Everyone who possesses culture is, in fact, saying: 'I see something higher and more human than myself above me. Help me, all of you, to reach it, as I will help every person who recognizes the same thing . . . so that finally the man may again come into being who feels himself infinite in knowing and living, in seeing and ability, and who with all his being is a part of nature" (p. 61). Nietzsche's ideal of the cultural community thus demanded of the individual an almost religious devotion to the task of overcoming his own egoistic existence to achieve a measure of unity with nature and his fellow man. This idea of culture "sets but one task for each of us: *to further the production of the philosopher, of the artist and of the saint within us and outside us, and thereby to work at the consummation of nature*" (p. 56). To the extent that the cultural community could bring forth such examples of genius it would provide further impetus to self-transcendence through imitation of these noble images. The genius thus occupied a central position in Nietzsche's cultural religion, "for the genius longs more deeply for holiness because he has seen, from his watchtower, further and more clearly into the reconciliation of knowledge and being, into the realm of peace and the negated will, over to the other shore of which the Indians speak" (p. 28). Nietzsche regarded Schopenhauer as such a genius who thus could serve as educator through the example of his life as well as through his ideas.

Nietzsche's ideal of the cultural community carried a number of important implications with respect to the immediate aims of those who shared his outlook. He had spoken of the first consecration of culture in which the individual devoted himself to some noble image of man, and he envisioned the possibility of an institution to further the work of the consecrated. "They themselves want, by means of a strong organization, to prevent themselves from being swept away and dispersed by the crowd. . . . These individuals must complete their work—that is the reason for their cohesiveness; and all who take part in the institution shall be concerned, through a continual purification and mutual care, with the birth of the genius and the fruition of his work" (p. 81). The community of the consecrated would answer the inner cry of men everywhere: "Come, help, complete, combine that which belongs together! We have an immeasurable longing to become whole!" (p. 62). In addition to this inner labor of self-transcendence the individual had to go through a second consecration of culture: "Culture demands from him not only inner experience . . . but finally and chiefly, action. This means fighting for culture and being hostile to the influences, laws and institutions in which he does not recognize his goal: the production of genius" (p. 56). Throughout this work Nietzsche emphasized the ideal of uniting thought with life and action, the ideal of the heroic life of a man who "fights against very great odds for what is beneficial to all" (p. 45).

As subsequent events were to demonstrate, the members of the Pernerstorfer circle had only to read Nietzsche's work to be convinced that they were ready for membership in his new cultural community. Their own circle had provided an almost perfect preparation for the kind of institution Nietzsche envisioned. It had allowed them to shape their innermost values in opposition to those of their time while providing a basis for combating the destructive influences of contemporary life. It had fostered an "inner examination" which also profited from the work of Schopenhauer. With respect to Nietzsche's ideal "images of man"—the one aspect of his theory which had no real precedent in the discussions and activities of the circle—even here the members of the circle had received a certain amount of psychological preparation. In discussing how Schopenhauer had overcome the many difficulties besetting his life, Nietzsche had placed great emphasis on the commanding influence of Schopenhauer's father, and this emphasis was closely tied to Nietzsche's basic attitude toward Schopenhauer, for at times he went beyond the conception of his mentor as an ideal image of man to refer to him unambiguously as a father figure. At one point (p. 13) he wrote,

> Schopenhauer speaks to himself, and if one wants to imagine a listener, let him think of a son whom his father is instructing. It is sincere, firm, good-natured speaking, before a listener who listens with love. Such writers are scarce. His power and well-being envelop us from the first sound of his voice; we feel as we do when we enter an Alpine forest, we take a deep breath and suddenly feel better.

Elsewhere he speaks of Schopenhauer as "the man who promised to make only those his heirs who . . . were capable of being more than just his readers: namely, his sons and pupils" (p. 17). In these passages Nietzsche gave expression to the same deep psychological needs that drove him to idolize Wagner, and these needs were highly relevant to those members of the circle who had experienced the intense generational conflicts to which Gruber and Adler testify. Nietzsche demonstrated a good understanding of these conflicts when he concluded, "Probably at all times fathers have most strongly resisted the philosophizing of their sons, considering it to be the greatest perversion." But even though he expressed the hope that "some father will learn something from what has been said," the whole thrust of his work was to offer a father surrogate to those sons who philosophized in spite of their fathers (p. 93). While it is impossible to know how strong an influence this psychological factor exercised in the circle's enthusiastic response to Nietzsche's work, it does seem probable that it played a significant role.

Similarly, the religious aura surrounding Nietzsche's mighty community of the consecrated made it resemble nothing so much as the monastic order responsible for the early education of the Telynen, and this similarity may well have encouraged their response to Nietzsche's ideas. Just as cultural and religious forces merged in the philosopher's community, so had they also in the tradition of this Benedictine order. Just as the members of Nietzsche's community incurred the dual obligations of personal self-transcendence and social activism, so had the students of the Schottengymnasium been taught not only to strive for individual excellence in attaining the good, the true, and the beautiful, but also to work for the realization of these ideals in the outer world of politics and society. Just as Nietzsche's first consecration of culture offered the individual the reassurance of a guiding fatherly image, so in Pernerstorfer's memories of the Schottengymnasium it was the "picture of our teachers which we recall and which fills our hearts with respect and gratitude." Where Nietzsche's encounter with a fatherly Schopenhauer was like breathing the refershing air of an Alpine forest, the Schotten student Alfred von Berger had the feeling in conversations with Father Hugo Mareta or Father Sigismund Gschwandner that he breathed the air of lower Austrian pine needles, vine blossoms, and beech trees. The terrain was somewhat different, but the fatherly reassurance was essentially the same.

As a result of reading Nietzsche's work, the members of the Pernerstorfer circle at once set about preparing themselves for the first consecration of culture, and since only he who had given his heart to some great man could receive this consecration, they decided to give their hearts to Nietzsche. Lipiner sent a copy of his *Unbound Prometheus* to the philosopher, and in the summer of 1877 set out for Jena where Volkelt was able to introduce him to Nietzsche's friend Erwin Rhode. In June 1877 Rhode mentioned Lipiner in a letter to Nietzsche, referring to the "not unsympathetic, shy, sensitive, lines of his face. He is a great admirer of your writings and is a member of a Nietzsche Society in Vienna. He is tremendously enthusiastic about you and says he has sent you his book, *The Unbound Prometheus*."[21] Two months later Nietzsche replied: "Only just recently I experienced a true day of consecration through *The Unbound Prometheus*. If the author is not a veritable genius, then I no longer know what one is."[22] Nietzsche wrote Lipiner expressing his admiration, and a correspondence between the two began.

Under these favorable auspices, the members of the Pernerstorfer circle next addressed a collective letter to Nietzsche on the occasion of his birthday (18 October 1877).[23] It began, "A small band of

21. Nietzsche, *Briefe*, vol. 2, p. 535.

22. Ibid., p. 538.

23. This letter and the accompanying one from Lipiner can be found in the Lipiner-Nietzsche correspondence of the Nietzsche Nachlass, now preserved in the Goethe-Schiller Archiv in Weimar.

young men, who have long desired an opportunity to express to you their sincere respect and heartfelt gratitude, draws near you today on your birthday." After expressing their good wishes for the occasion, they continued,

> We believe we are acting entirely on your principles when, instead of trying to describe in words how deeply your writings have moved, us, we rather give you the assurance that this emotion has strengthened in each of us the firm resolve to follow you as our luminous and transporting guide, and—as far as our abilities allow—to strive like you with the most powerful will, selflessly and honestly for the realization of that ideal which you have delineated in your writings, particularly your *Schopenhauer as Educator*. We say this in full consciousness of the heavy responsibility which we thereby take upon ourselves, for none of us would endure the thought of any sort of desire or action which would make us ashamed before an image such as yours which lives within us as a mighty presence.

The image of Nietzsche would thus serve the circle's members as a spur to the hard work of self-transcendence—exactly the process the philosopher had recommended for the first consecration of culture. After further expressions of gratitude the letter concluded with the signatures of Lipiner, Max Gruber, Pernerstorfer, Victor and Sigmund Adler, and Heinrich Braun (Victor Adler's brother-in-law). In a separate personal letter accompanying the collective one, Lipiner asked Nietzsche if it pleased him and declared, "It is intended very seriously. We could have had many signatures if we had taken it less strictly." Evidently the letter did please Nietzsche, and he responded favorably to the circle. In Lipiner's next letter to the philosopher he thanked him for the "lovely words which have moved and strengthened all of us."[24] Nietzsche had apparently accepted his disciples.

Unfortunately, this success seems to have overheated Lipiner's ambitions, and his persistent attentions soon ran afoul of the deeply private strain in Nietzsche's character. After a series of unsuccessful attempts by Lipiner to induce the philosopher to spend the summer in the Austrian Saltzkammergut—with Lipiner handling all the arrangements and costs—Nietzsche's enthusiasm for the young poet

24. Lipiner to Nietzsche, 3 Nov. 1877, Nietzsche Nachlass.

began to cool noticeably.[25] By the summer of 1878 the brief relationship had ended, and Lipiner embarked on an equally tantalizing and unsuccessful effort to win the friendship of Richard Wagner.[26]

Having undergone the first consecration of culture, the members of the Pernerstorfer circle did not forget the need for the second consecration of action, and during the period of preoccupation with Nietzschean cultural theory, their primary instrument for action, the Leseverein, had attained a position of unprecedented influence within the university community and beyond. The organizational and financial stability achieved by the society during its fourth year (1874–75) provided the resources for an expanded role in student life during the following years. As the fifth annual report declared, it was the society's goal "not only to maintain and strengthen the achieved position among the student body but to prove flatly that the Leseverein was the chosen agent and representative of the German student body of the Vienna universities."[27]

One means by which the society attempted to accomplish this aim was by organizing celebrations in honor of the distinguished living German poets, and since both of the poets honored in 1876, Joseph Scheffel and Anastasius Grün, had been active in the 1848 revolution these celebrations suited the society's increased political militancy during the period following the Ofenheim scandal. Apparently the society hoped that the celebrations would excite the interest of the entire student body and attract some of the students who were not members. The first of these affairs was held on 11 February 1876, in honor of Joseph Scheffel, and it attracted almost eight hundred students; the second, held in honor of Anastasius Grün on 16 March, was attended by some two thousand students, a figure representing about 40 percent of the total student body.[28] Anastasius Grün, whose real name was Anton von Auersperg, was a man who had

25. See Lipiner to Nietzsche, 20 April 1878, Nietzsche Nachlass; and Nietzsche to his mother and sister, 13 Aug. 1878, *Briefe,* vol. 2, p. 377. Since Lipiner was himself impoverished it is difficult to understand how he could have paid Nietzche's expenses unless he hoped to get the money from the Leseverein or perhaps from Victor Adler.

26. Carl F. Glasenapp, *Das Leben Richard Wagners* (Leipzig, 1911), vol. 6, p. 143, n. 3.

27. Quoted in Hiller, "Der Leseverein der deutschen Studenten" (Vienna, 1912), p. 16.

28. Ibid., pp. 17–18. The percentage is based on figures given in the student newspaper, which indicates that the student body numbered about 5,000 at that time. *Alma Mater, Organ für Hoch-schulen,* ed. Max Breitenstein, Jg. 2, p. 309.

frequently expressed his deep faith in the mission of German culture,[29] and this faith was the main theme of the speech in his honor delivered by Pernerstorfer. As he gazed down at Vienna from the Kahlenberg, the hill where the celebration was held, Pernerstorfer was "overcome by a doleful feeling of backward-looking longing. In the distant twilight we see the Ostmark and recall its struggles, and in us the memory arises of all the German blood that has been shed for the magnificence of the German name over the course of centuries." Pernerstorfer believed these struggles demonstrated that Austria's German population was "a not entirely unworthy member of the great community." Once again Pernerstorfer gave expression to the ideal he had imbibed in the Schottengymnasium lessons on the *Nibelungenlied*—the heroic community of the German nation. Pernerstorfer hailed Grün as a poet of youth who skillfully gave realistic expression to mankind's highest ideals: "And so he is an image of the two most noble aspects which our Austrian-German branch of the nation has to show. He has always begun from nature and always finally returned to nature."[30] Here too the standards inculcated by the Benedictine fathers and developed further by Nietzsche and Wagner manifested themselves in the belief that the ideal world of art must never lose touch with the real world of nature.

Pernerstorfer also took active part in another affair in which the Leseverein was able to make itself the spokesman for the student body as a whole. This concerned the question of whether lecture fees at the university should be abolished. The government supported the abolition, while most students opposed the measure, fearing that it would damage the relationship between professors and students. The Leseverein formed an agitation committee and on 17 January 1876 Pernerstorfer led a student rally in the University Aula. The students then circulated a petition, and after obtaining 1062 signatures, sent it to the Parliament which was considering the question.[31]

By means of such activities the Leseverein was able, in large part, to achieve the position it desired as a representative of student

29. Castle, *Geschichte der deutschen Literature,* vol. 2, pp. 12, 446.

30. *Gedenkblätter zu Ehren der 70. Geburtsfeier des am 11. April 1806 geborenen vaterländischen Dichter Anastasius Grün (Anton Alexander Graf von Auersperg),* ed. Jürg Simani (Vienna, 1876), pp. 3–4. Most of the speech is given in *N. F. P.* (17 March 1876), pp. 5–6. Since both Grün and Scheffel were active in the 1848 revolutions this revolutionary precedent was probably also being implicitly honored in these celebrations.

31. Hiller, "Der Leseverein," pp. 19–20.

interests and concerns. In its subsequent annual report (for the academic year 1876–77) it spoke of itself with assurance as the "social and intellectual center of Vienna's German students,"[32] and claimed that a description of the society's activities would in itself be a sketch of the life and aspirations of Vienna's students.

One unwanted testimony to the society's success came in the form of increased opposition from the government, which late in 1876 fostered the creation of a new, patriotic German-Austrian Reading Society (*Deutsch-österreichischer Leseverein*) to compete with the German nationalist Leseverein. A new student newspaper, *Alma Mater*, was also established to lend support to the campaign against the nationalistic society.[33] Within the Leseverein der deutschen Studenten itself, one of the most prized luminaries of Viennese liberalism's salon society, Franz Brentano, spoke out against the kind of philosophy that the Pernerstorfer circle was beginning to propagate. Brentano defended the ideal of scholarly learning and argued that philosophy had profited from the influences of the natural sciences—exactly the reverse of the position taken by Schopenhauer and Nietzsche.[34] While the foes of the student movement put up a vigorous struggle in defense of their interests and ideals, they met with little success. "In spite of the constantly increasing attacks against the Leseverein and its tendencies, the society's activity increased sharply. Its membership and book collection grew; the events it sponsored were popular and excellently attended; the association with the professoriate remained an intimate one."[35]

With the solidification of its position within the university, the Leseverein also commanded considerably greater attention from beyond the boundaries of the academic community. During this sixth year of its existence (1876–77) no fewer than twelve parliamentary deputies joined the society as supporting members, and at the same time the society began to establish a particularly close relationship with Georg von Schönerer, the deputy who eventually became their most ardent champion.[36]

32. *Jahresbericht* 1876–77, p. 3.

33. Beurle, *Beiträge* pp. 37–38.

34. Franz Brentano, "Was für ein Philosoph manchmal Epoche macht," *D.Z.*(16 April 1876), pp. 1–3.

35. Hiller, p. 23. See also Beurle, p. 39.

36. *Jahresbericht* 1876–77, pp. 20–21. They were Nicolaus Dumba, Friedrich Dittes, Julius Gomperz, Georg Granitsch, Ignatz Kaiser, Max Menger, Karl Russ, Georg von

While Pernerstorfer worked through the Leseverein to encourage increased political militance within the academic community, another member of the circle, Heinrich Friedjung, carried the campaign directly into the national political arena with the publication in 1877 of his *Ausgleich mit Ungarn* (*Settlement with Hungary*), the first work to give mature expression to the circle's political outlook. Unlike most of the Telynen, Friedjung had spent the greater part of his university career in Prague and Berlin rather than Vienna, and for a time this had limited his participation in the activities of the circle. Even so, he did maintain a lively correspondence with the group, and on his return to Vienna in 1873 he resumed active participation and also joined the Leseverein.[37] Perhaps because he was academically the senior member, Friedjung had always played the role of responsible elder statesman within the group, and this may account for the fact that he failed to sign their collective letter to Nietzsche. He might well have considered this kind of hero worship demeaning to his status as a professor at Vienna's School of Commerce. Nonetheless, even though Friedjung eschewed the more cultish aspects of Nietzsche's and Wagner's crusade for cultural regeneration, his *Ausgleich* did bring the basic ideas of this movement to bear on the specific political problems of Austria, and in so doing provided the foundations for the future political activity of the Pernerstorfer circle.

The occasion for Friedjung's work was the tenth anniversary of the agreement (Ausgleich) between Austria and Hungary, one of the events that kindled the feelings of radical German nationalism which Friedjung and his friends experienced during their days at the Schottengymnasium. Since the treaty between the two halves of the Empire became subject to renegotiation at this time, Friedjung called for a reversal of what he saw as a disastrous defeat for the German Volk. To achieve this end, however, required a degree of resolution foreign to the prevailing spirit of the day. "True, now as before, we reach hastily for the morning and evening paper; true, we discuss politics and intellectualize in restaurants and coffee-

---

Schönerer, K. F. Seutter von Lötzen, Eduard Sturm, Robert von Walterskirchen, Ludwig von Zschoch.

37. A number of the letters between Adler and Friedjung are in the Adler Archiv. For Friedjung's early career see A. J. P. Taylor's introduction to his translation of Friedjung's *The Struggle for Mastery in Germany* (New York, 1966).

houses, but we scarcely take firm sides in a matter; it is as if our will were hypnotized by the eternal oscillations in the direction of the machinery of state."[38] In Friedjung's eyes Vienna's coffeehouse culture symbolized the central failure of his time, the isolation of reason from the realm of action—the failure which the Leseverein's Rede Klub had also denounced and which Nietzsche and Wagner regarded as basic to the contemporary liberal's excess faith in reason. Friedjung also followed this line of thought in his characterization of Dr. Eduard Herbst, the liberal leader of the Bohemian Germans: "Thought joins thought in logical sequence; no place is allowed for emotion in political questions; only at the conclusion does one heartfelt tone always break through: 'We are, and will remain, Austrians.' " As Friedjung pointed out, this final assertion could be motivated only by a degree of inner uncertainty about its validity. "Did a Frenchman ever close his speech with the assurance that he was French?" No, Friedjung argued, Herbst closed his speeches with this thought because he wanted to "repress the German emotion which could alienate a portion of his heart from the consciousness of the state." According to Friedjung, "Herbst, as a logical sort, has attempted to close off a feeling which threatened to disturb his political orbit." Friedjung thus attributed the political impotence of his culture to this state of inner conflict in which a rational commitment to the Austrian state held in check the heart's feelings for the German nation (pp. 26–27).

In the terms of his socio-psychological model, Friedjung proposed to solve this problem by fostering a massive return of the repressed. "If it is now the highest duty of the political writer to exert an influence on that obscure first cause of the history of all peoples, on the national character, . . . then we must introduce a powerful new motive into public life: national feeling [*Nationalgefühl*]." More specifically he argued, "The only party which will be able to breathe new life into our fatherland is that one which rules Austria from a nationalistic point of view, which brings into being an alliance with Germany, which holds down the [other] nationalities and which reaches an agreement with Hungary that both states will rule themselves separately and independently of each other." Friedjung promised that such a program would call forth "a multitude of slum-

38. Heinrich Friedjung, *Der Ausgleich mit Ungarn,* 3rd ed. (Leipzig, 1878), p. 1.

bering forces," but he also warned that this would occur only when "every individual of our *entire* nation, filled with noble aims, joins actively in its regeneration" (pp. 28–31).

In the parallel which Friedjung developed between the psychological wholeness of the individual and the political wholeness of the nation he followed closely the approach to cultural analysis taken by Wagnerians generally, as he did also in tying both politics and psychology to art. Referring to Austria's artistic creativity, he noted that "our people [*Stamm*] has created for the German folk a great part of the musical works which are its pride." While Austria had contributed nothing to the development of German philosophy "our great composers have expressed the emotions of the German nation through tone." Citing the example of Mozart, he concluded, "We Austrians can say with pride that at the time of its philosophic and poetic flowering, Germany found the most beautiful completion of its nature through us." Friedjung evidently believed that rejoining the two Germanic peoples would restore national vitality by uniting the rational and emotional elements of German cultural life, for whereas the music of Mozart grew out of the healthy vitality of the folk, "poetry and art never bloom when the force of the folk spirit fails to develop unimpeded." It was this manly aesthetic power which allowed artistic genius to take impressions of this world, "and form them into another, greater one, which lifts us above the wretchedness of the world" (pp. 98–99).

Although the folk he envisioned for the future was more that of Wagner than of Mozart, Friedjung spoke repeatedly of the folk soul or spirit as an almost mystical entity of which man could only dimly perceive himself a part, but which might somehow be revitalized to surge into purposeful life. To achieve this end he called for a political movement to activate the dormant folk spirit: "Such a party would bring thousands of Austrians to a consciousness of what is now buried within them: that they are Germans above all" (p. 28).

Friedjung also suggested that such a movement could evoke men's emotions only by shifting from a politics of learning to a politics of art. The passive role of the man of learning, habituated to observation, to the reception of external impressions, contrasted with the active role of the poet. Where the scholar or scientist had to watch and listen, the artist was a source of expression and free creation. It was this more "masculine" artistic spirit which "must express itself not in the isolated poet; it must express itself in the whole nation, in every expression of its life, above all in its political activity" (p. 99). Friedjung also followed Wagner and Nietzsche in invoking the spirit of music, the most purely emotional of the arts, to enlist the masses in the task of cultural regeneration. "Orpheus only dared to walk with his lyre among the powers of the underworld because he knew there lives in the obscure masses a feeling, a dark presentiment [*Ahnen*] that will be awakened to thundering emotion by a full tone" (p. 1). Friedjung thus hoped to supplant an apathetic and overly rational liberal politics with a poetic politics which would arouse the emotions of the masses by sounding the full tone of German nationalism.

Friedjung's work produced a variety of reactions from various sources. As might be expected, the other members of the Pernerstorfer circle greeted it with jubilation. Writing from Berlin, where he was attending classes for a semester, Victor Adler spoke of his joy on reading it a first and then a second time: "You have elevated some, consoled some and shown some the way. . . . You have delivered us from the endless coquetry about the goal."[39] With respect to the more nationalistic, progressive wing of the liberal movement, the work evoked some interest but little action.[40] So far as the government was concerned, the work fostered a dangerous increase in nationalistic tensions, and when the first Taaffe government took office early in 1879 it secured Friedjung's dismissal from his academic position.

Following his own advice, Friedjung did not confine his call for action to the printed page. At a gathering of the Leseverein members on 10 December 1877 he marked the anniversary of the society's establishment, by urging students to concern themselves more actively with the problems of the time. Friedjung evidently ignored the practice of veiling political discussion in allegory or generality and thus precipitated the dissolution of the meeting by the police.[41] This was the attitude of total engagement which elicited from the political champion of the Leseverein, Georg von Schönerer, the admiring

39. Adler to Friedjung, 12 Dec. 1877, Adler Archiv.

40. Friedjung mentions the interest of various liberal political societies in the preface to the third edition of *Der Ausgleich mit Ungarn*.

41. *N.F.P.* (12 Dec. 1877), p. 7; (13 Dec. 1877), p. 6; *Jahresbericht* 1877–78, p. 4. The actual statement that brought about police action is not clear; it may simply have been the suggestion that students take a greater interest in political affairs.

statement, "Nicht Friedjung—Kampfjung soll er heissen"[42] ("He should be named War-youth—not Peace-youth").

In attempting to increase student political activity, Pernerstorfer and Friedjung received constant support from the activities of the Leseverein. One indication of the society's deepening political involvement during the seventh and final year of its existence can be seen in the fact that the number of parliamentary deputies belonging to the society rose from twelve to twenty-three.[43] In addition, the society, in conjunction with the fraternities, established a yearly pension of five hundred florins for Anton Füster, the former chaplain of the 1848 revolution's Academic Legion who had recently returned impoverished from his exile in America. In honoring Füster the students not only paid homage to the revolutionary spirit of 1848, the spirit which pervaded much of the Leseverein's activity, but they also reaffirmed the principle that students should be actively involved in politics. On 21 March 1878 the society made both Füster and Schönerer honorary members, an action which only increased the hostility of the authorities toward the Leseverein.[44]

Within the Leseverein, the members of the Pernerstorfer circle continued to use the Rede Klub to subject the intellectual foundations of contemporary liberal culture to critical examination. On 17 November 1877, Max Gruber spoke on Friedrich Albert Lange's *Geschichte des Materialismus* (*History of Materialism*), a work which had recently aroused interest. Lange attempted to lay bare the emptiness of the materialistic outlook and to show that periods of materialistic faith were usually followed by periods of reaction against materialism. To encourage such a reaction, he espoused an aesthetic idealism. "Once the principle is conceded that we should shape ourselves in the spirit of a more beautiful and perfect world than the world of reality, then one will certainly also have to allow the validity of myth—as myth." Lange's work also struck an idealistic note of social protest similar to that which had drawn the approval of the Pernerstorfer circle in the past. He noted the urgent nature of the social question and predicted that a peaceful solution would be possible only in a communal context, "which sweeps away egotism and re-

42. Quoted by Pernerstorfer, "Von Schönerer bis Wolf," *Der Kampf* 4 (Oct. 1910—Sept. 1911): 390.

43. *Jahresbericht* 1877–78, pp. 13–15.

44. Beurle, *Beiträge* p. 41.

places ceaseless work aiming only at personal advantage with a new goal of human perfection in human comradeship."[45]

Another of the Rede Klub lectures, given by Pernerstorfer in January 1878, reveals the circle's continuing concern with socialism and the social question. This talk concerned the work of Franz Michael Felder, a novelist of the Vorarlberg who had died eleven years before, after a brief but promising career.[46] Felder's stories were set in the villages and forests of his native province, but his theme was the social question. He had studied the writings of socialists such as Ferdinand Lassalle, and he attempted to apply their ideas to his own work. His final novel, *Reich und Arm* (*Rich and Poor*) attempted "to illuminate the chasm between rich and poor [and] the demoralization which the social contrast produced even in the simplest people."[47]

The most important of the Rede Klub lectures given by members of the circle during this final year was Siegfried Lipiner's "On the Elements of a Renewal of Religious Ideas in the Present." In this address Lipiner attempted to synthesize a coherent outlook from the various philosophical systems which the circle had studied. Schopenhauer, Nietzsche, Wagner, and Lange all contributed to Lipiner's metaphysics. Lipiner began by explaining, "I call religious everything that transcends the common conceptual world [*Vorstellungswelt*] of the human species, the so-called reality, *in so far as it is emotionally experienced*." Having equated religion with transcendent emotion, Lipiner went on to echo Wagnerian doctrine in calling for a revival of emotional experience as a step to the restoration of man's wholeness. "For man cannot split himself; there is not a moment in which his entire being might not be engaged; and the mightier a man is, all the more energetically do all the elements of his nature join together and yearn as a whole for a unified impression." As Friedjung had traced political apathy to this lack of wholeness, Lipiner blamed it for religious indifference. He also denounced arrogant rationalism which "rebuffs the longing emotion with the demand that everything to be believed and felt must be declared valid and binding by it [reason], the final judge."[48]

45. *Jahresbericht* 1877–78, p. 25. Friedrich Albert Lange, *Geschichte des Materialismus und Kritik seiner Bedeutung in der Gegenwart* (Iserlohn, 1873), vol. 2, pp. vi, 561–62.

46. *Jahresbericht* 1877–78, p. 25.

47. *Castle, Geschichte der deutschen Literatur,* vol. 2, p. 476.

48. *Jahresbericht* 1877–78, p. 25. Siegfried Lipiner, *Uber die Elemente einer Erneuerung*

Lipiner attempted to survey the prospects for a revival of religious feeling. He found one important source of encouragement in philosophy, specifically citing the works of Kant and Friedrich Albert Lange as immediately relevant to the problem. These two thinkers, said Lipiner, had shown that reality was simply a mental construct and that learning could claim to say nothing about the essence of things. Since they had shown the emptiness of materialism's basic assumption, he concluded that anyone who studied their work would turn from the empirical, materialistic outlook to one of artistic and religious feeling. Lipiner also saw a hopeful sign in the decline of religious form and dogma, for he believed that the growing skepticism about miracles would prepare the way for the acceptance of myth "as the artistic presentation of that which is beyond reality." The third source to which Lipiner looked was art, and for his discussion he drew heavily on the ideas of Nietzsche's *Birth of Tragedy.* He believed that where realistic art merely showed life as it existed, tragedy offered man the possibility of moving beyond the narrow limits of reality, "for in tragic art he sees himself as he destroys reality." It was this process that prepared the way for an important change within the individual. By participating in the suffering of the tragedy, the observer was "torn free from his transitory individuality" to find unity with all of nature. "We only grasp the true and stern pantheism when we see this nature from within, . . . when we have ceased to know and feel ourselves as individual beings: then are we Pan, the all-one and then are we Theos, the divine. . . . Yes, we must transform, transform, and be transformed."

After supporting his theories with a lengthy passage from Wagner's recently published *Parsifal,* Lipiner concluded his lecture on a note of poetic rapture as he depicted the possible consequences of a revival of religious ideas:[49]

> And if, with the renewal of religious ideas, all the other bases of our existence should also be renewed; if a *second Renaissance* should ascend, glowing above us like a sun, and disperse the oppressive twilight fog of our time; then, not unworthy of this redemption, we will greet the hour of rebirth and the young day,

religiöser Ideen in der Gegenwart (Vienna, 1878), p. 1. This work will henceforth be cited as *Elemente.*

49. *Elemente,* pp. 7–18, passim.

> and ourselves reborn, powerfully lift our hands to join in constructing the edifice of the new life.

As it had done three years before with Volkelt's talk on Kant, the Leseverein approved Lipiner's ideas by according his lecture the rare honor of publication, and a comparison of these two documents reveals the intellectual distance the society had traveled in these three years. Volkelt's address in 1875 had invoked Kantian idealism to inspire the still unformed social order that would replace the cynical morality of an Ofenheim, but it had focused far more attention on cataloguing the various failures of liberal culture. By the time of Lipiner's lecture three years later, the intellectual outlines of the new order were much clearer. Where Volkelt had only indicated skepticism about the ability of reason and science to solve all the problems of society, Lipiner, drawing on the theories of Wagner and Nietzsche, proposed to overthrow the tyranny of reason by emphasizing the life of feeling. In their search for new principles to replace the inadequate materialistic assumptions of liberal culture, the members of the Pernerstorfer circle had followed the Kantian path indicated by Volkelt, but their interest in Schopenhauer and Nietzsche strongly influenced their understanding of Kant. They saw his work as proof that even though reason could grasp the phenomenal world, it could never penetrate the essence of nature, the thing-in-itself. For Schopenhauer the *Ding-an-sich* was the will, and the phenomenal world was the realm in which reason usually operated in the service of the will. This belief, which inspired Schopenhauer's pessimism, was cheerfully affirmed by Wagner and Nietzsche who saw it as a source of hope. They believed that feeling (which they regarded as an aspect of the will) would not be subject to the phenomenal limitations of reason, and that it would open to the whole man a relationship to nature as a whole, a relationship to the thing-in-itself. The Wagnerites of the Leseverein accepted this viewpoint, and Lipiner's speech indicates his belief that he had found the tools necessary for constructing this new life of wholeness (*Ganzheit*). Philosophy would continue the necessary work of destruction in eliminating the erroneous suppositions of the previous world view, while art could begin the constructive task of carrying man beyond the limits of the phenomenal world through an appeal to his religious or emotional nature. Overcoming man's phenomenal self would restore his original unity with his fellow man and with nature. Lipiner's work thus provided the aesthetic and metaphysical analogue to Friedjung's poetic politics with its emphasis on emotion as a means of evoking the unity of the Volk.

The further task of constructing the life of wholeness, however, did not take place within the Leseverein. On 18 December 1878, the government declared the Leseverein dissolved on the grounds that it represented a danger to the state and that it had overstepped the limits of its charter in assuming a political character. Several days later the members of the society presented a petition protesting the action to the Reichsrath deputy Dr. Sturm, who introduced it into Parliament.[50] Schönerer, the political champion of the society, also addressed Parliament in its defense. By pointing out that the membership of the society had included a hundred and thirty-five professors, among them eighteen imperial counselors (*Hofräte*) as well as twenty-four members of Parliament, he implied that if the Leseverein was actually a danger to the state, then the state was in perilous condition indeed.[51] In spite of these appeals, the government refused to rescind its action.

In dissolving the Leseverein, the government succeeded only in multiplying its troubles, for its action greatly increased student sympathy for the society's cause. Moreover, since the society was easily the largest of the various student reading societies, it had more than enough members to take control of competing organizations by simply joining them and voting the incumbents out. During the next few years this fate first befell the Academic Reading Room and when it was dissolved, the German-Austrian Reading Society. By the time the final society was dissolved in 1882, virtually the entire student population had enlisted in the radical cause.[52] The members of the Pernerstorfer circle, however, did not join the struggle between government and students. Although the dissolution of the Leseverein robbed them of their intellectual sounding board, it also served the goals they had set for themselves by forcing them out of their primarily academic environment and into the professional worlds of

50. *N.F.P.* (20 Dec. 1878), p. 6. Specifically the government cited the Leseverein's cultivation of nationalism as dangerous. *N.F.P.* (22 Dec. 1878), p. 3.

51. Eduard Pichl [Herwig, pseud.] *Georg Schönerer und die Entwicklung des Alldeutschtumes in der Ostmark* (Vienna, 1921), vol. 3, p. 49. Hereafter referred to as *Schönerer*.

52. William J. McGrath, "Student Radicalism in Vienna," *Journal of Contemporary History* 2 (July 1967): 194–97.

art and politics where they could test their theories in more concrete form.

The intellectual and political efforts of the Telynen during their student years prepared them well for carrying on their crusade for cultural renewal within the variety of professional activities to which they now turned. The ideas of the various thinkers they studied, including Schopenhauer, Wagner, and most particularly Nietzsche, provided them with the ingredients for an all-embracing outlook based on a belief in the coherence of the arts and cultural unity of art and society. Moreover, Nietzsche had given them something even more valuable. In *Ecce Homo* Nietzsche says that "in *Schopenhauer as Educator* my innermost history, my becoming, is inscribed,"[53] and the Telynen clearly read the work with that understanding. In explicitly accepting Nietzsche as their *Erzieher* (educator) the Telynen pledged themselves to a life of self-overcoming on the model set forth in that work, the model of Nietzsche's own becoming. There Nietzsche calls for the members of the cultural community "to further the production of the philosopher, of the artist, and of the saint within us and outside us,"[54] and the circle's members devoted themselves to this task with both energy and success. In pursuing this cultural mission within their chosen fields they displayed a vigorous spirit of self-overcoming, which manifests itself directly in the process of intellectual maturation observable in the history of the circle's outlook as it develops through various preliminary metamorphoses to find realization in achievements of true artistic and political genius.

53. Friedrich Nietzsche, *On the Genealogy of Morals,* trans. Walter Kaufmann and R. J. Hollingdale; *Ecce Homo,* trans. Walter Kaufman, (New York, 1969), p. 281.

54. Nietzsche, *Schopenhauer as Educator,* p. 56.

Part II: In Search of the Poet Priest

It comes to pass that the middle class fails to succeed in incorporating its own intellectuals into the middle class order, and in its midst the number of the disillusioned . . . who are tormented by the dream of a higher, heroic life, challenging to the whole man, increases. Of these disillusioned and dream-drunk members of the middle class, some go into the proletariat which sets about destroying the middle class world in order to replace it with a humane one. Other of these disillusioned or dream-drunk ones (more peaceful or perhaps only to find momentary refuge) . . . see in art that life of the whole man denied them in the reductions of the middle class world order. Their procession is led by Beethoven, followed by Wagner and the young Nietzsche.

HERMANN BAHR

3. Aesthetes and Activists

Taken together, the demise of the Leseverein and the emergence of Siegfried Lipiner as the dominant intellectual force within the Pernerstorfer circle marked the opening of a new phase in its development. Through 1878 the members of the circle had been deeply and successfully involved in student politics; but with the dissolution of the Leseverein, their most important vehicle for exercising direct political influence was destroyed. Furthermore, the effects of this loss were reinforced within the circle by changes in its nature and composition. Not only was Lipiner's interest focused more on the possibility of an indirect religious–aesthetic cure for the degeneration of liberal culture than on the immediate political and economic goals of Pernerstorfer and Adler, but also the new members who were drawn to the circle through Lipiner were similarly inclined. Since all members of the group believed that politics and art were intimately related, the divergence was initially only one of emphasis, but as the quietistic implications of Wagner's new aesthetic religion became more and more obvious, there was an increasing tendency for the activists to withdraw to more practical concerns. With the eventual division of the circle, the Lipiner fragment abandoned any further interest in politics in favor of an attempt to evolve an art form which would constitute in itself an immediate religious and communitarian experience. After much unsuccessful experimentation, this attempt found fulfillment in the creation of one of the most complex and profound musical compositions of nineteenth-century Austria.

In developing his religious–aesthetic theories, Lipiner was assisted by a number of new members who joined the circle during and after 1878. Richard von Kralik and Gustav Mahler, both of whom were particularly close to Lipiner, were perhaps the most significant of the new members; Hugo Wolf and Friedrich Eckstein became more loosely associated with the group at a somewhat later period. Kralik's significance for the history of the Pernerstorfer circle stems not from the merits of his own aesthetic, religious, and political efforts, but rather from his intensely self-conscious preoccupation with his own intellectual development. Since Kralik felt obliged to record and preserve his detailed impressions of the circle's activities, his memoirs provide a vivid picture of the direction in which the group was moving during the period of Lipiner's leadership. Kralik had been a member of the Leseverein from its founding in 1871 until his graduation from the university five years later, but it was only in 1878 that Lipiner brought him into the circle.[1] During his years at the university he had wavered between a career in law and one in writing and he was eventually to publish innumerable works in such diverse fields as music, history, poetry, drama, literary history, and political propaganda.[2] Kralik's intellectual development fitted him admirably for participation in the circle's discussions. Like most of its members, he too had been impressed by the lectures of Lorenz von Stein, and by the philosophical outlook of Kantian idealism. Kralik also became interested in Wagner's works at an early age, and by 1876 this interest embraced the latter's musical compositions as well as his cultural program. Late in 1876 Kralik decided to continue his education at the University of Berlin, where he studied under Theodor Mommsen and heard lectures by Treitschke and Hermann Grimm. His year in Berlin also made a socialist of him: "I visited party meetings; I purchased the chief works of party literature. Thus I also assembled Lassalle's collected writings."[3] Kralik, who was later rather embarrassed by his socialist phase, explained the lapse by observing, "In my youth almost all people of the same age, rich and poor, were socialistic in the Marxian sense."[4] With this background in Kantian idealism, Wagnerism, and socialism, Kralik was ripe for admission to the Pernerstorfer circle, and when he became a member in 1878, Lipiner added the final necessary philosophical ingredient by introducing him to Nietzsche's writings.[5] Kralik's memoirs indicate that at least during the early

1. *Jahresbericht* 1871–72, p. 14; 1873–74, p. 19; 1874–75, p. 18.

2. Richard von Kralik, *Tage und Werke, Lebenserinnerungen* (Vienna, 1922), p. 37. This work will henceforth be cited as *Tage*. Castle, *Geschichte der deutschen Literatur* (Vienna, n.d.), pp. 1600–20, 1625–29.

3. Kralik, *Tage*, pp. 31–45.

4. Richard von Kralik, "Geschichte und Gestalten—Victor Adler und Pernerstorfer," Handschriften Sammlung, Wiener Stadtbibliothek, Ms. I.N. 106.071, fol. 1r. This essay will henceforth be cited as "gestalten."

5. Kralik, *Tage*, p. 61.

period of his membership, political concerns still played a very significant role for all the circle's members. One of his most remarkable descriptions is of a meeting at which Adler, Friedjung, Pernerstorfer, and the others joined in singing *Deutschland, Deutschland über Alles!* to the piano accompaniment of *O du Deutschland, ich muss marschieren.* Most remarkable of all, the pianist for this double dose of German nationalism was Gustav Mahler.[6]

Mahler was brought into contact with the Pernerstorfer circle in 1878 through Sigfried Lipiner whom Mahler had met at the home of his childhood friend Albert Spiegler. Since Spiegler's sister Josephine was married to Victor Adler's brother-in-law Heinrich Braun, Mahler soon met and became friendly with Adler, who took a particularly warm interest in his welfare. In their letter to Nietzsche the members of the Pernerstorfer circle had pledged themselves to encourage genius wherever they found it, and it seems highly likely that they regarded Mahler in this light, for after the young composer became a regular participant in the meetings at the Adler home, Adler went to the considerable expense of buying the best piano he could find so that Mahler could practice on it. Adler also threw himself into the task of finding pupils for the hours of piano instruction that provided Mahler's chief livelihood during his years as a student at the Vienna Conservatory.[7]

Although Wagner's music and his philosophical, aesthetic, and religious theories had been the subject of discussion and admiration within the circle years before Kralik and Mahler became members in 1878, a decidedly different tone began to characterize the circle's relationship to the composer at about that time. In part this change can be attributed to Wagner himself, for from the mid-1870s to his death in 1883 he became increasingly involved in religious mysticism, which was paralleled by increasingly ambitious attempts to establish himself as the revered prophet of a new religion combining Schopenhauerian philosophy, musical theory, and Christian mysticism. Although some members of the circle were eventually to follow Nietzsche in rejecting this development, the initial response to the new religious sect was highly favorable and the circle soon began to display most of the trappings of a mystical cult.

One aspect of the new faith was the practice of making pilgrimages

6. Kralik, "Gestalten," fol. 2r.
7. Braunthal, *Victor und Friedrich Adler,* p. 35.

to Bayreuth, both to participate in performances of Wagner's works and to bask in the presence of the Master himself. As early as 1876 Victor Adler had undertaken such a trip, but whereas his description of the experience was cast in the terms of a pleasant and interesting outing, the experiences of later pilgrims were almost always surrounded with a religious aura.[8] Certainly the visit of Lipiner to Bayreuth in 1878 was viewed in far more serious terms by the circle, for his was the rare honor of being summoned by the Master himself. Wagner's interest in Lipiner had been aroused by the recommendations of Malvida von Meysenbug, a friend of both Nietzsche and Wagner. Lipiner's blend of Wagnerian, Nietzschean, and Schopenhauerian ideas in his *Unbound Prometheus* had apparently created the expectation that he would be the ideal person to undertake the task of translating Wagner's prose works into popular form for publication in the *Bayreuther Blätter*.[9] Tact, however, was not one of Lipiner's gifts, and when in Wagner's presence he raised some minor objections to certain of Schopenhauer's ideas, the Master decided to look for someone else to undertake the task.[10] However brief his personal relationship with Wagner may have been, Lipiner's regard for Wagner's ideas remained undiminished, and the simple fact that he had been in "the presence" enormously enhanced his standing among his colleagues in the Pernerstorfer circle.

Although Lipiner did not obtain the desired position with the *Bayreuther Blätter,* this publication, which first appeared in January 1878 under the editorship of Hans von Wolzogen and "with the cooperation of Richard Wagner," played an extremely important role in molding the outlook of the Pernerstorfer circle and that of Wagnerians throughout Europe. It was in the pages of this monthly that the doctrines of Wagner's new aesthetic religion were elaborated; usually an issue would contain an article by the Master himself, several commentaries or explications of his works, and frequently an article on "The Philosopher" (Schopenhauer). Perhaps the most important single issue of this magazine appeared in October 1880, for in this number Wagner set out in clearer terms than ever before the exact nature of his aesthetic religion. In contrast to the customary

8. Adler to Pernerstorfer, Bayreuth, 8 Aug. 1876, Adler Archiv.
9. Hartungen, *Der Dichter Siegfried Lipiner,* p. 6.
10. Kralik, *Tage,* pp. 61–62.

practice, the entire issue was devoted to a single essay, Wagner's "Religion and Art" which was supplemented in several following issues.

Although few of the ideas presented were new, the essay did mark an important shift of emphasis from such writings as his *Art and Revolution* (1849) and *Beethoven* (1870). In the course of the thirty years spanned by these works, Wagner had steadfastly maintained his goal of cultural regeneration, but his hopes of finding an operative force to implement this process had shifted, first from politics to art and then from art to religion. By 1880 he could declare in "Religion and Art": "We have only to fortify ourselves thoroughly in one conviction: namely that all real drive and all effective power for realization of the great Regeneration can spring only from the deep soil of a true religion."[11] Not surprisingly, Wagner's definition of true religion involved a large admixture of politics and art, but religious conviction had now come to play the central role in these various concerns.

As was the case in his *Beethoven,* Wagner based the most important points of his religious metaphysics on the philosophy of Schopenhauer. He declared, "As guide to an independent pursuit of the path of true hope, nothing better can be recommended in our present state than to make Schopenhauer's philosophy, in every way, the basis of all further intellectual and moral culture" (*Schriften,* vol. 10, p. 257). The crucial element of Schopenhauer's philosophy for Wagner's new religion was his concept of a single world will, of which all living creatures were defective manifestations—defective because their failure to realize this unity of being brought them into constant conflict with other creatures. Wagner repeatedly called for a "recognition of the unity of all that lives, and of the delusion of our physical senses which present this unity to us as inconceivably complex multitude and total diversity." He stated his conviction that "the beast differed from man only in the degree of its intellectual endowment; that what precedes all intellectual equipment, what desires and suffers in them, is the same will-to-live as in the most reason-gifted man" (pp. 224–25). In Wagner's view, then, the importance of Christ lay primarily in the fact that Christ was aware of this unity of being and was able to express it in his life as well as his teachings; the greatest of all miracles possible was the turning of the

11. Wagner, *Schriften,* vol. 10, p. 243.

individual will on itself—the denial of the will-to-live by itself in recognition of the illusory nature of its separation from all other wills. This act would end the conflict of the will with itself and restore it to the harmony it had enjoyed before its appearance in the physical world had reduced it to a state of painful fragmentation. Christ, then, was taken as a living example, "inspiring one to the highest pity, to worship of suffering, to imitation through breaking of all self-seeking will" (p. 215).

The immediate conclusion Wagner drew from this conviction was that the killing and eating of animals was simply another form of cannibalism. If man shared the same world-will as the animals, their destruction was in part self-destruction, and Wagner called for all those who truly desired the regeneration of man to become strict vegetarians at once. In Wagner's mind there was no doubt that prehistoric man had realized his true relationship to all living creatures and that his carnivorous habits had been formed later. In tracing man's fall from this state of primal innocence, Wagner emphasized the relative purity of the Aryan peoples in this matter; they, at least, had preserved in mythic and religious forms the realization of their fall, whereas the Jews had only furthered the process of decay (pp. 226–28, 231–33). Wagner's racial nationalism was thus closely tied to his religious convictions.

When he turned to the question of how man could be redeemed from his debased state, Wagner called for more than simply a return to vegetarianism. The basic evil lay in the nature of the fragmented will itself, and this was an evil man shared with all living creatures. Nonetheless, man's deepest significance in the universal scheme of things was that in him the will first gained the capacity for becoming conscious of itself and thus for understanding both its apparent phenomenal fragmentation and its more basic unity with all living things (p. 231). It was the faculty of self-consciousness which Wagner believed could lead the individual will to turn and deny itself in its particularity, finding peace in its original unity; and he felt that art could play a crucial role in this process. Art could penetrate the veil of illusion and present things in their basic oneness. Wagner cast his description of the artist's role in openly religious terms: "The Poet-Priest, the only one who never lied, was always sent to mankind in the crucial periods of its most frightful confusion as mediating friend: us too, will he lead over to that reborn life" (p. 247). By recovering the truths buried in the ancient folk myths, the artist could show man his relationship to the hierarchy of being and through sympathy lead him to salvation.

In the course of his discussion, Wagner also suggested one immediate step that could be taken to further the crusade for man's regeneration. He believed there was enough common ground among the vegetarian associations, the humane societies, the temperance leagues, and the socialists to allow them to unite in battle against the corrupt egoism of their society (p. 231). A common front would, of course, require a marked change of attitude on the part of the socialists—particularly on religious matters—but if this could be accomplished, Wagner felt that a potent force would be available to the cause.

Bizarre as Wagner's ideas may seem today, their impact on the members of the Pernerstorfer circle was profound. A month after the article appeared in October 1880, Mahler wrote to his friend Dr. Emil Freund: "I have been a complete vegetarian for a month. The moral effect of this way of life resulting from the voluntary servitude of my body and the resulting freedom from wants is immense. You can imagine how convinced of it I am when I expect a *regeneration* of the human race from it."[12] Mahler then advised Freund to return to this natural way of life in order to discover its benefits. Kralik's memoirs also testify to the impact of Wagner's new religion on members of the circle; he later observed, "Already in preparation for the coming perfection, one practiced vegetarianism and spiritualism as the religion of the future which could and would experimentally, scientifically solve all of the previously obscure riddles of existence, or of the great beyond."[13] While Victor Adler was more skeptical of vegetarianism than Mahler or Kralik, he was induced to try it by his brother-in-law Heinrich Braun, who was quite enthusiastic about the possibility of using it as an instrument for social reconciliation.

According to the testimony of Friedrich Eckstein, Adler and Heinrich's brother Adolf became convinced that "vegetarianism was undoubtedly a meaningful prospect for the future of the human race," but they also felt that whether or not it "was at that time

12. Gustav Mahler, *Briefe, 1879–1911,* ed. Alma Maria Mahler (Berlin, 1925), pp. 14–15.

13. Kralik, "Gestalten," fol. 1r.

advantageous for winning the workers and the masses of the proletariat to them was very questionable and carefully to be considered."[14] Adler noted that since workers were far too poor to be able to afford meat anyhow, vegetarianism could offer them little that was new or appealing. If Wagner's call for a united front of socialists and vegetarians met with a hesitant response from Adler and Braun, his more general goal of infusing socialism with a religious spirit did find a response in Kralik, who actually set about attempting to create a new socialistic religion. He even went so far as to compose the necessary hymns, gospels, and epistles for the new proletarian Christianity. A typical hymn began, "My people, you are my God; I believe only in you. You are my Lord. I belong only to you. You are beloved; you are my bride."[15] Although Lipiner was delighted with these efforts and began spreading the gospel by reading from these works at a lecture on his own religious philosophy, this experiment was soon abandoned.

Kralik testifies that Lipiner was also the motivating force behind the interest in spiritualism which began to manifest itself in the circle at this time. Kralik testifies that "he and an even more mystically inclined friend led me into the seances of a spiritualist where we observed some writing mediums." Before long, however, the members of the circle lost interest in attending seances. Kralik relates, "We also read the chief works of this movement, but did not find ourselves inclined to pursue these questionable attempts further." The growing inclination to mysticism inspired by Wagner's "Religion and Art" as well as by his final opera, *Parsifal*, was pushed still farther by Lipiner's espousal of the works of Gustav Theodor Fechner.[16] In this cause as in so many others, Lipiner had the advantage of speaking as a chosen disciple, for in the summer of 1876 he had studied philosophy at Leipzig under Fechner. Like Wagner and Nietzsche, Fechner seems to have regarded Lipiner as a genius, and he followed the education of the young man with the greatest interest.[17] Lipiner's efforts eventually succeeded in inspiring both

14. Friedrich Eckstein, *Alte unnennbare Tage. Erinnerungen siebzig Lehr- und Wanderjahren* (Vienna, 1936), p. 107.

15. Although these hymns were eliminated from the published copy of *Tage und Werke* they appear in the original manuscript of the work, Wiener Stadtbibliothek, Ms. 1b. 119.627, pp. 260–63. This work will henceforth be cited as Tage manuscript.

16. Kralik, *Tage*, pp. 67, 60–61.

17. Hartungen, *Lipiner*, p. 3.

Kralik and Mahler to a lasting interest in the works of this mystical psychologist.

While Wagner's proposed union of socialists, vegetarians, temperance groups, and humane societies was never formally realized even among his followers in Vienna, there did exist an informal gathering point for the varieties of the Wagnerian faithful in the tiny vegetarian restaurant at the corner of the Wallnerstrasse and Fahnengasse. One entered this modest establishment through a small glass door which opened onto a flight of stone steps leading down into the cellar. Here, in a room lit by a few windows placed high in the wall and the flickering of gas flames which burned throughout the day, the members of the Pernerstorfer circle gathered for their meals and for intellectual communion with other groups. Here the circle came into contact with a Pythagorean group headed by Friedrich Eckstein.[18] In promulgating the doctrine of vegetarianism, Wagner had drawn attention to the Pythagorean precedent for this way of life: "No sage since [Pythagoras] has reflected on the essence of the world without returning to his teachings. Silent fellowships hidden from the world and its turmoil were founded to carry out this doctrine as a religious means of purification from sin and misery."[19] The picture Eckstein draws of the Pythagorean group indicates the intensity of its religious commitment to this doctrine. He relates that he and his friends had set for themselves the ideal of this sanctified life, and "according to the theses of Pythagoras always went about dressed completely in linen, summer and winter." Other friends appeared in hair shirts; and as Eckstein noted, "If one adds to this that most of us had hair reaching down to the shoulders and full beards, an occasional unprepared observer of our midday meal might well have been reminded in some ways of the famous painting by Leonardo."[20]

Although the Pythagorean group and the Pernerstorfer circle remained distinct, Eckstein himself did become closely associated with the circle, and certainly in his enthusiasm for Wagner's compositions and philosophy he was completely at one with its members. Eckstein's feelings were also shared by another newcomer to the circle, Hugo Wolf. How Wolf came into contact with the circle is

18. Eckstein, p. 105.
19. Wagner, *Schriften,* vol. 10, p. 230.
20. Eckstein, p. 105.

not known, but it seems most probable that it was through Mahler and Rudolf Krzyzanowski. Early in 1879 Wolf had shared a room on the Opernring with these two fellow students, and afterward he had continued in a friendly relationship with them for some time.[21] While Wolf was less enthusiastic about vegetarianism than some members of the circle, his reverence for Wagner was second to none, and his youthful expressions of this reverence testify to the religious awe in which the Master was held by that generation of students. Shortly after his arrival in Vienna in 1875, Wolf had attended several of Wagner's operas, and he immediately wrote home that he had become a Wagnerian. While Wagner was in Vienna, Wolf lingered outside the Hotel Imperial where the Master was staying, hoping to catch a glimpse of him. One day, when Wagner came out of the hotel bound for the Opera, Wolf rushed forward to open the door of his coach for him. Then, closing the door, he turned and raced the four long blocks to the theater where he arrived in time to open the coach door again for Wagner's exit. Eventually, by haunting his suite at the Imperial, Wolf was able to secure an interview with his idol, and although Wagner pleaded lack of time in declining to hear Wolf's compositions, he did treat his young follower kindly.[22]

With respect to enthusiasm for Wagner, Wolf clearly needed no instruction from the Pernerstorfer circle, but even though his participation in their meetings was never intense, it may well have contributed to a broadening of his interest in the secondary figures of the Wagnerian movement, Schopenhauer and Nietzsche. His letters indicate what proved to be a temporary interest in Schopenhauer beginning in 1880, about the time he came into contact with the circle; and Eckstein's memoirs tell of his lengthy discussions with Wolf about Nietzsche's works.[23]

Although the various Wagnerian fads adhered to by the patrons

21. Frank Walker, *Hugo Wolf, a Biography* (London, 1951), pp. 82–83, 92–93.

22. Hugo Wolf, *Eine Persönlichkeit in Briefen, Familienbriefe,* ed. Edmund Hellmer (Leipzig, 1912). This work will henceforth be cited as *Familienbriefe*; pp. 10–11, 13.

23. *Hugo Wolf in Maierling, Eine Idylle,* ed. Heinrich Werner (Leipzig, 1913), p. 13; *Familienbriefe,* p. 51; Eckstein, p. 194. According to Eckstein, Wolf was also one of several members of the circle who made a pilgrimage to Bayreuth in 1882 in order to see the first production of *Parsifal.* Once again Eckstein outdid the others in demonstrating Wagnerian piety. Instead of traveling by train, he chose to make the journey on foot, and (according to legend) in sandals à la *Tannhäuser.* During their stay in Bayreuth, Eckstein's various friends continued to assemble daily for their meatless meals at the vegetarian restaurant Frohsinn (Eckstein, p. 213).

of the vegetarian restaurant could all be strictly justified in the terms of the religious doctrines developed in "Religion and Art," the fact that Wagner had moved so far from the ideas he had espoused in the 1850s or even the 1870s introduced a considerable amount of confusion into the activities of his Viennese followers. Such members of the circle as Adler, Braun, Pernerstorfer, and Friedjung had first become interested in Wagner's ideas because they seemed to offer a viable alternative to the contemporary society which they rejected, and while their loyalty to Wagner led them to accept at least briefly some of the religious practices advocated in "Religion and Art," the central preoccupations of Wagner's final years were not of immediate relevance to their practical political activities. Wagner's aesthetic religion pointed in the direction of saintly or artistic withdrawal from the torments of reality, and while this might offer an individual solution to those so inclined, it did not offer immediate assistance to those who desired social and political change.

It is not surprising, then, that the passage of time should see a growing tendency for the circle to divide into aesthetes and activists, and this tendency was directly reflected in the cafés patronized by the members of the circle in the early 1880s. In addition to the vegetarian restaurant in the Wallnerstrasse, the Café Griensteidl, opposite the Hofburg, was also a favorite meeting place. The members who gathered here around their reserved table in a window niche included Lipiner, Eckstein, and occasionally Wolf, but on the whole, the café had a much more political tone than the restaurant.[24] In addition to the regular members of the circle, a number of foreign correspondents and lawyers would frequently take part in the discussions, and occasionally the political hero of the deutschnational students, Georg von Schönerer, would make an appearance.[25]

On the other hand, for those members of the circle who followed the aesthetic religious path suggested by Wagner's final works, political questions could only be regarded as futile, and this attitude became increasingly evident in the writings and activities of Kralik, Lipiner, and Mahler during the early 1880s. In Kralik's case, the rejection of social activism came suddenly at the end of 1880 in the form of a "revelation." Basically, Kralik's revelation was simply a

24. Eckstein, p. 129.

25. Max Ermers, *Victor Adler, Aufstieg und Grösse einer sozialistischen Partei* (Vienna, 1932), p. 100.

failure of nerve on the issue of life's meaningfulness and an assertion that life should be lived as a giant game. He declared, "On the earth we have nothing to create, no mission, nothing to strive for; it is unthinkable that things could change in essence, and that essence is that of our own free will we grapple with one another like Olympic contestants."[26] In the extremity of his new revelation, Kralik even went so far as to reject the existence of a more perfect reality beyond the purposeless phenomenal world, and this aspect of his vision greatly disturbed the other members of the circle. Lipiner wrote to Nietzsche, Fechner, and Lagarde asking that they intervene personally to change Kralik's mind.[27] Although only Lagarde actually replied, Kralik was persuaded to modify this aspect of his revelation in an essay written in December 1880 or January 1881. Here he returned to the conception of an ideal realm beyond everyday reality, but he also made clear his belief that their only relationship was the artistic one embodied in Germanic myth and symbol which he believed could suggest the ideal within the framework of the real. With respect to political activism, he simply restated his previous position: "also the statesman and social politician must know that he can indeed struggle but can attain nothing, unless it be a small branch like the Olympic victor."[28]

Although Lipiner did not undergo the dramatic conversion to social nihilism that Kralik experienced, his writings do reveal a clear rejection of sociopolitical goals by the early 1880s. In a letter to Kralik written in October 1880, Lipiner granted the lack of a meaningful alternative to imperfect reality, but went on to argue that such an ideal reality, or heaven, could be created by the strong. He made it clear, however, that this was to be a heaven for its architects, not for society in general; he observed that it was comfortless for the weak but meaningful for the strong and good.[29] Increasingly, the thoughts of Kralik and Lipiner were dominated by the vision of the heroic brother-band who would do battle for the ideal reality after the manner of medieval knights. Lipiner himself was never tempted

26. The letter was written in Vienna on 31 Oct. 1880; the person to whom it was written is unknown. Wiener Stadtbibliothek, Ms. I.N. 96670, fol. 3r–v.

27. Kralik, Tage manuscript, p. 323.

28. Richard von Kralik, "Moltke und R. Wagner," Wiener Stadtbibliothek, Ms. I.N. 105.478, pp. 3, 7–8. The essay is dated "1880?"; internal evidence indicates that it was written either in December 1880 or January 1881.

29. Castle, *Geschichte der deutschen Literatur,* vol. 2, p. 1567.

to go beyond the battlefield of literary and musical aesthetics, but his heroic stance did lead him to affirm the ideal of war which Richard Wagner had attacked in a dispute with Field Marshall von Moltke. In an essay entitled "Ewige Friede," Lipiner wrote, "Yes, Moltke is right: war is a source of the most noble power. Civilization does not make it dispensable—no, it is just that which first makes it necessary."[30] While this defense of war proved to be a passing phase in Lipiner's development, the basic motivation for his stand—the desire to evoke the ideals of the heroic warrior society of medieval Germany—found even fuller expression in the new Saga Society formed by Kralik, Lipiner, and Mahler late in 1881.

In directing their attention to the path of artistic or religious redemption open to the strong individual, the circle's artists prepared the way for the final dissolution of the group. While the aesthetes had moved toward a total rejection of the political and social realm, the activists—Adler, Pernerstorfer, Friedjung, and the Brauns—had begun to make considerable progress in just those fields. Under these circumstances it is not surprising that Heinrich Braun should react strongly to the stand outlined by Lipiner in "Ewige Friede." Looking forward to what he expected to be a most unpleasant reunion with Lipiner, he wrote to his friend Paul Natorp, "Specifically, I believe it will come to discussions between me and him which will inwardly alienate us." Noting that until recently he had believed himself to be in total agreement with Lipiner's ideas, he explained that his belief had been destroyed by Lipiner's article on Moltke: "The entire execution of that essay proves that the conception of war which Lipiner gives is not of an incidental nature, but stands in the most intimate association with all of his other opinions. In this case, however, I would have to become Lipiner's most determined opponent and attack no viewpoint more passionately than his." Although the encounter was far more pleasant than Braun had expected and an open break between the two friends was avoided, no basic agreement on the world view could be reached.[31] From this point on, the paths of the activists and the aesthetes diverged.

30. Siegfried Lipiner, "Der Ewige Friede," *D.Z.* (9 March 1881), pp. 1–2.
31. Quoted in Julie Braun-Vogelstein, *Heinrich Braun* (Tübingen, 1932), pp. 73–74.

4. The Saga Society

In choosing to pursue the crusade for cultural regeneration by the aesthetic-religious path mapped out in Wagner's final works, Lipiner and his friends would have rejected the suggestion that their choice involved a flight from reality into art. As Lipiner had written in an article for the *Deutsche Zeitung*, "For us, the kingdom of forms is no longer a wonderful fairy world into which we flee from 'life.' For us it is nothing—or it is *true life*."[1] The entire Wagnerian metaphysics pointed in the direction of this medieval assumption that true reality lay in the realm beyond the palpable physical world. Nonetheless, the immediate problem of living in the physical world remained, and it was here that Lipiner and his friends would find the cultural mission of Wagner's Poet-Priest most relevant. As Kralik observed, "It appeared to me that the most important duty of all was to secure for our nation the same epic cultural foundation as the Greeks and certainly the Indians and Persians had and have. To that end, I would have to bring into a unity the inherited sagas of gods and heroes just as Homer, Hesiod, or Ferdusi had done."[2]

This observation follows closely the theory elaborated in Wagner's "Religion and Art" that the Aryan peoples (primarily Indians, Persians, Greeks, and Germans) had preserved in their folk myths the knowledge of their fall from a primitive paradisal state, and that these religious–aesthetic myths were the key to a return to the garden of the unindividuated will. Kralik himself drew attention to this aspect of Wagner's thought. In a review of the Vienna Opera's 1883 Wagner cycle, he posed the question: Which of Wagner's many great accomplishments was the most important? "I am inclined to lay the greatest weight on the use of saga, for saga is the deciding point from which everything else follows, the only [point] from which it would once again be possible after centuries to establish a true—

1. Siegfried Lipiner, "Die künstlerische Neuerung in Goethe's *Faust*," *D.Z.* (30 June 1881), pp. 1–2.
2. Kralik, *Tage*, p. 84.

which is to say, unitary—art."[3] The artistic task which Kralik here acknowledged to be the starting point for any regeneration of German Volk culture was the same as that assigned by Wagner to his mystic Poet-Priest, and to fulfill this task Kralik and his friends established a new club which they christened the Saga Society.

The moving spirits were Kralik and Lipiner, and in a letter of 1 October 1881, Kralik enthusiastically summarized the aims and outlook of the group: "I believe that never in the history of the world has one been so delighted, elevated, understood, completed; [never has one] discussed such intelligent things." The group of friends had already accomplished a great deal: "The task of this association was to discuss [and] work through the entire world. That has already happened." Having completed this task, the group now wanted to get down to details. Kralik wrote, "I propose that the new society which is to be created be called the Saga Society [Sagengesellschaft] and that we set ourselves the goal of living, thinking, and working in myths, gods, and heroes, as, say, the ancient Greeks or the ancient Germans." He believed that such activity would yield dramatic results: "A new world view should come into being, an artistic, poetic one opposed to the modern scientific one. Life should become nature; nature should become life and spirit. Inspiration and will may compensate temporarily for lack of clarity and logic. Thus we want to found a whole [culture], a new and magnificent culture."[4]

The membership of the new society included a number of Kralik's college and family friends as well as the group from the Pernerstorfer circle. Heinrich Friedjung occasionally attended the meetings, which were usually held at Kralik's house. In tracing her friendship with Mahler, Natalie Bauer-Lechner relates that one of their first lengthy encounters was at Kralik's house where Mahler played the overture to Wagner's *Die Meistersinger* so grandly "that an entire orchestra seemed to sound forth from his hands."[5] For the earlier gatherings of the Pernerstorfer circle, Mahler had provided *O du Deutschland, ich muss marschieren,* while the new Sagengesellschaft demanded *Meistersinger*—the respective choices could hardly be more apt.

Kralik relates that at the meetings music was cultivated as much as literature. They listened to Wagner and practiced the choir music

3. *Deutsche Wochenschrift* 1 (9 Dec. 1883), p. 6.
4. Kralik, *Tage,* pp. 97–88.
5. Natalie Bauer-Lechner, *Erinnerungen an Gustav Mahler* (Leipzig, 1923), p. 2.

of Palestrina (which Wagner praised highly), as well as holding communal recitations of old German sagas including the *Nibelungenlied*, the *Gudrun*, the *Edda*, and many others.[6] The cultural regeneration prophesied by Wagner and Nietzsche demanded the union of Apollonian myth with Dionysian music, and the members of the Saga Society did their best to achieve this end. Indeed, their efforts eventually reached a somewhat sour fruition in the creation of several works of art. Lipiner's offering to Orpheus was the libretto for Carl Goldmark's opera *Merlin*, published in 1886 and performed at the Vienna Opera on 19 November 1886; two days later Hugo Wolf reviewed it in the *Salonblatt*.[7] After discussing the artistic richness of the Merlin saga, Wolf observed, "From this fantastic and symbolically moving saga, Lipiner has drained off a banal opera libretto." Wolf's basic complaint was that Lipiner had neglected the opportunity for a psychological study of Merlin's split personality in favor of staging meaningless battle scenes and triumphs. Wolf also found fault with the music, claiming that it was all too obviously derived from *Tristan* and other of Wagner's works such as the *Ring*, *Meistersinger*, and *Lohengrin*.[8]

Kralik's foray into the world of music was far more ambitious and even less successful than Lipiner's. In addition to the librettos and song texts which he provided for his sister Mathilde, who studied under Bruckner, he attempted composition on his own.[9] His boldest effort in this direction was his Easter festival play entitled *The Mystery of the Life and Sufferings of the Saviour*. This work consisted of three plays to be performed in three successive days complete with songs and choral music all provided by Kralik. Since Wolf had given up his position as music critic by the time this particular work was published in 1895, his evaluation is not available, but some ten years earlier he had virtually predicted its creation in one of his reviews. In discussing modish compositions in which poetry "extends a sisterly hand to her musical ally," he had suggested the alarming possibility that Richard von Kralik might one day attempt the composition of

6. Kralik, *Tage*, p. 98; Tage manuscript, p. 358.

7. Hartungen, *Der Dichter Siegfried Lipiner*, p. 48.

8. Hugo Wolf, *Musikalische Kritiken*, ed. Richard Batka and Heinrich Werner (Leipzig, 1911), pp. 300–04. This work will henceforth be cited as *Kritiken*.

9. Castle, *Geschichte der deutschen Literatur*, p. 1603.

a sacred festival play (*Buhnenweihefestspiel*). With acid irony, Wolf observed: "Music and poetry most intimately related and united—what a comforting prospect for the music of the future—Oh Wagner!—"[10]

However insignificant in its own right, Kralik's long and varied career offers a striking illustration of the tenacity with which so many of the Wagnerians pursued the Master's goal of renewing the Volk's religious mythic substance. One of his first efforts in this direction was an attempt to revive the medieval mystery play. His *Adam*, published in 1883, was designed for presentation on the mystery stage, the three levels of which were intended to represent heaven, earth, and hell.[11] An offhand comment in Kralik's essay "Moltke and R. Wagner" clearly reveals his purpose in using the mystery stage. In discussing the dichotomy between the phenomenal world of time and space and the essence of reality existing in a world beyond time and space, Kralik noted that the poet could simultaneously present both worlds only by use of symbols, unless the old mystery stage became available to him.[12] Evidently Kralik himself was not completely satisfied with the mystery stage as a vehicle for revealing the relationship between phenomenal reality and the world beyond time and space, for *Adam* was the only part of his *Human Tragedy* (intended as a dramatic inversion of the *Divine Comedy*) that he published.

Another contribution to the crusade for cultural regeneration began when he started work on his *Deutsche Götter- und Heldenbuch* (*Book of German Gods and Heroes*), intended to bring together all the Germanic myths and sagas. During this same period he began to edit his *Das Volkesschauspiel vom Doktor Faust*, an attempt to restore the Faust myth to its original form.[13] When the play was published in 1895, Kralik explained in his introduction that his purpose (as in the renewal of the mysteries) was not to satisfy simple historical curiosity or fashionable archaism but "to maintain and protect for the nation [Volk] its most personal, vital, sound, and powerful pos-

10. Wolf, *Kritiken*, p. 38.
11. Castle, p. 1599.
12. Kralik, "Moltke und R. Wagner," Wiener Stadtbibliothek, Ms. I.N. 105.478, p. 8.
13. Castle, pp. 1606–07.

session."[14] Since the folk would understand at once this expression of its spirit, Kralik disdained to barricade the way with a "learned or critical apparatus." Just as Friedjung tried to arouse politically the pure folk spirit uncorrupted by the excesses of reason, so Kralik believed that this spirit, expressed in natural myth, would provide the soundest basis for the renewal of art. Both men looked to the folk as a source of purifying simplicity and feeling.[15]

Although Kralik was active in innumerable fields throughout his lifetime, his most important and influential work was furthering the Catholic literary movement. Once he had settled upon Catholicism as the only religion that could provide the basis for cultural regeneration, he gave increasing attention to the revival of those medieval myths and sagas which expressed not only the Germanic folk spirit but also that of early Christianity. During the period from 1889 to 1892 he devoted himself to the creation of such works as *Kriemhildens Rache, Hildebrands Heimkehr, Merlin, Mabus, Balders Tod, Schwanhild,* and *Kraka.* In 1905, his efforts led to the establishment of the *Gralbund* (the Grail Brotherhood), a society of poets and writers dedicated to the creation of artistic works expressing the spirit of romantic Catholicism. The following year the society established a monthly journal, *Der Gral*, to publish its literary output.[16]

A typical product of this period was *Die Gralsage* (*Saga of the Grail*), and in an introduction Kralik explained its primary importance. The reason he had "collected, renewed, and explained" the old Grail myths was that he wanted "to contribute to the construction of that unified splendid edifice of modern culture which always hovers before me as a goal." Kralik again stated his belief that a popular national culture would have to be based on these mythic treasures of the past, and he took comfort in the fact that such names as Parsifal, Lohengrin, Tristan, Isolde, Arthur, and Merlin had become an integral part of modern education. "Just in our time poetry, music, plastic art, and philosophy have found the most vital impulse here [and] have been inspired to love for these symbols of the highest ideas." Kralik's ideal remained that of a regenerated culture inspired by myth to a symbolic comprehension of the realm

14. Richard von Kralik, *Das Volkesschauspiel vom Doktor Faust* (Vienna, 1895), p. 3 of preface.

15. For Friedjung see chapter 2.

16. Castle, pp. 1608, 1621.

beyond phenomenal reality. He felt that his work would not only illuminate the medieval masterpieces and those of Richard Wagner, but that it would also provide firm ground for future poetic efforts just as that of Homer, Hesiod, and Dante had done. Kralik regarded his work in renewing the nation's mythic substance as only a small part of a campaign to replace what he described as a Faust-culture, characterized by blind insatiable striving, with a Grail culture, the symbol of which would be Parsifal. "This is also more or less the goal of this and all my works and efforts, however insignificant . . . the work of an individual may be with respect to the great mission."[17] The shallow rationalism of his culture was to be transcended in a Grail culture where religious faith would point the way to the realm beyond phenomenal reality. These were the ideas Kralik expressed time and again, and they were all drawn with but slight modification from the tenets of Wagnerism.

Externally, Lipiner's career was almost the mirror image of Kralik's. Where Kralik achieved widespread recognition only after decades of ceaseless publication, Lipiner was widely regarded as a new Goethe on the basis of his *Unbound Prometheus*, published before he was twenty. But even though this work had led such figures as Nietzsche, Wagner, and Fechner to hail him as one of the most promising writers of the age, his subsequent artistic works were disappointing both in quality and quantity. After the mid-1880s, his publications were confined to a few translations, and by the time of his death in 1911, his work had been almost completely forgotten. Two years later, Lipiner's friend Paul Natorp attempted to revive interest in his work by publishing two plays which Lipiner had completed before his death, but this effort too was only momentarily successful.

While Lipiner's claim to enduring literary accomplishment is scarcely greater than Kralik's, the works of this "new Goethe" do offer a much deeper insight into the complex metaphysics of the Wagnerian aesthetes. Where Kralik devoted himself to accomplishing the most obvious of the Master's goals, Lipiner took on the more difficult task of creating a consistent theoretical framework from the religious, philosophical, and aesthetic theories of Schopenhauer and Nietzsche as well as Wagner. Indeed, in terms of

17. Richard von Kralik, *Die Gralsage* (Regensburg, 1907), pp. iv, xiv.

style and temperament, Lipiner often found himself closer to Nietzsche than to Wagner. In an essay written for the *Deutsche Zeitung* in February 1881, Lipiner characterized the typical Philistine in thoroughly Nietzschean terms. He ridiculed him for never allowing himself to be inspired by the "fire of a truly great will" and for always preaching objectivity and cool wisdom.[18] Lipiner's aesthetic principles demanded just the opposite. In an essay on Gottfried Keller's poetry, he criticized those naturalistic parts of the poet's work which, because they were confined to mere observation, failed to stir the heart. In Lipiner's view, Keller's poems expressed true life only when "*emotion* holds sway and the excited inner being [*Innere*] is manifested."[19] Behind this criticism was the assumption, shared by Schopenhauer, Wagner, and Nietzsche, that man's emotional component is much closer to the essence of reality than is his intellect.

These beliefs were closely related to the artistic principles that informed almost all of Lipiner's own work. In his lecture on the renewal of religion, Lipiner had suggested the possibility that "art was simply a symbolic abbreviation of life,"[20] and this idea was repeated a decade later (1887) in the introduction to his translation of Mickiewicz' *Festival for the Dead*.[21] At the same time, Lipiner attributed an even more profound significance to these artistic symbols of life, for life itself was a manifestation of the world of forms beyond phenomenal reality. The lens of true art, then, was bifocal: it examined the basic forces of human life, but it could also look beyond them to the essence of reality which was the world of forms. It is in this sense that the symbolism of Lipiner's plays must be understood.

In essence, the central problem of Lipiner's two final plays, *Adam* and *Hippolytos*, is that of Wagner's "Religion and Art." After tracing the history of man's fall, Wagner observed, "As we initially followed in broadest outline the successes which this human beast of prey evidenced in world history, so it may now be useful to examine more closely the efforts to counter these successes through a rediscovery of the lost Paradise."[22] In Lipiner's *Adam*, the central

18. Siegfried Lipiner, "Apologie der Philister," *D.Z.* (20 February 1881), p. 2.
19. Siegfried Lipiner, "Ueber Gottfried Kellers Gedichte," *Deutsche Wochenschrift* 1, no. 3, 18 Nov. 1883, p. 3.
20. Lipiner, *Elemente*, p. 9.
21. Adam Mickiewicz, *Todtenfeier*, trans. Siegfried Lipiner (Leipzig, 1887), p. xiv.
22. Wagner, *Schriften*, vol. 10, p. 238.

theme, the search for the lost paradise, is raised in its opening words. Eve declares, "It was there, / . . . it lay far far to the east/ . . . beyond the wilderness/ it was there that the Garden lay." In answer to Adam's impatient response, she adds "stillness—still joy—Yes, there was peace there!" Soon Adam, too, is caught up in this longing for the lost garden:

> Beyond the wilderness is eternal rest:
> Is it *there* indeed your thoughts and longings go?
> Yes if I could go *there*, neither the thorns of the forest
> Nor night and dread would bar my way
> Where neither sun nor moon nor stars existed
> Neither peace nor discord—neither
> I nor you."[23]

Adam's description of paradise, then, goes beyond that of the Bible to identify it with the Schopenhauerian notion of a prephenomenal existence in which neither physical reality nor human individuation existed. In this world the will's painful conflict with itself would not exist and peace would reign supreme. The principal symbol, which Lipiner juxtaposes to that of the lost garden, is the animal, which is equated with *Trieb*—a word meaning instinct, passion, or germinating force, all of which are closely related to the Schopenhauerian concept of Will. Immediately after expressing his longing for the garden, Adam describes the animal world with horror: "And the eternal animal,/ Instinct [Trieb], the stupid—in the bodies of thousands upon thousands/ . . . He sinks his teeth into his groaning flesh."[24] The image of the Will constantly devouring itself in the phenomenal realm was one that was familiar to all followers of Schopenhauer, and when Mahler read Lipiner's completed manuscript of the play, he made a point of noting the "magnificent-mystical sense" in which Lipiner treated the concept of Trieb.[25] In essence, then, the problem posed at the outset of the play is that of recovering the peace and unity of being, lost through the will's manifestation of itself in phenomenal, fragmented form.

The third important symbol, which Lipiner presents in the opening scene of his play, is sunlight, the traditional representative of

23. Siegfried Lipiner, *Adam, Ein Vorspiel; Hippolytos* (Stuttgart, 1913), pp. 17–18.
24. Ibid., p. 20.
25. Mahler, *Briefe*, p. 279, (June 1898).

human intellect. Adam, reminiscing on the moments before the Fall, recalls the divine command, "You shall not know what is good and evil," and complains that God wanted to keep him in "beloved darkness." Instead, he had eaten fruit: "Shrouded in deepest night/I found myself rash—and rashly sundered [*zerriss*] /The night!" When, at this point, Eve cries "Woe!", Adam rebukes her and declares,

> I am chosen for the light,
> And this eye will bore into the sun
> And fill itself with its day
> Until it is blinded or endures
> And I will spy and trace and investigate.[26]

Intellect appears in an ambiguous light from the beginning of the play, for it is both Adam's pride and also the curse which drives him from the Garden.

Lipiner's aesthetic search for a return to the Garden focuses on the relationship between intellect and passion (Trieb) in each of the three principals: Adam, Cain, and Abel (the character of Eve is not well developed). In Adam, intellect and emotion are sharply separated, indeed so sharply that he has something of a Dr. Jekyll–Mr. Hyde personality. In the reasonable light of day, he lectures his sons on the value of obeying the law of God and of repressing Trieb: "Instinct is evil, and even if it drives you to the good." However, when evening falls, a change comes over Adam's character; his reason begins to falter under the impact of increasing emotion: "I must collect them, collect them,/ The racing thoughts—where do they run?/Back to me, for I am your Lord!—/It was the evening twilight—it began then—." At night Adam is a different man who secretly goes into the wilderness to commune with the wild beasts and snakes; then he becomes a "night friend of the wolves," as Cain calls him later in a moment of rage (*Adam*, pp. 25, 42, 74). Lipiner thus depicts the father of mankind as a good nineteenth-century burgher whose passions are kept under strict control during the day and are expressed only in the secrecy of the night.

Cain is fashioned very much after his father's image. He has dutifully obeyed Adam's command: "Vanquish your flesh and tame your lusts—;/I do, I do;—obedient is/My poor flesh, I constrain my

26. Lipiner, *Adam*, pp. 19–20.

desire." Cain is presented as the archetype of the repressed man who believes he has eliminated the passional element from his nature. "I have eradicated the sin from my blood,/ And removed the animal from my body,/ And I myself know how to choose between good and evil—" (pp. 24, 25). Another indication of Cain's completely repressed nature is his fear and hatred of animals. As he explains to Abel (p. 32),

> They are mute, deaf—and their nature is foreign
> To the word in which the spirit reveals itself; . . .
> Instinct peers out their sockets, seeking fodder,
> Fodder and sensual pleasure. Feeling, without soul!

The full extent of Cain's loathing for the animal is manifest in his belief that it is necessary to wash one's hands after touching one; he also takes great pleasure in killing and torturing animals. Like his father, then, Cain is a psychic cripple, but unlike his father, he does not benefit from the periodic releases of passion which Adam enjoys on his nightly excursions.

Where Cain embodies Adam's daylight ideals, Abel expresses his father's nocturnal passional qualities. Cain describes him as a dreamy youth who goes his own way unconscious of either God's commands or those of Adam (p. 24). Unlike Milton's Abel, he is definitely not a good shepherd, for while he daydreams, the flock wanders away. Then, when he discovers what has happened, he is enraged:

> Now he plunges away, strikes with his staff
> At random, blind with rage as he is;
> And how he screams, no jackal screams so wildly
> And sinful, the way he curses and swears. [p. 21]

Cain's description of his brother elicits only a chuckle of knowing indulgence from his father. Abel, then, is presented as the completely unrepressed man, the man in whom emotion expresses itself freely. Where Adam and Cain despise animals, the symbols of Trieb, Abel loves them. Although he often curses the animals of his flock, he also likes to sleep with them. On one occasion when he comes to join his family, he is accompanied by a wolf and an eagle. Cain drives them off in horror. Abel's attitude toward knowledge is also opposed to that of Adam and Cain. Where they believe in it, he rejects it: "No, I don't know: I don't want to know; No, no!" (pp. 30, 38).

Taken together, then, the father and his sons represent three possible psychic relationships of intellect and passion: the guiding force in Adam oscillates between the two; in Cain, passion is held in iron bondage to the service of the Word; in Abel, passion is the ruling force, and intellect is but lightly regarded.

The action of the play makes clear which of these alternatives is the most promising in the quest for the lost peace and unity of the G rden. The crucial issue is the growing antagonism between the brothers, and the incident that sets off the conflict is Abel's appearance in the company of the wolf and eagle. This inspires Cain to give him a lecture on the wickedness of all animals, to which Abel responds with an account of how he had come into contact with them. In the course of the day, he had wandered into an unfamiliar region, and moved by an unknown impulse, he had gone still farther. Soon he found himself accompanied on his journey by a multitude of birds which fluttered about his head and animals which followed at his heels. Then, when he paused and looked up, a ray of light struck him and all the animals disappeared except the wolf and eagle, which, after looking at him carefully, also turned away. Abel, feeling that he had been rejected, then returned home only to discover that the two animals had accompanied him as far as the hut (pp. 30–33).

Adam's excited response to his son's description of the path he took leaves no doubt in the mind of the reader that Abel has indeed stumbled on the path leading back to the Garden. The symbolism of the incident is, in fact, too clear to be aesthetically satisfying, but it does reveal the message that Lipiner is attempting to convey. It is Abel who momentarily finds the path, because unlike Adam or Cain, he disdains the knowledge of good and evil and lives a passional life in common with the animals. As Schopenhauer and Wagner had taught, the path back to the primal oneness lay within the individual in the form of the will. The intellect, with its reliance on the word, could never restore the unity of being essential to salvation.

Lipiner also follows Wagner and Schopenhauer in making clear his belief that although the key to man's salvation lay in the passional side of his nature, it did not lie in the unchecked expression of these animal-like passions. Man's Trieb was good because it was the quality that united him with all other beings, but the assertion of Trieb or will was also the source of all pain and evil in the world, for it was this that drove creatures to devour each other, and thus unknowingly to devour themselves. Later in the first act (p. 43) Abel moves to a full realization of this truth; in a prayer to God he bewails the fallen state of man and nature:

> Can they not flourish in peace,
> Speak, must one die through another?
> Have you given breath to the bird
> That it may smother in the throat of the snake?

Then, as a good Schopenhauerian pessimist, Abel calls upon the Lord to take his life and end the pain which it inevitably entails. Soon thereafter, Abel's faith is rewarded by a divine vision (p. 60):

> And see how small everything became to my senses—
> Forest, rocks, and heaven and the flames of the sun;
> All dissolved and flowed together
> Everything became small—and I also became so
> small within myself.

The crucial line in this passage is the third, in which Abel relates that everything dissolved and flowed together, for this indicates that he has miraculously transcended his individuation to regain the unity of the world-will.

Immediately after relating the vision to his brother, the bonds of restraint snap within Cain, and in a jealous rage he kills Abel. His first words after the deed are "Free! free! I breathe! Oh how well, how free!" Cain's joy, however, is brief. A lifetime of repression cannot be undone by a single deed, and he is soon tortured by his conscience. "Like the animals I also have torn to pieces,/But I know it —and fire consumes my bones." His proudest possession, knowledge, thus becomes his curse. In rage, he tells his father, "How I hate you! You gave me knowledge—/What am I now? I am a knowing beast" (pp. 62, 75). In the play's final action, Adam goes into the wilderness to find Cain and exact vengeance, but shortly after encountering his son, he is himself caught and torn to pieces by the wild animals.[27]

27. Schopenhauer and Nietzche had found in the myth of Dionysos the perfect symbolic representation of the theory that man's individuation was the source of all his misery. In having Adam suffer the Dionysian fate of dismemberment, Lipiner was drawing on this association to point ahead to the salvation of man which would be achieved when Christ once again brought these individual fragments into oneness.

Cain thus escapes vengeance to find the greatest possible punishment in continued life with a guilt-wracked conscience. Eve retires to a cave to nurture the unborn child who is to be the hope of the future.

While Lipiner's *Adam* is not a great artistic success, it does provide a revealing treatment of the metaphysics of the Wagnerian religion to which the artist adhered. The assumption of a pantheistic unity of will, lost through the will's fragmented manifestation in the phenomenal world and retrievable only through a surmounting of the will's individuation, is transposed into biblical terms and related as the opening play of a great human drama. Since Abel's redemption was only momentary, the play does not reveal Lipiner's full solution to the problem of transcending the will, but the broad lines of his metaphysics are clear.

Important as the philosophical content of Lipiner's play may have been, the peculiar nature of this work of art was even more significant in the eyes of Gustav Mahler—perhaps the only reader who shared Lipiner's beliefs fully enough to understand it completely. Mahler was transported with joy over the play, and in a letter to Lipiner he declared,

> It is a truly Dionysian work! Believe me, no living person understands that besides me . . . What is it then that gives all living creatures into the power of Dionysos? The wine intoxicates and elevates the condition of the drinker! But *what* is the wine? Dramatic presentation has never yet succeeded in conveying what exists of itself in every note of music. *This* music wafts from your poetry! It is really unique in the world.—It does not speak of wine and describe its effects—but it *is* the wine, it is Dionysos!"[28]

The point that Mahler makes in this letter is of crucial importance in understanding both Lipiner's plays and Mahler's own compositions. The reference to the incapacity of drama to present what music conveys in every note is based on Schopenhauer's doctrine that music is the direct and immediate portrayal of the world-will, while drama is but a presentation of will in its phenomenal, fragmented form. Mahler thus believed that like music, Lipiner's verse communicated the essence of reality to the reader in an unmediated form,

28. Mahler, *Briefe,* p. 279.

and in this belief Mahler was echoing ideas expressed in Nietzsche's *Birth of Tragedy*. In this work, Nietzsche made an important observation about the nature of the relationship existing between the audience and the work of art being presented in the primitive religious prototragedy of ancient Greece. "What must be kept in mind . . . is that the audience of Attic tragedy discovered *itself* in the chorus of the orchestra. Audience and chorus were never fundamentally set over against each other: all was one grand chorus of dancing, singing satyrs, and of those who let themselves be represented by them." The basis of this unity of the audience with the chorus, that "living wall against the onset of reality,"[29] lay in the religious nature of the performance; the prototragedy celebrated the unity of the chorus and the aesthetically participating audience with the god Dionysos, the unitary essence of being.

This was also one of the most important criteria on which Nietzsche based his praise of Wagner's works. Like the ancient Greek tragedies, they were intended to draw the audience into the work of art as in a religious celebration. Wagner, too, wrote extensively on this subject, and his decision to call *Parsifal* a *Buhnenweihefestspiel* (sacred festival play) indicates the seriousness of his religious intent. In describing Lipiner's play as a Dionysian work, then, Mahler was paying his friend the highest possible compliment, and when he added that "it appears to me in addition that the figure of Dionysos among the ancients was precisely *instinct* [*der Trieb*] in the mystic-magnificent sense in which you conceive it!", Mahler was expressing his conviction that the play had succeeded in its *religious* purpose. The play was itself a religious sacrament—"It *is* the wine, it *is* Dionysos"—and the audience of Lipiner's play would participate in divinity just as the audience of the Greek prototragedy had done. It is understandable that Mahler could write in a second letter to Lipiner, "I have made myself completely at home in your *Adam* and have found that life only begins here above in these regions . . . I have known this region for a long time, and so I have borne the trip better than many others will succeed in doing."[30] These words were written a year after the completion of Mahler's *Third Symphony*, a work which was intimately related to Lipiner's in its aesthetic-religious intent.

Since Lipiner's *Adam* was but the first part of a planned tetralogy,

29. Friedrich Nietzsche, *The Birth of Tragedy*, trans. Francis Golffing, pp. 54, 53.
30. Mahler, *Briefe*, p. 279 (June 1898); p. 280 (June 1898).

it cannot be expected to contain a full solution to the central problem of the transcendence of the individual will. Throughout the play there are events and symbols which point to a resolution in the remaining works of the series, the most significant of these being the dismemberment of Adam by the beasts in the final scene. This is one of many obvious allusions to Dionysos which point forward to the time when the unity of the fragmented deity (or will) would be restored, and in Lipiner's original plan, the crucial figure in this process would be Christ. An equally important problem left unresolved by *Adam* was that of how the individual will could turn and deny itself in its quest for reunion with the divine essence. In his essay "Religion and Art," Wagner had pointed to the example of Christ as proof that the miracle of the will's transcendence could be achieved, and with respect to his own day, he had suggested that art would play a crucial role in this process. Mahler's comments on *Adam* certainly indicate that he believed the audience would be religiously moved by this work, but clearly, the actual miracle of transcendence would be appropriate only to one of the later plays. Thus, both in terms of the actual story related in the plays as well as the anticipated transmogrification of the audience, the process of transformation remained unfulfilled.

How Lipiner would have attempted to accomplish this task must remain a mystery since he was never able to complete the remaining three plays, but the themes of his final play, *Hippolytos,* suggest that he may have intended this work as an ideological surrogate for the larger task which he found he could not finish. In any case, the play does resolve some of the unanswered problems of *Adam.* As in the earlier play, the quest for peace and salvation is examined through the theme of psychic fragments seeking wholeness and, as was the case in all of his works, Lipiner drew heavily on the precedents of Wagnerian literature in establishing his symbols. In this instance, it was Nietzsche's *Birth of Tragedy* upon which he relied most heavily, but Wagner's *Götterdämmerung* and *Tristan und Isolde* also exercised a clearly visible influence. Lipiner wove these and other borrowings together to produce a work in which the quest for wholeness proceeds on at least three levels: the personal-psychological, the political, and the metaphysical.

As the play begins, Phaedra is presented as the embodiment of pure physical striving. She calls herself "the enchained one of the abyss" whose limbs are riven with pain: "How they struggle upwards, upwards/Struggle groaning."[31] Hippolytos, on the other hand, is depicted as a serene contemplative youth in whom the force of will or passion finds no expression, and as Hartmut von Hartungen has observed, the structure is clearly intended to reflect Nietzsche's Dionysian–Apollonian duality.[32] In the context of the play, this is suggested by making Phaedra a devotee of Aphrodite, and Hippolytos a follower of Artemis, but yet another divine dichotomy is added by using Phaedra as a symbol of the Dionysian Titanic rebels against the Olympian gods represented by Hippolytos, Artemis, and Apollo. Phaedra's description of herself as the enchained one of the abyss, then, is intended to identify her as one of the imprisoned Titans.

Within this jungle of symbology, the action of the play proceeds to the second act where the crucial change in Phaedra's character occurs. Up to that point Phaedra had been completely the creature of her irresistible passion for the pure Hippolytos, while Hippolytos himself had remained completely ignorant of her feelings. Indeed, Phaedra had been so successful in concealing her feelings that Hippolytos had come to think of her as the ideal of feminine purity. Then as Hippolytos prepares to depart on a military expedition, he is suddenly transfixed by a vision. His lieutenants assume that Artemis has appeared to assure him of victory, but actually, his idealization of Phaedra has allowed him to identify her with Artemis in his vision.[33]

> Phaedra
> Shining in the birghtness of the sunrise
> At her feet
> Like the power of restrained beasts
> The troubled Waves grow calm.
>
> Be pure! Be bold! I saw the words
> Hover on her lips . . .
> No longer a child of the earth!—Oh woman [*Weib*]—
> All women [*Frauen*] are sanctified in you.
> All thoughts, like birds beating their wings, soar to you!

31. Lipiner, *Adam, ein Vorspiel; Hippolytos,* p. 94.

32. Hartungen, *Lipiner,* p. 62.

33. Compare Lipiner, *Hippolytos,* p. 108, where the soldiers assume Artemis has appeared to Hippolytos, with his following description of Phaedra (p. 113).

Phaedra unintentionally overhears the speech, but the imminence of Hippolytos' departure finally causes her passion to burst forth, and she confesses it to him. Hippolytos is shattered and immediately begins to revile her, but this only intensifies her rage and frustration. At the height of her passionate outburst she pictures herself as the first of the repressed Titans who will overthrow the rule of Hippolytos' beloved Olympians. The sons of the earth mother will destroy the measured and balanced Olympian realm (p. 117).

> You fierce sufferers,
> You dull thinkers,
> Rise up! Throw over! . . .
> In your gullet of flames—
> Pillars and columns and roof and beams.
> Fire in Heaven!—

But, then, when her passion has finally begun to spend its force, she begins to recall Hippolytos' earlier idealization of her, and this initiates a transmutation of her character. Slowly repeating fragments of Hippolytos' speech, she begins to identify with his idealized view of her. Hippolytos notices the change at once and urges her on (p. 119):

> For you are chosen for the heights
> Victorious power bears you
> To the highest, purest heights
> Purest cloud and clearest blue
> Open, open wide your soul!

Soon Phaedra's Trieb or will has been transmuted to a pure love, and she can say of her former self, "Away with her! She is no longer, she never existed—!" Whereas at the beginning of the play she dwelt in a crevasse and observed Hippolytos far above her, she has now identified with his symbol of her and she is above him: "Beneath me his eyes look up./ Over the waves he spreads/His arms toward me!" (p. 120).

While this scene is not artistically convincing, it does reveal clearly Lipiner's attempt to realize the Nietzschean ideal of tragedy in the most literal possible sense. Nietzsche had argued that the great Greek tragedies and indeed the greatness of Greek culture in general had resulted from a brotherly union of the Dionysian and Apollonian forces. He believed that the Dionysian force (particularly music) could inspire a symbolic (and thus Apollonian) intuition of Dionysian universality, and that this symbol or myth then had the power to push the world of appearance "to its limits, where it denies itself, and seeks to escape back into the world of primordial reality."[34] This is exactly what occurs in the second act of *Hippolytos:* Phaedra, the embodiment of the Dionysian spirit, inspires the Apollonian spirit Hippolytos to an intuition of Dionysian universality. He makes a symbol of her; she becomes the essence of the universal woman: "No longer a child of the earth!—Oh woman—/All women are sanctified in you." Then this Apollonian symbol of myth transports Phaedra, the prisoner of the phenomenal world, to the boundary of that world, where she renounces it and merges with the "real" world of forms. Since, in the course of the emotional interchange of the second act Hippolytos describes Phaedra as "drunk with crime! Possessed by madness [*Wahnbesessene*]" and she speaks of him as Artemis' brother (Apollo) in connection with his idealization of her, there can be little doubt that the Nietzschean relationship between Dionysian and Apollonian forces was specifically what Lipiner was attempting to convey. After Phaedra goes through the transformation involved in the identification with Hippolytos' symbol of her, her escape from the phenomenal realm is complete: "Mine, mine/the eternal height/And the Garden of the blessed."[35] Lipiner then goes on in the remainder of the play to reinforce this central message by examining the changes in Hippolytos, the political interaction between Theseus and Menestheus (who represents political passion) and, on the divine level, the further actions of Artemis and Aphrodite. In all cases, however, the plot moves toward the fruitful union of these formerly opposed forces.

The search for the lost Garden of the unindividuated will which began in Lipiner's *Adam* is thus crowned with success in *Hippolytos,* and from the latter play emerges a fairly clear picture of how the poet felt this was achieved. As in *Adam,* the total affirmation of the passional element of the human psyche over the narrowly rational is the essential initial step. Just as Lipiner could say in his poem "Vergessen," "No pain shall die in my bosom,/No sigh shall escape my breast," so Phaedra must reject the offer of Aphrodite to ease

34. Nietzsche, *Birth of Tragedy,* p. 132.
35. Lipiner, *Hippolytos,* pp. 113, 116, 120.

her pain with forgetfulness.[36] As Wagner had indicated in his many essays, passion and the will were the source of mankind's pain, but they were also the key to transcendence. In the actual process of transcendence which Lipiner depicts, the Poet-Priest plays the crucial role that Wagner suggested in his "Religion and Art." After the explosion of Phaedra's passion (accompanied symbolically by the rebellion of the passionate Titans against the restrained Olympians) the symbol of the Poet-God Apollo (speaking through Hippolytos) transmutes Phaedra's striving will and allows its entry into the divine kingdom of forms. Lipiner thus sees the path of the will as leading through passionate aspiration to transcendence and then to divine reconciliation, and while the theoretical basis for this metaphysical schema was primarily Nietzschean, it was the young Nietzsche of the *Birth of Tragedy,* the Nietzsche who revered Schopenhauer and Wagner, rather than the author of *Zarathustra,* who assumed that the striving of the human will was inescapable.

While Lipiner's *Hippolytos* does depict the role of the Poet-Priest in helping the will transcend its individuated form, Wagner had clearly indicated that this was but part of the artist's essential task. Not only was it necessary for the work of art to show the relationship of the individual will to the universal will (a process which Lipiner accomplished by showing Phaedra's subsumption into the symbol of the universal woman), but it was also necessary that the work of art should itself exert the direct emotional impact necessary to move the audience to a similar transcendence of the will. Only if this were accomplished would the art work serve the religious function that Nietzsche had found in the prototragedies of ancient Greece and the modern operas of Richard Wagner.

Although Mahler had specifically attributed this accomplishment to *Adam* in saying that the play "*was* Dionysos," his praise of *Hippolytos* was somewhat more restrained. In a letter to Lipiner, he combined a certain amount of technical criticism with the statement that "one thing has again forcefully appeared to me in your art: a new profound relationship of your work with your musical nature. I understand still more many half-humorous remarks of yours when you thunder at the Gods for giving you no music. My dear Siegfried,

36. Ibid., p. 106. "Vergessen" is from his *Buch der Freude* (Leipzig, 1880); quoted in Hartungen, *Siegfried Lipiner,* p. 40.

you are composing music!"[37] Since it was the musical aspect of the Greek prototragedies and Wagner's operas which gave them the emotional power to pull the audience into the religious celebration of the work, the attribution by Mahler of musicality to Lipiner's work was probably intended to suggest that Lipiner had succeeded in the essential act of the Poet-Priest, but one must suspect that the depth of Mahler's friendship had distorted his critical sense. However profound their metaphysics, the aesthetic power of Lipiner's works is slight. To find a full realization of the goals of the Poet-Priest, one must examine Gustav Mahler's own compositions.

37. Mahler, *Briefe,* p. 283.

5. The Metamusical Cosmos of Gustav Mahler

In his brief but penetrating essay on Mahler, Hans Redlich observed, "One of the many clichés with which Mahler was described during his lifetime runs: Mahler writes 'philosophical music.' "[1] While Redlich prefers the term metaphysical to philosophical, he is essentially in agreement with this description; but with few exceptions, subsequent critics have tended to treat this dimension of Mahler's work as a matter of almost incidental importance to the music itself. A similar attitude has prevailed with respect to the related matter of Mahler's lifelong friendship with Lipiner.[2] The friendship itself, as well as Mahler's repeated declarations that his music was more closely related to Lipiner's plays than anyone could ever know, has more often than not been taken as evidence for the timeworn adage that no one is less capable of judging aesthetic merit than the artist himself. Actually, Mahler knew exactly what he was saying, for it was precisely the metaphysics of his music which he shared with Lipiner, and for Mahler himself this was certainly one of the most important dimensions of his work. While one can not assume that Mahler's compositions necessarily convey his metaphysical intent, it seems a violation of common sense to

1. Hans Redlich, *Gustav Mahler, eine Erkenntnis* (Nuremberg, 1919), p. 25.

2. Donald Mitchell, in his *Gustav Mahler, the Early Years* (London, 1958) does discuss Lipiner as a source of Nietzschean influence (pp. 98–103), but he does not take the matter seriously enough to pursue it to a fruitful conclusion. Dika Newlin in *Bruckner, Mahler, Schoenberg* (New York, 1947), also raises these issues but also fails to develop them. Mahler's contemporaries understood the philosophy of his music much more fully, but they did not possess the memoirs and letters that allow an insight into its genesis. An invaluable guide to Mahler's symphonies is Paul Bekker's *Gustav Mahlers Sinfonien* (Berlin, 1921). Although somewhat impressionistic, Paul Stefan's *Gustav Mahler* (Munich, 1920) also contains some extremely valuable insights. The slender essay by Redlich, *Gustav Mahler, eine Erkenntnis,* is of the greatest value in understanding the intellectual context of Mahler's work. Neville Cardus' *Gustav Mahler, His Mind and His Music* (London, 1965) attempts to provide for English readers the kind of musical guide to the early symphonies that Bekker had furnished to Germans, but Bekker's work is clearly superior. The series of essays on Mahler in *Anbruch* Jg. 12, vol. 1 (March 1930) also deserve mention for their generally high quality; it includes essays by Theodor Adorno, Hans Redlich, Paul Stefan, Erwin Stein, Hanns Gutman, and Egon Wellesz.

treat it as irrelevant. As will be seen, no one was more aware than Mahler of the difficulty of expressing metaphysical concepts in musical terms, or of expressing verbally the content of his music; it is perhaps because of this realization that he succeeds as well as he does at both. In any case, with respect to Mahler's position in the intellectual history of his time, his aesthetic intentions and his own conceptions of his work are of great importance in themselves.

Although Lipiner's plays do much to illuminate the religious metaphysics he shared with Mahler, its full understanding requires a further examination of the Wagnerian sources on which both artists drew. Mahler's relationship to Nietzsche was not as close as Lipiner's had been, but there is nevertheless considerable evidence to indicate that the influence of this philosopher was quite important, most significant of all the simple fact that Mahler uses one of Nietzsche's poems in his *Third Symphony*. In a letter to Bertha Lohr (January 1891), the sister of his friend Fritz Lohr, Mahler declared, "I wrote Fritz today, and later today a volume of Nietzsche will be sent off to you. Hopefully you will then stop bombarding me with common obscenities." While the reference is not made clear, Mahler's interest in Nietzsche is. Far more significant, however, was the letter three years later (1894) to Emil Freund when Mahler wrote of Nietzsche, "Also in these recent weeks I have finished such remarkable readings that they indeed appear to be exercising an *epoch-making* influence on my life.[3] Unfortunately, neither the letter itself nor the editorial comments make clear which of Nietzsche's works are involved. With respect to Wagner, the evidence is more specific. As has been seen, Mahler reacted instantly to the vegetarian injunctions of Wagner's "Religion and Art" when it was published in the *Bayreuther Blätter* in 1880, so it is highly likely that he was familiar with that work. More significant still is a reference to Wagner's *Beethoven* in a letter from Mahler to Arnold Berliner (June 15, 1892). Mahler had given Berliner a copy of the work, and in the letter he asked, "What is *Beethoven* doing?" Alma Mahler explained the reference in the following note: "Mahler had often said that except for Wagner in *Beethoven*, only Schopenhauer in *The World as Will and Idea* had had anything worthwhile to say about the *essence* of music. Berliner once heard him describe the section in

3. Mahler, *Briefe*, pp. 485, 151.

The World as Will and Idea as, to his knowledge, the most profound thing ever written."[4]

Since Wagner's *Beethoven* (published in 1870) summarizes and then extends this portion of Schopenhauer's philosophy, it is perhaps through this work that Mahler's Wagnerian metaphysics is best approached. Wagner began by explaining some of the difficulties that confronted an attempt to understand those processes of musical creation which, in contrast to the conscious creative methods characteristic of sculptors and (to a certain extent) poets, sprang "from the dark soil of the subconscious [*Unbewusstsein*]." This dichotomy between the conscious and subconscious (which was linked with the Kantian thing-in-itself) was central to Wagner's thought, and for its development he summarized a number of ideas he had adapted from Schopenhauer's philosophy. He argued that since music was an immediate manifestation of the will, a consideration of the nature of the will (or unconscious) and its relationship to the conscious was necessary to an understanding of music. While the inner world of the will could not communicate directly with the conscious world, Wagner, following Schopenhauer, did believe that it manifested itself indirectly through dreams, which were brought to consciousness by the function of what was called a dream organ (*Traumorgan*). And, "since the dream organ cannot be roused to activity through external stimulations, to which the brain is now completely closed, this can only occur through happenings in the inner organism, happenings which our waking consciousness perceives only as dark emotions." Due to the temporal and spatial limitations of conscious perception, Wagner believed it was only through the individual unconscious that man could approach the timeless and spaceless all-inclusive will (or thing-in-itself), and this position led him to the implicitly pantheistic conclusion that through the inner realm man was related to the whole of nature.[5]

Wagner went on to argue that music performed a role similar to that of the dream as a means of communication between the inner subjective realm of the unconscious and the outer objective world. Since this inner passional world was not bound by the Kantian categories of time and space which formed perception in the outer world, the problem of explaining how music could provide a communicative

4. Mahler, *Briefe,* p. 126.
5. Wagner, *Schriften,* vol. 9, pp. 65–69.

link between the two spheres was extremely important. Wagner attempted to solve the problem by making a distinction which corresponded to the dichotomy between conscious and unconscious. He said that sound, in its most elementary form, the cry of terror, was an immediate expression of the anguished will, and he believed that the hearer of such a cry was directly affected on an emotional level. Since reason did not enter into the process, he felt that these sounds were not subject to the Kantian categories that bound conscious perception. He then reasoned that music was built up through combinations and modifications of such elemental sounds and was able to link the inner unconscious world of the subject to the external unconscious of the object.[6]

There was another element of music that provided a link with the conscious world of reason. Wagner believed that whereas the most basic component of music, harmony, was independent of time and space, rhythm was based on a sequential ordering in time, and thus, by means of this element, music "so to speak extends the hand of understanding to the waking world of appearances." Focusing still more closely on the crucial role of rhythm in music, Wagner defined what he regarded as one of the great artistic problems of the period of Beethoven's life—the secularization of music. He pointed out that in Palestrina's music, rhythm, in the sense of a symmetrical succession in time, had no independent existence, but came into being only as a result of the polyphonic interplay of the different voices. Under these circumstances, music remained true to its spiritual nature, but subsequently it had become infected with a secular spirit characterized by a regular and repetitious rhythmic pattern which gave to melody an insistent, catchy quality. Since secular music was bound by the category of time, it was closely tied to the outer world of appearances, to the conscious world of reason, and was thus alienated from its true nature and purpose. Wagner felt that the real villain in this development was reason. It was reason which dictated the "banal repetition of phrases and flourishes, with an exact division of loud and soft, with the prescribed, regular, grave introduction of just so many bars through the gate, of just so many half-closes to the sanctifying uproar of the final cadence."[7]

Wagner thought that this destructive rationalistic spirit was a

6. Ibid., pp. 69–71.
7. Ibid., pp. 76–84 passim.

foreign influence which had penetrated Germany from France and Italy, and he felt that Beethoven's greatness lay in the fact that he had transcended these rigid rationalistic forms to return music to the inner world of feeling where it belonged. Wagner was convinced that once the German spirit (as symbolized by Beethoven) had achieved victory over sterile foreign influences in the sphere of music, the new Germanic music could lead the way to a general cultural rebirth by overthrowing the stultifying dictates of rational convention. He believed that imitation of these conventions poisoned all levels of contemporary life, and this malaise was ascribed to the influence of the French and the journalistic world[8] (one of his many synonyms for liberalism).[9] The program of cultural regeneration which Wagnerianism proclaimed sought through music to redirect attention to the inner spiritual realm of the emotions, and thus to redress the imbalance which liberal culture had created through its overemphasis of man's rational element. This, it was hoped, would restore to man the unity (*Ganzheit*) that was essential if he was to live in harmony with nature.[10]

Mahler's comments on the role of reason with respect to music and the forces of the unconscious reveal an attitude very close to that elaborated in this essay. In a letter written to his wife in June 1909, Mahler spoke of reason as the limited but necessary means for communicating with the phenomenal world:

> The rational, that is to say, that which can be analyzed by the understanding, is almost always the inessential and actually a veil which disguises the form [*Gestalt*]. But insofar as a soul needs a body—there is nothing that can be said against that—the artist must pick out his means for presentation from the rational world. There where he himself has not yet achieved clarity, or actually wholeness [*Ganzheit*], the rational will stifle the artistic unconscious and demand too much explanation.[11]

At the same time, Mahler also followed the Wagnerian demand for an organic fusion of word and tone. Wagner believed this was neces-

8. Ibid., pp. 113–16.
9. For this identification see his "Publikum und Popularität," *Schriften,* vol. 10, p. 87.
10. Wagner, "Kunstwerk der Zukunft," *Schriften,* vol. 3, p. 66.
11. *Gustav Mahler im eigenen Wort—im Worte der Freunde,* ed. Willi Reich (Zürich, 1958), p. 57.

sary to bring about that reunification of the arts which was to prepare the way for a general cultural revival. While music had the power to appeal directly to the emotions without mediation by reason, it could not, according to Wagner, define sharply the object of feeling and emotion.[12] For this it was necessary to use words, but the relationship of the words to the music could not be what had so often obtained in the past, when, as Wagner put it, the words provided merely the explanatory label beneath the painting. In the organic relationship for which Wagner argued, the music would express the emotional element of a given verbal passage. The words would thus precede the music chronologically, even though they were not primary in ultimate significance.[13]

Mahler adhered closely to this principle, as he indicated to Natalie Bauer-Lechner. He aked:

> Have you noticed that with me the melody always proceeds [*ausgeht*] from the word, which, so to speak, creates it for itself, never the reverse? It is that way with Beethoven and Wagner. And . . . only in this way is there created what one would like to describe as the identity of word and tone. The reverse, where any sort of words must arbitrarily try to accommodate themselves to a melody, is a conventional association, but no organic fusion of the two.[14]

However, Mahler also believed that "the text actually constitutes only a suggestion of the more profound content which is to be brought out, of the treasure which is to be raised."[15] Thus, with Mahler as with Wagner, the word held a position of primacy only in the sense that this was the necessary means by which the more important musical, suprarational world could communicate its wisdom to the phenomenal world of man.

Mahler followed Wagner in developing his view of the relationship between word and tone within the context of the idea of wholeness (Ganzheit). In a letter to Bruno Walter (1906), Mahler wrote,

> That our music involves the "purely human" (everything that

12. Wagner, "Eine Mitteilung an meine Freunde," *Schriften,* vol. 4, p. 318.
13. Wagner, "Oper und Drama," *Schriften,* vol. 4, pp. 113, 318, 102–03.
14. Bauer-Lechner, *Erinnerungen,* p. 30.
15. Ibid., p. 10. The date of the conversation is around July 1893.

> belongs thereto, thus also the "intellectual") cannot be denied. It depends, as in all art, on the pure means of the expression, etc. If one wants to make music one must not want to paint, to write poetry, or to describe. But *what* one makes into music [*musiziert*] is still only the whole (thus feeling, thinking, breathing, suffering) man. There is indeed nothing further to object to about a "program" (even if it is not the highest step of the ladder)—but a *composer* must express himself in it and not a writer, philosopher, or painter (all of which are contained in a composer).[16]

Even though Mahler rejects the idea of a program as the central point of a composition, he does allow it a secondary descriptive role, a view which reflects his more specific ideas on the relationship of world and tone. Mahler felt the full range of man's being should be expressed in music, and even though the words dictated the subject of the music in any vocal composition, it was still the music itself that conveyed the ultimate meaning. Thus a program could be taken as a partial guide to the whole; it was not incidental or inaccurate, but simply incomplete.

To understand the nature of the musical world which Mahler felt to exist beyond the reach of reason, it is necessary to examine his music itself, using his comments on his work as guideposts into this ultimately unfathomable metaphysical realm. Since it was in the *Third Symphony* that Mahler first achieved and fully expressed a clear vision of higher spiritual reality, it is to this work, composed during the two successive summers of 1895 and 1896, that we now turn.

One of the first problems confronting an attempt to understand the Third is that posed by the structure of the work. The symphony is divided into two parts, the first containing one movement lasting almost thirty-five minutes and the second containing five movements lasting about an hour. This highly unconventional structure was not what Mahler had initially intended, and the gradual evolution of the unusual form is itself the product of a crucial development in Mahler's view of his art and of himself as artist. The importance of this process to Mahler personally is seen in the extraordinary number of comments on the work which he made in letters and conversations

16. Mahler, *Briefe,* p. 277.

during and after its composition. As Paul Bekker has observed, "Even later, Mahler appears to have written and spoken about no composition with the readiness and explicitness that he did of the Third. . . . On this work a remarkably abundant selection of revealing comments by Mahler has been preserved while on many others scarcely a word has been reported."[17] To discover the nature of this important event in Mahler's life one must trace his changing conceptions of the Third during the twelve-month period in which he composed it.

Initially, Mahler had intended this work to provide a respite from the intense emotional demands of his first two symphonies. This would be a joyous, comic work. As he jokingly remarked to Natalie Bauer-Lechner, "With it I hope to win applause and money." He went on to declare in an allusion to Nietzsche, "I will call the whole thing *My Joyous Wisdom* [*Meine frohliche Wissenschaft*]—that is what it is."[18] One of his sketches contains an alternative title expressive of the same mood; it would be called *The Happy Life, a Summer Night's Dream* (*Das glückliche Leben, ein Sommernachtstraum*). To the title Mahler added the comment "(not from Shakespeare, note of a critic)."[19]

Although the earliest proposed programs for the work vary considerably in detail, the one Mahler related to Natalie Bauer-Lechner in the summer of 1895 is representative of his overall intent and mood. There would be seven movements entitled:

1. Summer marches in
2. What the flowers in the meadow tell me
3. What the animals in the forest tell me
4. What the night tells me (the man)
5. What the morning bells tell me (the angels)
6. What love tells me
7. What the child tells me[20]

The first movement, which would be "thoroughly humorous" would depict the defeat of winter by summer and then a triumphant victory

17. Bekker, *Mahlers Sinfonien,* p. 106.

18. Bauer-Lechner, *Erinnerungen,* pp. 19, 20. The latter remark is an obvious allusion to Nietzsche's work.

19. Bekker, p. 106.

20. Bauer-Lechner, *Erinnerungen,* p. 20

march. In the following movements the messages of the various creatures and forces of nature would be expressed. By August of 1895 Mahler had completed the sketches for the last six movements, and during the following months he worked on the orchestration of this portion of the work.[21] Mahler put off all work on the first movement until the following summer.

At the close of the conducting season in June 1896, Mahler retired to his cabin at Steinbach am Attersee in the Salzkammergut. Here he could wander among lakes and pine-covered mountains as he worked out the problems of his composition. Natalie Bauer-Lechner, who often accompanied him on these excursions, noted in her recollections (*Erinnerungen*) his complete absorption in his work. "One sees that, when walking or bicycling with him, he is always completely lost in himself or he has stopped to draw out his musical notebook and write something in it" (p. 47). When not lost in thought, Mahler eagerly poured out his ideas and feelings about the work in letters to Anna Bahr-Mildenburg and in conversations with Natalie Bauer-Lechner. Both women were accomplished musicians, so he could expect that his most sophisticated musical conceptions would be understood and appreciated. Since Natalie Bauer-Lechner regularly transcribed the conversations in her diary and the letters to Anna Bahr-Mildenburg have also been preserved, it is possible to obtain a rare degree of insight into the process by which Mahler's work came into being.

The structure of the symphony which Mahler envisioned as he again took up his work in June 1896 was only slightly altered from the program of August 1895. Mahler now planned an introduction to precede the first movement, and his work on the introduction had caused him to alter the title for the as yet unwritten first movement. "The title *Summer Marches In* is no longer appropriate to this arrangement of things in the introduction; perhaps instead *Pan's Procession*—not *Procession of Dionysos!* It is not a Dionysian mood, but rather there are Satyrs and other such coarse creatures of nature roaming about" (p. 41). The mood of the movement was still to be humorous.

On 28 June Mahler excitedly announced to Natalie Bauer-Lechner that he had completed the sketches for the movement—weeks before he had thought it possible. In addition, he had chosen a title for the

21. Mahler, *Briefe*, p. 108.

introduction: "Pan Awakens" (*"Pans Erwachen"*), and he could exclaim to her with delight, "Well, what will become of it? It is the wildest thing that I have ever written" (p. 42). During the following days Mahler found the instrumentation much easier than expected, and his work proceeded rapidly.

Then on 4 July Mahler's work brought him to what can only be described as a mystical experience. Bauer-Lechner notes: "Today, when Mahler came from his work to my studio to fetch me for a walk before dinner, he was completely exhausted and yet as if intoxicated." The conversation she then recorded is the longest and probably the most significant of the entire diary. Mahler began, "It is fearful the way this movement has caused me to grow beyond everything that I have ever composed." He felt it was so much larger than life that everything human collapsed to the level of a pygmy empire. "I am literally gripped with terror when I see where the path ordained for music leads and that it has become my terrifying office [*schreckliche Amt*] to be the bearer of this gigantic work [*Träger dieses Riesenwerkes*]." Mahler then described the experience he had undergone:

> Just as something which you have long known [*Gekanntes*] often becomes illuminated and clear through a personal experience, so today it suddenly came over me in a flash: Christ on the Mount of Olives, who must—and desires—to drain the cup of sorrows to the dregs. He who is chosen for this cup can and will not turn it back; still at times a deathly fear must come over him when he thinks of what stands before him. I have such a feeling about this movement and the prospect of what I will have to suffer on its account in order not even to live to see that it is recognized and acknowledged."

Mahler went on to say that while the contents of the other movements of the symphony could be indicated or described in words to a certain extent, that was not possible in this case. "You must sink with me into Nature herself which is grasped so deeply at the roots by music as by no art and no science. And I believe that no artist must suffer from her secret lessons [*Mystik*] as much as the composer when she seizes him" (p. 44).

While Mahler's feelings at this moment can be conveyed only in religious or perhaps musical terms, an understanding of his Wagnerian background does much to illuminate the nature of his experience.

Perhaps the most basic single idea of the Wagnerian movement was that enunciated by Schopenhauer and repeated by Nietzsche—the idea that music is an exact copy of the world-will, the essence of reality. Schopenhauer had even gone so far as to say that one could as well call everything a manifestation of music as of will. This seems to be the idea Mahler had "long known" but which had been palpably realized in his own experience. In writing his work he had suddenly felt himself in contact with this ultimate reality. More significant still are his references to Christ, for this suggests that Mahler has to a certain extent identified with him in his role as artist. In speaking of the *schreckliche Amt* which he must fill, and of himself as the *Träger dieses Riesenwerkes,* the sufferings and burdens of Christ immediately come to mind. In terms of the Wagnerian metaphysics, this too is understandable, for in his "Religion and Art" Wagner had attributed essentially the same significance to Christ's sacrifice as he did to the message of the Poet-Priest who would convey the religious lessons of the transcendence of the will in his art.[22] This was the dual task which Mahler had assumed to be his own.

Dramatic as was Mahler's call to the role of Poet-Priest, the genesis of this experience is perhaps even more remarkable. The original subject envisioned for the first movement was "Summer Marches In," the triumph of Summer's vitality over the still death of Winter, and implicit in this choice was a perhaps accidental parallel with Mahler's own creative rhythm. Because of the demands of conducting, Mahler was forced to save all his creative work for the summer. In this instance he had composed the last five movements in the summer of 1895 and had then been forced to put off work on the first—the subject of which was to be the birth and triumph of the creative force in nature—until the following summer. The coincidence of his own experience as an artist with the subject of his art was thus complete, and Mahler seems to have realized this in his July fourth conversation with Natalie Bauer-Lechner. Speaking of his work he declared, "It is irresistibly carrying me forward. It is as if the stream of creation [*Strom des Schaffens*] had become so massively swollen through a year-long damming that there is no possibility of outrunning it."[23] Later he speaks of the birth pangs of the

22. Wagner, *Schriften,* vol. 10, pp. 215, 247.
23. *Erinnerungen,* p. 46.

work. In both instances the artistic process is related to a natural creative process, and thus when Mahler speaks of understanding the first movement by sinking into a nature which is grasped in its essence by music, he is making a complete identification of the process of musical composition with the divine forces of natural growth.[24] Given this identification, Mahler's position was clearly that of a mediator of divine wisdom and his identification of his role with that of Christ becomes understandable.

Mahler's decision to name the introduction to his work "Pan Awakes" and the first movement "Pan's Procession" (*Pans Zug*) are also highly significant in this context, for Pan was traditionally a god of music, a patron god of pastoral poets, and the god of natural growth and fertility. The personification of the abstract concept of the arrival of summer in the form of this musical nature-god may well have been the essential step in the process by which Mahler so dramatically came to identify himself with the subject of his composition. It is small wonder that he could observe to Natalie Bauer-Lechner that this work had caused the problems of his *Second Symphony*, the human question of man's purpose and his immortality, to become irrelevant. "Can a spirit who rethinks [*nachdenkt*] the eternal creative thoughts of the godhead in a symphony such as this die?"[25] In the Third, Mahler was able to achieve the most reassuring answer to this question. Even though the diaries of Natalie Bauer-Lechner so essential to understanding the process by which Mahler's *Third Symphony* was created, were not available when Paul Bekker wrote his brilliant analysis of the work, he realized fully what an important event in Mahler's life it represented: "Here for the first time he had penetrated to the essence of his own nature and directed himself to it with the passionate intensity of the achieved consciousness of personality."[26]

Considering the enormous importance of this experience for Mahler's personal world view, it is not surprising that it should produce a significant impact on the work that had inspired it. The "thoroughly humorous" movement which Mahler had set out to

24. As Bekker observes of the first movement, "In sie hinein tönt der Weckruf Pans, des Erdengottes, oder des Sommers, oder—wenn das Symbol in noch weiterem Sinne efasst werden soll—des Künstlers. Er beseelt die fühllose Materie, weckt sie zum Bewusstsein, macht sie fruchtbar" (*Mahlers Sinfonien*, p. 109).

25. *Erinnerungen*, p. 45.

26. Bekker, p. 112.

compose led him to a dramatic religious experience that brought home the realization that Pan's role as well as that of the Poet-Priest entailed profound suffering as well as joy. As he wrote a short time later (18 November 1896) in a letter to Dr. Richard Batka, "That this nature hides within it everything that is terrifying [*schauerlich*], magnificent and also lovable . . . of that naturally no one learns anything. It always strikes me as odd that most people, when they speak of 'Nature,' always think only of flowers, little birds, the perfume of the forest, etc. No one knows the god Dionysos, the great Pan."[27] It was this fearful deity whom Mahler had encountered in his mystical experience and, as the letter to Batka indicates, Mahler's initial intention that the movement express "no Dionysian" mood had given way to a musical conception in which Pan and Dionysos became closely related. The mood of the finished movement was one that incorporated the fearsome aspects of the godhead as well as the humorous. In the course of his July fourth conversation with Natalie Bauer-Lechner, Mahler also announced his intention to restructure the work so that the first movement would by itself comprise a separate part, followed by a pause; in addition, he decided that the entire work would be entitled "Pan, Symphonic Poems."[28] In Mahler's eyes, Pan was now the central figure in the symphony and in deciding to call it symphonic poems, he was expressing his belief in the importance of the metaphysical structure underlying the work; by describing it as poetry, attention would be shifted from the musical to the intellectual connectives. This structure, which is essentially that of the completed symphony, could provide the form and scope necessary to express the vastly deepened conception of nature which Mahler now hoped to convey.

After his revelation, Mahler continued his labors, secure in the conviction of his religious mission. In a letter to Anna Bahr-Mildenburg he told her that his work demanded so much of him "that one is as dead to the outer world. Now just think of such a huge work in which the entire world is actually reflected—one is oneself, so to say, only an instrument on which the universe plays." As he revealed in another letter to Anna Bahr-Mildenburg, he found that the universe could also play jokes on him. "When your letter arrived, a strange thing happened. As usual, I looked at the postmark, and noticed this time instead of Malborghet, only P.A.N. (beneath it

27. Mahler, *Briefe*, pp. 214–15.
28. *Erinnerungen*, pp. 42, 45.

was also a 30 which, however, I didn't see)." He then told her that he had just decided to call his work "Pan" and continued, "Now you can imagine what a surprise these three inscrutable letters were to me at first, which I afterward deciphered as Post Office No. 30 [*Post Amt Nr.* 30]."[29] Another time he told Natalie Bauer-Lechner of a strange occurrence. He had been worried about a technical problem in his composition for days; "Then today in my sleep a voice called to me (it was that of Beethoven or Wagner, with whom I am now generally accustomed to having nightly intercourse—not bad company): 'Just let the horns come in three bars later!' and with that, the most difficult part was resolved in the most simple and wonderful way, so that I didn't trust my eyes!"[30] It is clear, then, that Mahler's vision of himself as the mediating instrument of divine musical wisdom remained with him throughout the period of composition.

Although the explosion of Mahler's vision into his work does much to explain the vast size of the first movement, it does not fully explain his decision to constitute the movement as a separate section, but if the content of Mahler's vision is examined more closely, this too becomes apparent. In turning to the work itself, one is aided in an interpretation of the music both by the explicit and extensive comments with which Mahler loaded the score of his completed work as well as by a series of notes which were included in the manuscript and later eliminated from the published work.

The symphony begins with a stentorian theme (see musical extract A) announced by the eight horns.[31]

In the final manuscript the beginning of the theme is accompanied by the comment "Reveille" ("*Der Weckruf*"), which indicates that this theme should be taken, as Bekker has suggested, "as the first message [*Botschaft*] to the lifeless world."[32] This is the call that will

29. Mahler, *Briefe*, pp. 163, 162.

30. *Erinnerungen*, p. 48.

31. Gustav Mahler, *Symphony No. 3*, Universal Edition (Vienna, n.d.), p. 3. This will hereafter be cited as *Score*.

32. The manuscript notes are quoted in Paul Stefan, *Gustav Mahler*, pp. 125–26; Bekker, p. 113.

awaken the slumbering world to life. Bekker also argues that this triumphant theme is soon forcibly drawn down to its close by a "repressive power" ("*niederzwingende Kraft*") which he describes as representative of lifeless nature.[33] The group of themes representing lifeless nature makes its appearance beginning four bars before score no. 2, and soon develops into the characteristically ponderous configuration in extract B.

Mahler's directions in the printed score are, "Heavy and dull" ("*Schwer und dumpf*").[34]

While composing this section of the work, Mahler had remarked to Natalie Bauer-Lechner, "That is really almost no longer music, it is almost just nature sounds. And it is frightening the way in which from out of the soulless inflexible matter—I could also have called the movement 'What the rocks on the mountain tell me'—life gradually fights its way free."[35] The initial musical expression of this struggle is found in a developing dialogue between the strings and the horns (C). Finally, after about twenty-five measures, this dialogue leads to the birth of a significant theme (D) in the trumpets.[36] The process by which this theme comes into being, as well as the coincidence of its overall contour wiht that of the *Weckruf*, suggests it is intended to represent the answering call of the new life born out of dead nature.

33. Bekker, p. 114.
34. *Score*, pp. 5, 7.
35. *Erinnerungen*, p. 40.
36. *Score*, pp. 8, 10.

In the fourth movement where this theme is brought into specific relationship with certain words and concepts of Nietzsche's poem it becomes clear that the theme also symbolizes the striving will in a specific, Nietzschean-Schopenhauerian sense. It was this force which Wagnerians believed resides within all manifestations of life, so the term life-will seems the most appropriate title for the rising and falling motif which plays such a central role throughout the symphony. In another reference to this section of his work, Mahler himself suggests in Promethean imagery the tormented longing so characteristic of the life-will as described in the *Birth of Tragedy* and symbolized in that work's emblem of Prometheus bursting his chains. He notes how "the youth, the enchained life, striving for salvation, laments from the abyss of the still lifeless, immobile nature "[37]

After this brief appearance of the life-will motif, there is a fleeting allusion (E) to Pan's eventual appearance,[38] at which point the manuscript of the score bears the comment "the Herald."[39] After another exchange between the forces of lifeless nature and the Weckruf, the Pan-call is heard in the oboe and is answered by a variant of the life-will motif (F) in the double bass.[40]

37. *Erinnerungen*, p. 40.
38. *Score*, p. 16.
39. Stefan, *Mahler*, p. 125.
40. *Score*, p. 25.

The directions on the printed score read "As from a great distance." Exchanges between the forces of lifeless nature and the life–Pan complex continue until a final confrontation about two-thirds of the way through the movement leads to the complete victory of life. The victory is then celebrated by a Bacchic procession which (beginning at score no. 62) marches in steadily rising intensity of jubilation to the end of the movement.

It is at this point that the function of the first movement within the structure of the entire work can best be understood. As has been seen, Mahler toyed with the possibility of a number of different titles for his work in the course of its composition. One of his first ideas before any of the work was written was *The Happy Life, a Summer Night's Dream*. Then, after completing the closely related last five movements, he considered the possibility of calling it *Summer Morning's Dream*. Finally, after completing the first movement and deciding on the division into two separate parts, he came almost full circle in choosing *Summer Noontime's Dream*.[41] This is a highly significant choice in terms of the ancient Pan legend, in that Pan—himself regarded as an inspirer of dreams—traditionally slept and dreamt at midday.[42] It is clear, then, that the two parts of the symphony are intended to present the two different phases of Pan's experience. In the first, Pan's awakening symbolizes the newly born life-will struggling into existence against the forces of lifeless

41. Bekker, p. 106; Mahler, *Briefe*, p. 140 (letter of August 1895 to Arnold Berliner), and p. 198 (letter of 6 Aug. 1895 to Max Marschalk).

42. *Oxford Classical Dictionary* (Oxford, 1961), p. 640.

nature, and this is then followed by a Bacchic victory procession. In the second section the music communicates Pan's midday dream, inspired by the Dionysian intoxication of the procession.[43]

If this can be taken as the plot of Mahler's symphony, the most appropriate possible form for presenting the experiences of this Greek nature-god would be that of the ancient Greek religious proto-tragedy which Nietzsche had discussed in his *Birth of Tragedy*. The prototragedy consisted of a chorus of Satyrs whose Bacchic celebration first drew the aesthetically participating audience into the chorus, and then projected its Appollonian vision of the god into the center of the celebration. The effect of this, according to Nietzsche, was to make the individual aware of himself as a part of all being (the assumption into the chorus) and then to allow him to transcend willing and find peace in reunion with the All (the Apollonian vision).[44]

If Mahler did indeed model his symphony on the structure of a Greek prototragedy, a primary function of the Bacchic celebration at the close of the first movement would be to draw the audience into the chorus of celebrants; and a comparison of Mahler's comments on his work with the work itself yields evidence that this was his intention. One of the notes in the manuscript of the score consists of the words "The South Storm" ("*Der Südstorm*") at score no. 51, and it is followed by a tempestuous variation of the various Weckruf, Pan, and life-will themes.[45] Significantly, Mahler also used the image of the south storm at the close of the crucial July fourth conversation with Natalie Bauer-Lechner. In describing the movement he said,

> It rolls along frantically in the first movement like the south storm which in recent days has swept here and there and which —I am convinced—bears all fruitfulness in its womb, since it comes from distant fruitful-hot lands. . . . In a rapid march tempo it roars nearer and nearer, louder and louder, swelling like a landslide until the entire exaltation pours over you. In the midst of it there resounds in mystic harmony and like an

43. It is not surprising that Mahler should say in a letter written to Bruno Walter during the composition of the first movement that he imagined future critics would declare that in the symphony "one often seems to find onself in a winery or a stable." The date of the letter is 2 July 1896 (Mahler, *Briefe*, p. 220).

44. Friedrich Nietzsche, *The Birth of Tragedy and the Genealogy of Morals*, trans. Francis Golffing, pp. 40, 50, 54, 58, 132.

45. Stefan, *Mahler*, p. 125; *Score*, pp. 72 et seq.

> extremely strange, mysterious pause [*Ruhepunkt*]: "Oh man take heed!" ["*O Mensch, gib acht*!"][46]

The coincidence of Mahler's score note, "south storm," with the image of the conversation, as well as his reference to the mysterious *Ruhepunkt* make it possible to identify the portion of the movement that inspired his revelation and the ensuing conversation. This part of the movement begins with the south storm marked in the manuscript at score no. 51 and proceeds to the 37 measure Ruhepunkt between nos. 60 and 62. The latter section is completely different in tone from any other part of the first movement and is built around the life-will theme which follows the words "Oh man take heed!" in the fourth movement. It is clear, then, that this was the portion of his composition Mahler was describing in his conversation. Immediately following the Ruhepunkt the Bacchic victory celebration begins, and here too the words of Mahler's description ("In a rapid march tempo it roars nearer and nearer, louder and louder") fit the finished score precisely. The beginning of the Bacchic celebration (score no. 62) is in march tempo. and the note in the printed score is, "Again, everything approaching from a great distance."[47] The light that Mahler's conversation throws on this section of the work is extremely significant. The description of the south storm as the far from gentle bearer of fruitfulness coincides with the attributes of Pan, the nature-god Mahler is describing musically, and in characterizing the Bacchic procession as roaring ever closer and "swelling like a landslide until the entire tumult and the entire exaltation pours over you," he is suggesting exactly that absorption of the audience into the Satyric celebration which would be appropriate to the first part of a Greek prototragedy.

Most important of all, Mahler's own reaction to the music he was composing at this crucial point was exactly what Nietzsche described as the experience of one who has been drawn into the Satyrs' chorus by the power of Dionysian music. According to Nietzsche this communicated to the celebrant a feeling of his oneness with all being, and the essence of Mahler's "revelation" was just such an experience when he spoke of sinking into Nature herself which was grasped

46. *Erinnerungen,* pp. 46–47.
47. *Score,* pp. 82–84.

by music as by no other art or science. Whether this coincidence of Nietzschean theory with Mahlerian feeling attests to the wisdom of the philosopher's arguments or the susceptibility of the composer's emotions remains open to question, but it does seem clear that Mahler's own revelation—inspired by his work on the first movement—testifies strongly for the argument that this movement is intended to serve the same function as the first half of the Greek prototragedy described by Nietzsche.

Although Hans Redlich does not discuss the possibility that the *Third Symphony* is structured on the model of the ancient prototragedy, his comments on the affective power of Mahler's völkisch music strongly support this thesis. He observes, "For Mahler the 'people,' the 'mass' is naturally a Dionysian one. Where Mahler, as in the first movement of the Third Symphony, creates from a profound Dionysian fervor for the masses [*Masseninbrust*] the communal-forming [*Gemeinschaftbildende*] effect . . . is the strongest."[48] The observation that Mahler made about the movement to Natalie Bauer-Lechner in the fall of 1896 when he finally was able to play it for her in completed form on the piano—"I see ever more how much the colossal Greek conception of nature lies at the basis of it,"[49] — also suggests that the work be viewed as an attempt to recreate that feeling of man's unity with all of nature, which was the purpose of the Greek prototragedy.

In turning from the first to the second part of Mahler's symphony, one could hardly find a more appropriate characterization of the contrast in tone and mood than that noted by Nietzsche in the two halves of the prototragedy: "We may recognize a drastic stylistic opposition: language, color, pace, dynamics of speech are polarized into the Dionysiac poetry of the chorus on the one hand, and the Apollonian dream world of the scene on the other." In developing the nature of this dream world, Nietzsche noted that it was "very different from the continual interplay of shifting forces in the music of the chorus, from those powers deeply felt by the enthusiast, but which he is incapable of condensing into a clear image. The adept no longer obscurely senses the approach of the god: the god now

48. Redlich, *Mahler,* p. 29.
49. *Erinnerungen,* p. 60.

speaks to him from the proscenium.[50] In the second half of his symphony Mahler too was concerned with the presentation of a dream vision, and just as the nature-god of the Greek prototragedy spoke directly to the religious initiate through the dream, so too did he speak in Mahler's work. The composer wrote Anna Bahr-Mildenburg in July 1896 that in his new symphony "all of nature finds a voice and speaks such profound secrets as one perhaps intuits in dreams." In its final form, the specific titles Mahler suggested for the movement of this section were:[51]

II. What the flowers of the meadow tell me
III. What the animals of the forest tell me
IV. What man tells me
V. What the angels tell me
VI. What love tells me

Different as the two halves of Mahler's symphony are in form and tone, in terms of philosophical or religious content they are very closely related. The first movement had depicted the struggle through which the life-will had come into being, followed by its triumphant victory; the second section carries the evolution of the life force from this point to its highest possible expression. Mahler described it thus: "Gradually life fights its way free until it differentiates itself from step to step in ever higher forms of development: flowers, animals, man, into the realm of the spirits to the angels."[52] In the final "love" movement, Mahler is dealing with the divinity in its highest form, for as he observed to Anna Bahr-Mildenburg, "I could also call the movement 'What God tells me,' and indeed just in that sense, as indeed God can only be grasped as 'love.' "[53] In its completed form, then, the work presents a giant chain of being embracing the full hierarchy of God's creation.

Where the formal function of the first section of the work is the absorption of the audience into the Bacchic celebration, the purpose of the "dream" section is to convey the wisdom of the God to the celebrants; and to penetrate this wisdom, one must examine the content of the dream-vision. While the second and third movements

50. Nietzsche, *Birth of Tragedy,* pp. 58–59.
51. Mahler, *Briefe,* pp. 163, 198.
52. *Erinnerungen,* p. 40.
53. Mahler, *Briefe,* p. 161.

are essential to Mahler's aesthetic and religious purposes, it is possible to deal with them briefly in considering the philosophical or metaphysical significance of the work.

The second movement, "What the flowers of the meadow tell me," presents the life force in its most innocent form. This was the first part of the symphony which Mahler composed; according to Natalie Bauer-Lechner it was written at the very beginning of his summer vacation in 1895: "Immediately on the first afternoon, as he looked out from his cabin to the meadow where grass and flowers were thickly clustered, it was planned and completed without a break." Mahler described this as the most "untroubled" piece he had ever written, but he also observed to her: "As you can imagine, it does not end with harmless flower cheerfulness but suddenly becomes serious and heavy. It is like a storm wind that comes over the meadow shaking leaves and blossoms which moan and whimper on their stalks as if pleading for salvation [*Erlösung*] in a higher kingdom."[54]

On the next highest level of manifestation, the life force appears in animal form, and what the animals of the forest tell is definitely less innocent than the message of the flowers. Mahler later described it as both scurrilous and tragic. It was "as if all of nature cut capers and stuck out its tongue."[55] In the animal world the life principle or will often displayed a predatory brutal quality, and Mahler indicates this in his score notes. On one occasion the life-will theme is accompanied by the score direction "Rudely"! (*"Grob!"*).[56] The conclusion of the animal section (*Tierstück*) even sees a fleeting allusion to the elemental monotones which symbolized lifeless nature in the first movement (ten measures after score no. 33). Mahler observed of this passage that "the heavy shadow of lifeless nature, of still uncrystallized organic matter, once more falls on the conclusion of the 'animals.' Here, however, that has more the meaning of a relapse into the lower animal forms of being, before she [Nature] makes the mighty leap to the spirit of the highest earthly being, of man."[57]

54. *Erinnerungen,* p. 33.
55. Ibid., p.. 118
56. *Score,* p. 167.
57. *Erinnerungen,* p. 41.

With this mighty leap, Mahler reaches the fourth movement, the intellectual center of his work. Here, for the first time in the symphony, Mahler uses the human voice, and it is for the purpose of conveying a development of great metaphysical significance. Mahler himself said of this transition from the Tierstück scherzo, "The adagio follows upon it as a confused dream is followed by an awakening—or rather a gentle coming to consciousness of oneself [*sich-seiner-selbst-bewusst-werden*]."[58] At this point in the great chain of being, the intellect comes into play and is focused on the life force which has appeared in such various forms throughout the first three movements. Not only is this the first movement to employ words, it is also the movement in which the life-will motif finds its most elaborate development and explication. Musically, the subject of the movement is the dialogue between the life-will motif, the rising and falling theme representing the realm of feeling, and the human voice, the representative of intellect, a dialogue through which the will first becomes aware of its own nature, and then, as the dialogue becomes a duet, realizes the possibility of transcending that nature.

The text which Mahler chose to communicate this profoundly important idea was the *trunkene Lied* (drunken song) from Nietzsche's *Zarathustra,* but whatever Mahler may owe to Nietzsche in terms of the form and structure of his work, the message Mahler conveys with Nietzsche's words is one that significantly modifies the basic intent of Nietzsche's poem. It was a modification that the young Nietzsche, the devoted follower of Schopenhauer and Wagner, might have accepted, but it is more clearly the particular expression of Mahler's own Wagnerian faith. Mahler could use the poem because it spoke the same Wagnerian language, but in his union of word with tone a new dimension of meaning was added. Nietzsche's poem reads:[59]

O Man! Take heed!
What does deep Midnight speak?
"I was asleep—
I waken from a secret dream:—
The world is deep,
And deeper than the day has known.
Deep is her woe—
Desire—deeper still than heart's pain:

58. Ibid., p. 118 (June 1899).
59. The poem precedes the final chapter of the last part of *Also sprach Zarathustra.*

Woe speaks: Perish!
But all desire wants eternity—
—wants deep, deep eternity!"

O Mensch! Gib acht!
Was spricht die tiefe Mitternacht?
"Ich schlief, ich schlief—
Aus tiefen Traum bin ich erwacht:—
Die Welt ist tief,
Und tiefer als der Tag gedacht.
Tief ist ihr Weh—
Lust—tiefer noch als Herzeleid:
Weh spricht: Vergeh!
Doch alle Lust will Ewigkeit—
—will tiefe, tiefe Ewigkeit!"

The imagery of this poem represents the traditional Wagnerian dichotomy between the rational phenomenal world of day and the essential passional world of night. The poem is a statement of Nietzsche's belief that the world encompassed more than could be grasped by reason alone, and that even though the counsel of human misery (*Weh*) was to accept annihilation or resignation, the element which reason was unable to comprehend, the will, (represented here as desire, *Lust*) rejected this to affirm its desire for a deep eternity of willing. In setting the poem, Mahler follows Nietzsche's basic meaning up to the final two lines, where he introduces a highly significant modification.

The beginning of the movement contains the score note "Very slow, mysterious"; and the delivery by the alto solo of the first "Oh" in "Oh Man!" so nearly approaches the sound of a musical instrument as to convey the idea of an initially almost imperceptible difference between the ordinary musical sounds and this first manifestation of consciousness. Immediately after the isolated delivery of "Oh Man! Take heed!" the life-will motif makes its first appearance, a placement which suggests that his motif is to be the object of man's attention.[60] The setting of the next five lines, "What does deep Midnight speak?/I was asleep—/I waken from a secret dream:—/The world is deep,/ And deeper than the day has known," continues in the same mysterious isolation, but then, as in response

60. *Score,* p. 182.

to the idea expressed by these words, the will motif appears again in the violins. As the theme reaches its climax, the horns begin their own variation of the motif, and for a brief span the music expands to fill a broad range of orchestral expression (G).[61]

This would suggest that Mahler is attempting to convey musically the enormously rich depths of being which daylight thought could not penetrate. As he explained to Natalie Bauer-Lechner, this conviction was central to his conception of reality.

> That people always think nature lies on the surface! So far as the most superficial part of her is concerned, yes! But those who, in the face of nature, are not seized by all the terror of an endlessly mysterious divinity which we can only intuit [*ahnen*], not conceive or penetrate, have not gotten on the track of her.[62]

After suggesting the deep nature of the reality beyond the veil of phenomenal appearance, the music returns to the lonely, mysterious mood of the opening, and the invocation "Oh Man! Oh Man!" is repeated. These words introduce the most obviously didactic part of the movement. The words continue: "Deep, Deep/Deep is her woe [*Weh*]," and on this last phrase the notes of "is her woe" occupy the beginning of the upward scale of the will motif. To ensure that the similarity not be overlooked, the final A of "woe" is joined by an A in the solo violin, and this note in turn marks the beginning of a fully articulated repetition of the will motif (H).[63]

61. *Score*, p. 186.
62. *Erinnerungen*, p. 140.
63. *Score*, p. 189.

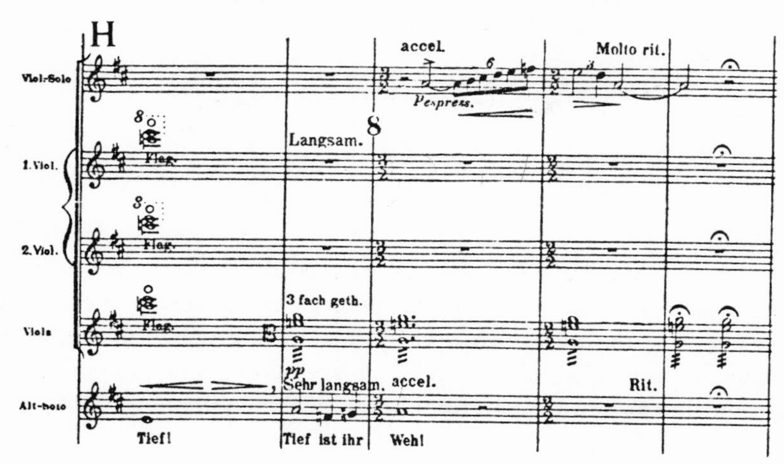

This treatment of "Deep is her woe" is then repeated in a slightly more intense version, thus solidifying the association Mahler is attempting to convey. In this phrase, words and tone combine in mutual instruction. The coincidence of human misery with the affirmative ascending portion of the will motif accurately reflects the conviction of Schopenhauer, Wagner, and at least the early Nietzsche that the affirmation of the individual will was the source of all human misery. As the words continue, "Desire, Desire, deeper still than the heart's pain," the will motif in the solo violin (I) echoes the rising feeling of desire:

The lesson continues with the words "Woe speaks: Perish [*Vergeh*]*!*" and in this phrase the syllables *"spricht: Vergeh!"* occupy the descending resignation half of the life-will motif. As before, the similarity of this "spricht: vergeh" fragment to that of the basic motif is made clear by the appearance of a variant of the will motif (J) in the solo violin immediately following "vergeh."

In terms of Mahler's Wagnerian background, the point is clear. These passages express the essence of Schopenhauer's pessimism: the answer to the misery caused by the striving will is annihilation.

After a repetition of this phrase, the voice and violins come together for the central and final lesson of the movement (K).[64]

Here the words "all desire wants" (*"alle Lust will"*) are stretched out to occupy the full rising scale of the will motif, while the word eternity (*Ewigkeit*) occupies the descending scale of the motif; the violins fully support the voice at each point of the phrase. It is here that Mahler's music begins most obviously to modify Nietzsche's meaning. In the concluding lines of Nietzsche's poem there is a clear shift toward the emphatic mood ("But all desire wants eternity—/—wants deep, deep eternity!") while in Mahler's symphony the emotional direction—and punctuation expressing it—is from affirmation to resignation ("But all desire wants eternity!—/—wants deep, deep eternity."). The significance of this change is made clear by the music. After the fairly concise three-measure statement of the entire will motif in the penultimate line, it expands to fill almost eight measures in the last line. The final "eternity" occupies almost

64. *Score*, p. 190.

three measures and in the first violin accompaniment the resignation half of the motif alone is extended in a slightly varied form for another four measures.[65] In this way Mahler places the final emphasis of the movement on the idea of resignation, and thus in both theme and tone points forward to the ultimate resolution of the will's striving in the concluding sixth movement.

Through the constant interaction between life-will motif and text, Mahler is able to make the metaphysical point of his symphony clear. The truths which deep midnight speaks concern the nature of the will; and as all Wagnerians believed, these were truths which lay beyond the ordinary capacity of reason to express. In his letter to Anna Bahr-Mildenburg, Mahler had stressed that the symphony imparted truths that could be intuited only in dreams, and the form of the second section of the work is that of a dream-vision through which the divinity speaks. Furthermore, it should be recalled that Mahler described the movement as a "gentle coming to consciousness" rather than a full awakening. It is clearly only the character of the work as a dream-vision that allows the deep truths about the nature of the will to be communicated. These truths which are "deeper than the day has known" are themselves rooted in Schopenhauer's philosophy: the superficial character of the ordinary world of appearance, the conviction that everything is a manifestation of will, the beliefs that the will's assertion is the source of human misery, that misery counsels annihilation, and that even so, the will itself desires nothing more than its own eternal assertion. All of these ideas are aspects of Schopenhauer's philosophy which reappear in this work, but nonethless the central point of the composition is more Mahlerian than Nietzschean or Schopenhauerian. The conclusion of the movement suggests Mahler's conviction that the striving will can finally find peace and salvation in reunion with God.

The course of instruction which Mahler offers in the movement also allows a much deeper understanding of the life-will motif itself. In its full form, it can now be seen to convey not only the assertion of the will but also the momentary relaxation that follows satiation. Although the emphasis is certainly on the ascending scale of the motif throughout the first four movements, the "resignation" segment is always present. Here, too, Schopenhauer's beliefs are relevant, for

65. *Score,* p. 191.

even though he argued that the will itself always desired its own assertion, he also saw a constant assertion–resignation rhythm in its ceaseless striving. One of the most painful characteristics of the will was the fact that the attainment of its object induced only boredom, relaxation, and then reassertion in a new direction.[66] With respect to the motif itself, then, resignation is definitely not final resolution or salvation. It may point in the direction of salvation, as in the Ruhepunkt (rest point) of the first movement and the final measures of the fourth, but in and of itself it implies no more than the regular satiation or relaxation of the will.

In the fifth movement, the mysterious portentous tone of the "O Mensch!" gives way to a mood of light jubilation. The message of the angels is a joyous, comic one. The argument that such humor was inappropriate following the deep seriousness of the fourth was answered by Mahler himself in a way that reveals a characteristic facet of his personality. Mahler told of a friend who posed this objection, "and in doing so failed to understand (what generally so few understand), that humor must be put into play here only for the highest, which otherwise could no longer be expressed."[67] Since the message of the fourth movement was by its own admission beyond rational expression, it is not surprising that the next highest stage should be even more difficult. A brief examination of this movement reveals the seriousness of Mahler's humor; here the text is provided by a poem from the *Knabenwunderhorn*. At first, the music expresses the untroubled cheerfulness of the opening lines of the poem:[68]

> Three angels sang so sweet a song,
> That heaven rang with joy.
> Their message merrily proclaimed
> That Peter was free from sin.
>
> Es sungen drei Engel einen süssen Gesang;
> Mit Freuden es selig in dem Himmel klang,
> Sie jauchzten fröhlich auch dabei,
> Dass Petrus sei von Sünden frei.

66. *Schopenhauer Selections,* ed. De Witt H. Parker (New York, 1956), p. 122.
67. *Erinnerungen*, p. 43.
68. *Score,* pp. 192–95.

However, with the final line telling of Peter's freedom from sin a more mysterious tone is conveyed by the music (L).[69]

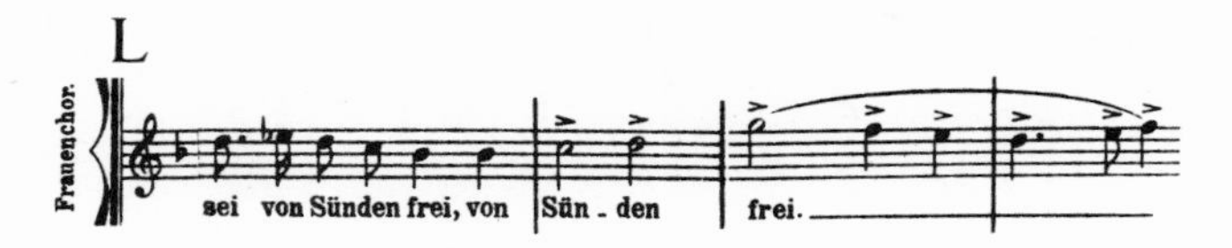

The cheerful tone of the beginning is then resumed, to the words:

> And when the Lord Jesus sat at the table,
> To dine with his twelve disciples:
> Then Jesus asked: Why are you here?
> When I see you I must weep!

> Und als der Herr Jesus zu Tische sass,
> Mit seinen zwölf Jüngern das Abendmahl ass:
> Da sprach der Herr Jesus: Was stehst du denn hier?
> Wenn ich dich anseh, so weinest du mir!

The object of the Lord's words is the alto solo who reappears in the symphony at this point and "bitterly" (as in a score note) sings:[70]

> And should I not weep, you gracious God.
> I have broken the ten commandments.
> I will go and weep most bitterly.

> Und sollt' ich nicht weinen, du gütiger Gott.
> Ich hab' ubertreten die zehn Gebot.
> Ich gehe und weine ja bitterlich.

The object of the fourth movement was the life-will's gentle coming to consciousness of itself. The essential part of the new consciousness was the knowledge of the will's constant and indeed necessary assertion of its own individuated form at the expense of other beings, and in violation of its more basic unity with all being. This was the essence of the Schopenhauerian-Nietzschean tragic view. In the fifth movement, then, the alto solo reappears armed with the knowledge of man's sins, but helpless to overcome them. Her next line "Oh

69. *Score,* pp. 194–95.
70. *Score,* pp. 195–200.

come and have mercy" introduces the crucial development of the movement (M).

This passage is obviously very closely related to the earlier "von Sünden frei" music, and perhaps more important, it is also a slightly altered inversion of the life-will motif (N).[71]

Immediately following this plea for compassion, the womens' and boys' choirs begin the bell-like "bimm, bamm, bimm, bamm" with which the movement started. In this case, however, the comic tone is replaced by one of mystic seriousness. The bell interlude is, in fact, the emotional climax of the movement, and in both tone and function it is reminiscent of the transformation music in Wagner's *Parsifal.* At the conclusion of this section (four bars after score no. 7), the cheerful tone returns and remains throughout the rest of the movement.

In terms of philosophical structure, the humorous fifth movement of Mahler's symphony occupies a position scarcely less important than that of the more serious fourth and sixth. The consciousness gained by the striving life-will in the fourth movement is only the first step in the process of its transcendence or redemption. Wagner had argued that the turning of the will on itself to deny itself was the greatest miracle conceivable, and as the embodiment of this miracle he had pointed to Christ, "inspiring one to the highest pity, to worship of suffering, to imitation through breaking of all self-seeking

71. *Score,* pp. 201, 190.

will."[72] In the fifth movement, then, the human soul, suffering bitterly from the knowledge of its sins, turns to Christ and pleads for the compassion that will allow the miraculous denial of its will to live. The allusion to Parsifal's transformation music and the words of the angel chorus provide the assurance that this miracle will occur.

The final movement is one of the most beautiful pieces of music Mahler composed. Its subject is the message of love, and its motto, as revealed in a letter to one of Mahler's oldest friends, Fritz Lohr, was a pair of lines from the *Knabenwunderhorn:* "Father, look upon my wounds!/Let no creature be lost!" ("Vater, sieh an die Wunden mein!/Kein Wesen lass verloren sein!").[73]

In a letter to Anna Bahr-Mildenburg (1 July 1896), Mahler quoted this motto to explain the meaning of the final movement: "With it the peak and highest level from which the world can be viewed is described. I could just as well call the movement 'What God tells me,' and indeed, just in the sense that God can only be grasped as Love."[74] In terms of the symphony's philosophic structure this is the movement in which the struggling life force at last finds rest, resolution, and salvation in reunion with the divine essence of nature. In the fifth movement, the repentant soul had appealed to Christ for mercy and had received the angelic assurance that the joy of heaven would be bestowed. As the motto of the final movement indicates, the suffering son of God now appeals to his father for the salvation of all creatures. However, as Mahler indicated to Fritz Lohr, even on this highest level of being, suffering and struggle are not absent: "'What love tells me' is a bringing together of my feeling toward all beings in which deeply painful paths of the soul cannot be avoided, but which, however, are gradually resolved in a blessed assurance: 'the joyous science' [*Zuversicht 'die fröhliche Wissenschaft'*]."[75]

Musically, this development is expressed through the interaction between the familiar life-will motif and the movement's serene opening theme built around a three-measure quotation from the adagio of Beethoven's opus 135 quartet (O).[76]

72. Wagner, *Schriften,* vol. 10, p. 215.
73. Mahler, *Briefe,* p. 108.
74. Ibid., p. 161.
75. Ibid., p. 107.
76. Mahler, *Score,* p. 210. I am indebted to Norman Rabkin for pointing out this quotation to me.

Gradually, the untroubled mood of this theme gives way to a more ambiguous tone, and shortly thereafter the life-will motif appears in a modest form in the second violin. Mahler's directions in the score (P) are, "Somewhat hesitant."

Two measures later it is reasserted by all the violins in a more fully articulated form; Mahler's score note is "Somewhat insistent" (*"etwas drängend"*). This is immediately followed by a final, even more forceful statement, to which Mahler notes "Passionately." After a transitional development, the opening theme is restated by the first violin, but this time the final measures of the theme (Q) are altered to incorporate the will motif within it.

The violins and flutes then immediately restate the will motif in a reversed and extended form (R).[77]

To this point the music seems to suggest the subject of the movement —the dichotomy between the love and will motifs—as well as its

77. *Score,* pp. 212, 214.

ultimate intention to bring together these two motifs. Although the second statement of the divine love theme does incorporate the will motif at its conclusion, this merely points the way to the final union of the two. (The first "indicative" joining of the themes is elaborated only in the first violin and is not supported by the remainder of the orchestra.)

In the middle section of the work, the will motif appears repeatedly in forms expressing constantly rising emotional intensity juxtaposed with equally intense reversals of the motif (at score nos. 18, five measures before 23 and at 23), and after the last of these climaxes, the motif makes its final unmodified appearances, first in the flute and then the piccolo. These most lofty and spiritualized of the many expressions of the will theme are delivered in almost complete isolation, and are followed immediately by the opening love motif in the trumpets (S).

The love motif is accompanied initially by an inverted form of the motif in the horns and concludes with a reversal of the will motif. From this point on, the tone of the movement is triumphant and joyous; the music builds to a climax in which the love motif in both its initial and inverted form is developed by the entire orchestra in constantly increasing intensity until it concludes with a vastly altered statement of the will motif (T).[78]

Here the fruitless surge and recession of passion which had characterized the initial life-will motif is transformed through the rhythm of the love (and also pity) motif into a joyously serene affirmation of faith. Here at last, the striving will has found resolu-

78. *Score*, pp. 225, 229.

T
30
1.2.3.4. Fl.
1.2.3.4. Ob.
1.2.3. Cl. in B.
1.2. Cl. in Es.
1.2.3. Fag.
Ctrfag.
1.2.7.8. Horn in F.
3.4.5.6.
1.2. Trmp in F.
3.4. Trmp in B.
1.2. Pos.
3.4.
zu 4
zu 3
zu 2
Schalltrichter in die Höhe.
molto cresc.
cresc.
4.

tion and salvation. This is followed shortly by an allusion to the fifth movement's themes (U) associated with the words "Come and have mercy" and "free from sin."[79]

Dominated by a drum beat reminiscent of Parsifal's transformation, the symphony then concludes.

In the final movement of this massive work, Mahler brings to an end the development that began in the first movement with the response of lifeless nature to the wakening call of the creative spirit. In comparing the first movement with the last, Mahler observed, "What is dull and stiff there has here achieved highest consciousness; the unarticulated sounds have reached the most refined articulation."[80] In the last movement, the life-will motif, which had originally appeared in its most elemental form, achieves first the most spiritualized expressions possible and then finally achieves that reversal of itself which allows its reunion with the divine essence. In his *World as Will and Idea,* Schopenhauer had spoken of those rare religious or aesthetic experiences that allowed the will to deny its own nature:[81]

> Then all at once the peace which we were always seeking, but which always fled from us on the former path of the desires comes to us of its own accord, and it is well with us. . . . We are for the moment set free from the miserable striving of the will; we keep the Sabbath of the penal servitude of willing; the wheel of Ixion stands still.

In one of his comments on the final movement, Mahler perhaps unconsciously acknowledged the importance of this philosophy for his work in declaring, "In the adagio everything is resolved in peace and being; the Ixion's wheel of appearance [*Erscheinung*] is finally brought to rest."[82] Of all his intellectual forebears, there was none whom Mahler resembled more in temperament and world view than

79. *Score,* p. 230; compare with pp. 194–201.
80. *Erinnerungen,* p. 41.
81. Parker, ed., *Schopenhauer Selections,* pp. 122–23.
82. *Erinnerungen,* pp. 50, 45.

Schopenhauer, and in his Third, Mahler felt he had captured the will-less serenity that his predecessor had so ardently sought and so rarely found. In the July fourth conversation following the revelatory experience in which he had suddenly perceived the full significance of his art as an instrument of divine mediation Mahler had said,

> Can a spirit who rethinks the eternal creative thoughts of the Godhead as in a symphony such as this one die? No, one receives the assurance [*Zuversicht*]: everything is eternally and immutably well created; and here also human suffering and sorrow have no place. The most sublime cheerfulness holds sway, an eternally brilliant day, admittedly for Gods, not for men.

This, then, is the "assurance of the joyous wisdom" ("*Zuversicht: die fröhliche Wissenschaft*") with which Mahler had told his friend Fritz Lohr the symphony concluded.[83]

Viewing the symphony as a whole in the light of its joyous conclusion, one can begin to understand more fully the aesthetic, religious, and cultural intent of Mahler's work. One of Mahler's descriptions of it says this: "Gradually life fights its way free until it differentiates itself from step to step in ever higher forms of development: flowers, animals, man, to the kingdom of the spirits, to the 'angels.' "[84] In its first movement, the symphony depicts this birth and struggle of the life-will in the form of a Dionysian celebration, a celebration intended to draw the audience into the Satyric chorus of celebrants. In the midst of the celebration, the god speaks to the celebrants in the form of an Apollonian dream-vision. The vision itself reveals both the relationship of the individual will to being in all its many forms and the path by which the human fragment of being can find its way back to the divine oneness.

The aim of the work, then, was that which Wagner ascribed to the Poet-Priest, who "was always sent to mankind in the crucial periods of its most frightful confusion, as mediating friend: he will also lead us over to that reborn life, to set before us there in ideal truth the 'image' of everything transitory ['*Gleichnis*' *alles Vergänglichen*]." In this remarkable passage from "Religion and Art," Wagner continues, "In solemn hours when all the world's phenomenal forms dissolve before us as in a prophetic dream, we seem already to feel ourselves a part of this redemption: we are no longer troubled by the

83. Mahler, *Briefe,* p 107.
84. *Erinnerungen,* p. 40.

image of that yawning abyss, of the gruesomely formed monster of the deep, of all jaundiced offspring of the self-lacerating will." In this state, the cry of Nature brought man the hope of salvation: "United in this cry, by it made conscious of its own high office of redemption of the whole, like suffering Nature, the soul of mankind soars from the abyss of semblances [*Abgrund der Erscheinungen*] and set free from all that awful sequence of rise and fall, the restless will feels fettered by itself alone, but from itself set free."[85]

The image of the restless will plays a crucial role in the artistic conceptions of both Mahler and his friend Lipiner. Mahler said of the first movement of his Third, "In the midst of it, the youth, the enchained life, striving for salvation laments from the abyss of still lifeless nature."[86] In "Religion and Art" Wagner had spoken of music as filling "each sphere of Nature with new life, teaching redemption-starved mankind a second speech in which the Infinite can voice itself with unmistakable definition."[87] Mahler had declared that in his symphony all of nature found a voice and told the deep secrets that one might intuit in dreams.[88]

Wagner's statement that the Poet-Priest was to show man the 'image' (*Gleichnis*) of everything transitory is relevant to Mahler's work in a way that touches the most basic nature of his outlook. Essentially, Mahler's Third is just such a Gleichnis in that it serves as a metaphorical reality relating everything transitory, every form of the striving will, to every other form. This explains why Mahler was constantly changing the titles and metaphors with which he described his symphony. As has been seen, some of the changes resulted from basic alterations in the nature of the work, but even after it was completed, the metaphors continued to change. As Natalie Bauer-Lechner observed of Mahler's comments on the first movement, "The manner in which he attempts to get on the trail of his creations after the event gives him first this, then that picture for it. 'It is Zeus who overthrows Kronos; the higher form which overcomes the lower.' " Then later, taking a still broader view of the work, Mahler said, "A magnificent picture for the artist [*den Schaffenden*] is Jacob who struggles with God until he blesses him."[89] All words and images for

85. Wagner, *Schriften,* vol. 10, pp. 247, 249.
86. *Erinnerungen,* p. 40.
87. Wagner, *Schriften,* vol. 10, p. 250.
88. Mahler, *Briefe,* p. 162.
89. *Erinnerungen,* p. 60.

Mahler were inadequate to describe music, just as the phenomenal world created by the rational faculty was itself but an inadequate metaphor for the essential reality of music or the will. For him as for Goethe, Schopenhauer, and Wagner, the statement "Alles vergängliche ist nur ein Gleichnis" ("Everything transitory is but a simile") was an explanation of the basic nature of reality. Clearly, all of Mahler's many statements on the Third must be understood in this context. No words and no single image could ever express the content of his music, but a series of metaphors or titles could suggest the outlines of the reality lying beyond reason; at one point Mahler referred to his program as a star map of the night sky.[90] By examining his comments and images, it is possible to describe the evolution of his symphony, and by setting these comments into the metaphysical structure of the Wagnerian heritage, it is possible to understand the religious, aesthetic, and cultural intent of the work, but clearly the religious-aesthetic experience itself lies only in the music. Mahler's awareness of this probably accounts for his final decision to omit all titles from the published version of the Third; from past experience, he was fearful that the Gleichnis would be taken for the thing-in-itself.

Perhaps the most revealing statement Mahler made on this matter was the comment to his close friend Arnold Berliner when he sent him a preliminary program for the Third. He wondered "if by means of the title I will bring the reader to the path which I will then walk with him."[91] Elsewhere he spoke of the titles as signposts and milestones. Mahler hoped that the program would set the context of his work clearly enough so that the music itself would be able to transport the hearer into its suprarational realm.

Once within the musical realm of the symphony it was equally important that the listener be made constantly aware of his relationship to the forms of the will presented to him musically as well as his relationship to all other members of the community formed by the audience. The structure of the work is crucial to this aim in that the passionate Dionysian celebration of the first movement is intended to create the emotional community essential to the redeeming Apollonian vision of unity. Mahler's treatment of themes and motifs is carefully directed toward leading the audience to this goal.

90. Mahler, *Briefe,* p. 188.
91. Ibid., p. 140.

The most important motifs are simple, and usually if two themes or a theme and a part of the text are being related, the relationship is made clear by repetition.

Another quality of Mahler's music, which has frequently been noted and is closely related to the need for the total engagement of the audience, is his use of musical quotations. The last movement of the symphony begins with a quotation from Beethoven and concludes with allusions to *Parsifal*. These references help direct the listener toward the goal inherent in the composition. Wagner had singled out Beethoven as the great musical innovator whose compositions (particularly the *Ninth Symphony*) shattered convention to achieve an effect which was at once more complete on the individual psychological level and more inclusive on the sociological level. In setting Schiller's *Ode to Joy*, Beethoven had spoken to the entire Volk in a way that aristocratic chamber music never could; in his hands, the symphony had become a vehicle for reaching a mass audience. Wagner himself had constantly stressed the importance of reaching the Volk through art, and in his operas he attempted to achieve the aims for which he praised Beethoven. His religious festival play *Parsifal*, first performed in the Bayreuth festival house built to accommodate a vastly larger audience than was customary, attempted to transcend the conventions of operatic composition so as to reach both the entire individual and the entire Volk. It was the capacity of music to create this psychological and sociological unity which had given Nietzsche and Wagner the hope that German culture could be regenerated through music just as the unity of religion, music, and drama had originally generated the forces which led to the great creations of the Athenian *polis*.

Mahler's quotation of Beethoven's last quartet should thus be taken as an acknowledgment of one of the composers whose work was so important to the Wagnerian crusade, but it is also more than that. Shortly after Mahler assumed the direction of the Vienna Philharmonic, he announced his plan to present the last Beethoven quartets in orchestral versions. He felt that the musical conceptions of these works could not be given proper expression with just four instruments:

> Indeed, to bring any quartet, which after all, is made for a room, into a hall would be risky and arbitrary—especially so, however, with the powerful compositions of Beethoven's last

> quartets, in which the four pitiful little men have long since been lost, and which, so far as the conception is concerned, should have had completely different dimensions and simply *demanded* a small string orchestra.[92]

Thus, in beginning the final adagio of the Third by quoting from the adagio of Beethoven's opus 135 string quartet, Mahler was at once paying tribute to Beethoven's accomplishments and attempting to realize the full orchestral power of this opening theme in a way that a quartet could never accomplish. Mahler's allusions to Beethoven and Wagner are thus very closely related to the purpose of the *Third Symphony* as a whole. Nietzsche had argued that religious prototragedies embodied the unity of the Greek *polis*; the Wagnerians could look to their music as a similar means of restoring the unity of a socially disintegrated Volk. In alluding to the two composers who, Wagnerians believed, had expressed this unity, Mahler was placing his work in this tradition.

In the light of this Wagnerian tradition Hans Redlich's conclusion that "for Mahler the '*Volk*,' the '*mass*,' is naturally a Dionysian one," would seem to be fully justified; and in this context Mahler's frequent use of folk melodies and folk poems can be seen to signify far more than just an attempt at local color. Along with the religious message of his work, the form of the composition, and the use of musical quotations they are intended to help restore the lost unity of the disintegrated Volk. It is this restoration to which Hans Redlich referred when he said, "I see . . . in the totality of Mahler's creations the symbol of a future, more ideal, more spiritual Austria."[93]

When one realizes the full extent of the religious, aesthetic, and cultural mission that Mahler attempted to accomplish in his Third, it becomes clear why he could say that in spite of its projected two-hour duration it was a work of the greatest conciseness. It also becomes clear why the work is so rarely performed and even more rarely understood. Mahler himself had known this would be the case; in his July fourth conversation with Natalie Bauer-Lechner, he said, "Only I will be able to direct it. I am not capable of imagining that anyone else would ever be able to, unless there are a few who hear it under me and understand it. I must almost fear that it will be too much for these few disciples and initiates [*Anhängern und Einge-*

92. *Erinnerungen,* p. 107.
93. Redlich, *Mahler,* pp. 29, 33.

weihten]."[94] For the work to be understood, the Poet-Priesthood would have to be passed on, and it was not.

In a sense, too, Mahler's work has suffered as a result of the very Wagnerian heritage which gave it birth. When Redlich argues that "Mahler's world is the antipodes of Wagner's," he is absolutely correct, although, as he goes on to point out, *Parsifal* is the only musical composition that is at all related to Mahler's work.[95] Even though Mahler was immersed in the theories of Wagner, Nietzsche, and Schopenhauer, and even though Mahler fervently admired Wagner and adopted many of his musical techniques, the content and sound of Mahler's music are nevertheless uniquely his own. There are, in fact, few composers whose work is so instantly recognizable. Moreover, the Volk of Mahler's music was no longer Wagner's Volk. Wagner's dream of a united German Volk had indeed inspired Mahler when he joined the other young Pan-Germans of the Pernerstorfer circle in singing *Deutschland, Deutschland über Alles,* but that was in 1880 before the political movement to which his friends gave birth had adopted the vicious anti-Semitism which was to make it so popular. After the rise of political anti-Semitism in Vienna, Mahler's Pan-German nationalism diminished to the vanishing point. What remained was a full knowledge of, and admiration for, the Wagnerian musical metaphysics, as well as a deep loyalty to Wagner himself—particularly to the Wagner of *Parsifal*. But even so, the völkisch quality of Mahler's music was Austrian rather than German. As Redlich has observed, "Mahler's art works are permeated in a completely unprecedented way by all the spiritual elements of the total Austrian complex."[96] They drew from the elements of Mahler's Slavic, Jewish, German, and Catholic background in a way that transcended any specifically German nationalism. Mahler's music was more universal and cosmopolitan than Wagner's, just as the Austrian Volk was more diverse than that of Bismarck's German Empire. Thus Redlich's argument that Wagner's domination of art during Mahler's lifetime lessened the appreciation of the latter's work might well be correct. Certainly the inverse problem—the complete ignorance of the entire Wagnerian metaphysics—has greatly lessened the possibility of understanding and appreciating Mahler's work in the period following his death.

94. *Erinnerungen*, pp. 45, 141.
95. Redlich, pp. 6, 30.
96. Ibid., p. 33.

In terms of its effect on the individual, Mahler's music moved beyond Wagner's, and again Redlich expressed this well: "Mahler's music itself lies between music and the cosmos in a metamusical plane. That is what is new: thus its effect is transcendental, while Wagner's affective power lies completely in the physical effect [*physis*] of the music."[97] While this may overly denigrate the effect of Wagner's music, it is certainly true for Mahler. As he had told Natalie Bauer-Lechner on the day of his great revelation, in his *Third Symphony* it was "the All itself into whose boundless abyss you descend, into whose eternal realms you ascend, so that the earth and human fate remain behind you like an unrecognizable small point and vanish."[98]

When Mahler completed this monumental work at the end of July 1896, he presented his sketches for the first movement to Natalie Bauer-Lechner with the inscription, "On July 28, 1896, occurred the singular event that I could present to my dear friend Natalie the seed of a tree which nonetheless blooms and grows in the world in full maturity with all its twigs, leaves, and fruits." After making one final alteration, he and Natalie set out to visit Lipiner who was living nearby in Berchtesgaden. After taking a train from Attersee to Salzburg they set out on bicycles early the next morning to travel the final twenty miles through the winding green valley of the Salzach. Mahler then spent the day in animated conversation with the friend whose work was so closely related to his own in overall conception and so distant from it in aesthetic realization.[99]

A few days later, Mahler set out on a second pilgrimage, this time to Bayreuth, the spiritual center of Wagnerism. The existing documents do not reveal what Mahler saw or felt on this journey, but when Anna Bahr-Mildenburg visited Bayreuth later that year, he wrote her a note that reveals something of what must have passed through his mind. "Soon you will stand in that realm [*Raum*] in which one of the most magnificent spirits who has walked among men held sway . . . Just always keep in mind: he is satisfied with you, for he looks into your heart and knows everything of which you are capable and which you desire. Now you go your way, armed as few have been.' "[100]

97. Ibid., p. 26.
98. *Erinnerungen*, pp. 44–45.
99. Ibid., pp. 50, 55.
100. Mahler, *Briefe*, p. 164.

PART III: In Search of a Poetic Politics

> To treat political ideas as the offspring of pure reason would be to assign them a parentage about as mythological as that of Pallas Athene. What matters most is the underlying emotions, the music, to which ideas are a mere libretto, often of a very inferior quality.
>
> L. B. NAMIER

6. The Linz Program

When the dissolution of the Leseverein drove the members of the Pernerstorfer circle from their well-established position at the university, they took refuge initially in the coffeehouses of Vienna where they found a congenial atmosphere in which to discuss vegetarianism, spiritualism, and the other fine points of Wagnerian theory. Idle intellectualization, however, was the very fault to which Friedjung had attributed so many of Austria's political ills, and in 1879 the members of the circle most interested in politics—Pernerstorfer, Adler, and Friedjung—joined with Georg von Schönerer to launch a political movement aimed at bringing into being the new order they had envisioned as students. They began their careers at a time when the political climate of Austria had begun to undergo a gradual but basic change. In that year the formation of Count Eduard Taaffe's government signaled the end of the brief period of liberal dominance in Austrian politics. Initially, the government included a strong liberal contingent, but by 1881 the Slavic-conservative alliance had taken full control and forced the liberals into opposition.[1] The members of the Pernerstorfer circle thus began their political activity in a situation dominated by the onset of liberal decline, a situation for which the antiliberal theories and experiences of their student days had prepared them well. The significance of this prior training in radicalism can be seen in one of the first and most important achievements of the new movement: the writing of the Linz program.

Although political and scholarly controversies surround the origins of the Linz program, there is general agreement that the men responsible for it exercised a profound influence on the politics of twentieth-century Austria. For example, Adam Wandruszka depicts the political forces of the Austrian Republic as divided into three camps, varying in strength at different times but maintaining their identity and continuity over a long period of time: the Social

1. William A. Jenks' *Austria under the Iron Ring 1879–1893* (Charlottesville, Va., 1965) offers a sympathetic and intelligent treatment of the Taaffe government.

Democrats, the Christian Socials, and the Pan-German nationalists. Wandruszka argues:[2]

> If one follows the three camps and their intellectual history back to their origins, an interesting fact emerges. Not only do the histories of all three groups reach back to the same time, the 1880s, but one can also observe that the further one traces back the pedigrees of the three camps the more intimate become the points of contact and mutual entanglement of the movements and their leading personalities, until one finally finds the "founding fathers" of all three camps—and thus of Austrian party and domestic history in the 20th century—gathered together in a single circle around the young Georg von Schönerer.

This was the circle that produced the Linz program as the charter of the deutschnational movement, and in addition to those members directly involved in writing the program, such as Schönerer, Friedjung, Pernerstorfer, and Adler, it also embraced in a looser way men like Karl Lueger, who did not help formulate it but did participate in other political activities sponsored by the movement.

As the historical significance of the Linz program became more obvious with the passage of time, a bitter partisan debate developed over the question of its authorship. Most writers of German nationalist persuasion, including Schönerer's uncritical biographer Eduard Pichl, gave the credit to Schönerer. After discussing the controversy, Pichl asserted categorically, *"Schönerer is the father of the Linz Program!"*[3] Others have emphasized the contributions of Pernerstorfer, Adler, or Friedjung. A. J. P. Taylor describes the program as "the work of Friedjung more than of any other one man."[4] Most of the bitter partisanship of the controversy stemmed from the violently anti-Semitic position which Schönerer and his followers in the German nationalist movement adopted after 1882. This made it desirable to minimize the role of such Jews as Friedjung and Adler in the formulation of their party platform.

2. Adam Wandruszka, "Oesterreichs politische Struktur," *Geschichte der Republic Oesterreich,* ed. Heinrich Benedikt (Munich, 1954), pp. 292–93.

3. Eduard Pichl [Herwig], *Georg Schönerer und die Entwicklung des Alldeutschtumes in der Ostmark,* vol. 1. p, 118.

4. Heinrich Friedjung, *The Struggle for Supremacy in Germany 1859–1860,* trans. A. J. P. Taylor and W. L. McElwee (New York, 1966), p. xv.

While the question of political credit for the Linz program needs no further discussion, the question of its authorship retains considerable importance to the extent that it illuminates the nature of the forces responsible for the destruction of Austrian liberalism. Moreover, since the three mass movements that accomplished this task also served Adolf Hitler as models in his infinitely more ambitious work of destruction, there is all the more reason for exploring the historical point of common origin to which Wandruszka has traced these three movements. The forces unleashed by the circle of the "founding fathers" provided potent tools for a twentieth-century politics of mass psychology, and by examining the way the Linz program evolved within the movement launched by this circle, the nature of these forces is greatly clarified.

The first step in this process occurred on 18 December 1879, the first anniversary of the Leseverein's dissolution, when a group of its former members established a new organization to carry on the political tradition of the student group. According to one of its founders, this new society—originally called the Deutscher Leseverein—"owed its establishment to the government's dissolution of the Akademischen Leseverein. This left behind a number of action-oriented young Ph.D.s, some books and furniture, an old attendant named Pöschl, and some debts—that is, a sufficiently broad basis for the founding of a new society."[5] The members of the Pernerstorfer circle played a leading role in the establishment of the new society, and at the outset even the aesthetic wing of the circle took part. An early membership list shows both Kralik and Lipiner as members in addition to Friedjung, Pernerstorfer, and Adler.[6] When the society chose its officers in January 1880, Friedjung became a member of the executive committee, along with Anton Haider, one of the most important leaders of the old Leseverein.[7]

5. This account, entitled "Die Entstehung des Linzer Programmes," appears in the *Egerer Zeitung* Jg. 55 (13 Feb. 1901), pp. 1–2. The author does not identify himself except as a participant in the events described. His account had appeared earlier in the *Deutsche Zeitung* of 31 Jan. 1901. In the passage cited, the author errs in referring to the dissolution of the Akademische Leseverein. Clearly he means the Leseverein der deutschen Studenten, for the Akademische Leseverein had been dissolved a full decade earlier and the Akademische Lesehalle had not yet been dissolved. This article will henceforth be cited as "Entstehung."

6. This list is in the Pichl Nachlass, Oesterreichisches Staatsarchiv, Allgemeines Verwaltungsarchiv, carton 35, folder 1. The collection will henceforth be cited as Pichl Nachlass.

7. *N.F.P.* (28 Jan. 1880), p. 6.

Unlike its predecessor, the new society was not a university organization, and it may have been to emphasize this fact and attract a wider membership that the society soon changed its name to the *Deutscher Klub*. In any case, soon after this change, the membership increased dramatically: "In addition to the founding members, who belonged exclusively to academic circles, new men appeared, predominantly manufacturers, railroad officials, and high school teachers. From political circles one should mention Schönerer, Weitlof, Walterskirchen, Weisenburg, Menger."[8] The Deutscher Klub, within which the Linz program was written, thus began its activity with a membership made up largely of young academics and technocrats, in addition to a few seasoned politicians.

The first important success for the members of the Deutscher Klub came almost immediately. As one of them later recalled, "We young people first inundated the *Deutscher Verein,* not particularly to the joy of the then chairman, Dr. Kopp; we then founded the most distinguished and lasting bulwark of German culture in Austria, the *Deutscher Schulverein*."[9] Although in its early days the Leseverein had established close ties with Dr. Kopp's Deutscher Verein, the student movement had subsequently become much more radical, so Kopp's displeasure stemmed from the fear that this large influx of young members might pose a threat to his more conservative leadership. With their own Deutscher Klub still in the initial stages of organization in December 1879, these young men used Kopp's society to raise an urgent problem. At a meeting on 20 December, Max Menger proposed the election of a committee to determine whether the boundaries of the German-speaking area in Austria were being reduced, and to make proposals for meeting this threat if it existed. The committee of seven members chosen at the meeting included Friedjung, Adler, and Pernerstorfer, with Pernerstorfer assigned the task of reporting on the South Tirol.[10] In his research on the question, he read a pamphlet by a Dr. Lotz describing the efforts made by a priest named Franz Mitterer to preserve Germanic culture in Proveis. This work evidently convinced Pernerstorfer that a great deal could be accomplished at relatively slight expense, and he formulated the idea of a society to protect and further German

8. "Entstehung," p. 1.
9. Ibid., pp. 1–2.
10. August von Wotawa, *Der deutsche Schulverein 1880–1905* (Vienna, 1905), p. 7.

education in border areas. A short time later he raised the issue in the newly established Deutscher Klub, which immediately accepted his proposal for the foundation of a Deutscher Schulverein.[11] The new society was established on 13 May 1880, and two months later it completed its permanent organization with Moritz Weitlof as chairman, Pernerstorfer as secretary, and Adler as a member of the executive committee. Five of the seven members of the committee were former members of the Leseverein.[12] The Deutscher Schulverein enjoyed spectacularly rapid growth from the outset. At the time of its formal organization in July 1880 it had about three thousand members and by the end of October 1884 there were some ninety thousand members scattered throughout Austria.[13] Among those who became officers in the society during these first years were Schönerer and Karl Lueger.[14]

Encouraged by the successful establishment of the Schulverein, the members of the Deutscher Klub next tried to enlist the more nationalistic, progressive wing of the liberal movement in an effort to establish a new German People's Party (*Volkspartei*), and as one anonymous participant later recalled, it was their first failure. This setback, which resulted at least in part from poor organization, occurred at the *Deutsch-österreichische Parteitag* (German-Austrian Party Convention) held in December 1880.[15]

> In the preliminary discussions of the convention, Dr. Steinwender, who had been entrusted with the task, explained the necessity for a strict nationalistic policy and an independent nationalistic party. The speaker presented the matter . . . too briefly, became distracted and was misunderstood. Paul von Pacher came to his rescue and was laughed down. Dr. Stengl from Krems, on whom we had counted but whom we had forgotten to inform, launched into solemn declarations of unity, and so they passed over us mischief makers to the day's agenda.

When the convention opened on the following day, "they noticed nothing of us young ones [*Jungen*] except for those young people at the entrance who were looked at askance as they passed out pam-

11. Robert Arthaber, *Neue oesterreichische Biographie,* p. 102.
12. Wotawa, p. 12. *Deutsche Worte,* (16 May 1882), p. 2.
13. Pichl, *George Schönerer,* vol. 2, p. 277.
14. *Mittheilungen des deutschen Schulvereines Wien,* no. 2 (1 Sept. 1881), p. 3.

phlets which were ignored."[15] However disappointing these results may have been to the Deutscher Klub members, their efforts ultimately made an important contribution to the Linz program, for the pamphlet they distributed provided the basis for the nationalistic segment of that program.

This pamphlet, containing the outline of a program for the German Volkspartei resulted largely from the efforts of the Pernerstorfer circle. It was written, set, and printed in one night after the failure at the preliminary session of the convention. "The author was Dr. Friedjung; the collaborators were Drs. Victor von Kraus, Serafin Bondi, and Victor Adler."[16] (Bondi was a long-standing if somewhat obscure member of the Pernerstorfer circle and Kraus was closely associated with most of its political activities.) Friedjung drew much of the program for the prospective people's party directly from his *Ausgleich mit Ungarn,* the political tract written three years earlier. Once again he called for reforms to sunder the remaining political ties with Hungary; by eliminating the Delegation (the body that controlled the common finances, army, and foreign affairs of Austria-Hungary), the control of these affairs for Austria would pass to the Austrian Reichsrath.[17] To ensure the Germanic character of the Austrian half of the Empire, he again called for granting autonomy to Galicia (which would remove the influential Polish votes from the Reichsrath), and for making Oesterreich the legal name of the state (instead of "the Kingdoms and lands represented in the Reichsrath"). Friedjung also added an important nationalistic point not included in his *Ausgleich mit Ungarn:* the demand that German be declared the national language and be required for all public offices and transactions.[18]

With respect to foreign affairs, Friedjung began his Volkspartei program by sounding a note of remorse familiar to the Telynen from their Gymnasium days on. "Since, among the Germans of Austria, the memory can never be extinguished that for a thousand years, until 1866, they formed a political unity with the other German tribes," the program demanded the maintenance of a close per-

15. "Entstehung," p. 2.
16. Ibid., p. 2.
17. Friedjung's program is printed in Pichl. vol. 1, pp. 104–05. Compare Friedjung. *Ausgleich,* pp. 20, 100.
18. Pichl, vol. 1, pp. 104–05. *Ausgleich,* pp. 100–01.

manent alliance with the German Empire. In this point, as in most of the foreign policy section, Friedjung's program merely repeated the ideas of his *Ausgleich*. He again called for the establishment of close economic ties with Germany, including co-ordination of currency and indirect taxes.[19] He also repeated the demand for a policy that would guarantee the independence of the Balkan states from Russia while renouncing any Austrian desire for conquest or annexation.[20] Friedjung's Volkspartei program also contained one foreign policy plank which had only been implicit in his earlier work: the demand for a customs union with Germany.

In the area of internal politics and socioeconomic problems, Friedjung's Volkspartei program departed substantially from his earlier work. Insofar as it touched on internal questions, his *Ausgleich* concentrated on the individual liberties traditionally prized by middle-class liberals—freedom of the press, the right of association, and the right to assemble. With a perfunctory repetition of these demands, the Volkspartei program directed attention to the problems of the working classes. "With respect to economics, the German Volkspartei will promote the kind of organization of the peasants, the middle classes, and the workers through which society's industrial and agricultural working classes will finally be given their fitting position in the state next to the great landowners and the capitalists who alone until now have exercised the dominant influence." To achieve this end, the program proposed "a constantly progressing expansion of the suffrage" as well as a complete overhaul of the tax system. Specifically, the program called for the abolition of taxes that discriminated against the poor, such as those on meat and grain, in favor of a progressive income tax, an inheritance tax, a luxury tax, and a tax on stock-market transactions.[21] In social terms, the Volkspartei program clearly aimed at reducing the privileges of the upper-middle class in order to assuage the conditions (and gain the support) of the peasants, the workers, and the lower-middle class.

In the scholarly and political controversy over the origins of the Linz program, one very important point of dispute concerns the

19. Pichl, vol. 1, p. 105. *Ausgleich*, p. 102.

20. Pichl, vol. 1, p. 105; *Ausgleich*, p. 101. Further annexations would only have increased the problems created by the numerical preponderance of the Slavs in the Austrian half of the Empire.

21. Pichl, vol. 1, p. 104.

relationship of Friedjung's Volkspartei program to the next political task undertaken by the Deutscher Klub, the proclamation of a Pan-German society. Recognizing the close similarity of the Linz program and this proclamation on the various German nationalist issues, Pichl treats the proclamation as almost exclusively the work of Schönerer and dismisses Friedjung's role as insignificant. He claims that "even a superficial comparison of Schönerer's two programs of June 1879 and January 1881 [the proclamation] with Friedjung's outline of 13 November 1880 [his Volkspartei program] reveals that by far the greatest part of the Linz program's contents originated in Schönerer's two programs." Although a superficial examination might well suggest this conclusion, a more careful scrutiny of the proclamation within its political context does not. The proclamation was one of three goals which the members of the Deutscher Klub set for themselves at a meeting called the day after their defeat at the German-Austrian Party Convention. Besides proclaiming a deutschnational society, they also proposed the establishment of a party newspaper and the promulgation of a comprehensive and detailed political program. To accomplish these tasks it established a committee of some fifteen members with Schönerer as chairman and including among others Pernerstorfer, Friedjung, Adler, Serafin Bondi, Otto Steinwender, and Victor von Kraus. Although the actual formation of the deutschnational society did not occur until mid-1882, the committee completed work on the proclamation in short order and issued it in January 1881 in Schönerer's name "and in the name of numerous political friends."[22]

Given Schönerer's chairmanship of the committee in addition to the advantages of a stubborn and aggressive personality, there is no reason to doubt that he played an important role in the proclamation of the deutschnational society; in the words of one participant, "he provided most of the money and moral support."[23] Nor is there any reason, on the other hand, to doubt the claim by Pernerstorfer that Friedjung's Volkspartei program provided the basis for the proclamation. A comparison of the two documents strongly supports this assertion.[24] The principal German nationalist planks were identical:

22. Ibid., pp. 100, 103–05.

23. "Entstehung," p. 2.

24. Engelbert Pernerstorfer, "Von Schönerer bis Wolf," *Der Kampf* 4 (1910–11): 391. This article will henceforth be cited as "Schönerer."

German as the national language, autonomy for Galicia, and a close alliance and customs union with Germany. In addition, many of the political, social, and economic proposals echoed points in Friedjung's program: a constantly progressive expansion of the suffrage; the rights to associate and to assemble; the freedom of the press; the corporate organization of the producing classes; the various tax reforms, including the progressive income tax.[25] Furthermore, even the language and phraseology of the two documents are strikingly similar. As Erich Zailer demonstrates in his dissertation on Friedjung, there are far too many examples of parallel formulation to accept the argument that Schönerer's proclamation did not rely heavily on Friedjung's Volkspartei program.[26]

Nonetheless, the proclamation did depart from Friedjung's program in a variety of new proposals expressing a wide range of socioeconomic interests. It called for rapid and cheap justice, nationalization of the railroads, factory laws and reform of working conditions, restrictions on the powers of the church, regulations to ensure the independence and character of parliamentary deputies, and laws to prevent stock swindles. In addition, the provisions for the corporate organization of the producing classes were considerably more detailed and complex in the proclamation than in Friedjung's program.[27] Pernerstorfer later explained the motley character of the proclamation by noting that while the members of the Deutscher Klub agreed in their democratic convictions, they differed radically on economic questions: "Next to radical demands for a social policy friendly to the workers there were also voices extremely partisan to guilds [*extremzunftlerische*] as well as the voices of agrarian reactionaries. Every single point was voted on, and thus, completely contradictory points were accepted with changing majorities."[28]

It seems clear that the proclamation was a collective document expressing a variety of outlooks within the Deutscher Klub rather than the product of Schönerer alone, as Pichl strongly suggests. The members of the Pernerstorfer circle, particularly Friedjung, played an extremely important role in the deliberations, but given

25. Compare Pichl, vol. 1, pp. 104–05 with pp. 100–01.

26. Erich Zailer, *Heinrich Friedjung unter besonderer Berücksichtigung seiner politischen Entwicklung* (Ph.D. dissertation, University of Vienna, 1949), pp. 51–52.

27. Pichl, vol. 1, pp. 100–01.

28. Pernerstorfer, "Schönerer," p. 391.

the past history of the circle there is no reason to suppose that they attempted to challenge Schönerer's leadership in any way. Throughout their long association with the Leseverein as well as their involvement in the creation of the Schulverein, the circle had always avoided official positions of leadership in favor of a dominant role in the shaping of ideology and institutions. The available evidence strongly indicates that their role in the proclamation of the deutschnational society followed this pattern. While they seem to have provided most of the material for the nationalistic planks as well as many of the political and socioeconomic points, the dominant personality of Georg von Schönerer furnished the leadership necessary to synthesize these proposals with those of the Deutscher Klub factions which held basically different outlooks on economic issues.

Several months after the publication of the proclamation, the committee of the Deutscher Klub accomplished the second of the three tasks assigned to it by the society—the establishment of a party newspaper. On May Day 1881, the first issue of the *Deutsche Worte* appeared, edited by Pernerstorfer and including articles by the leading members of the club: Adler, Pernerstorfer, Friedjung, Schönerer, and Steinwender. The lead article by Pernerstorfer struck the familiar notes of German nationalism, social concern, and contempt for the liberal order. He described past liberal governments as "governments which conducted their business in the interest of the liberal parties and which no more had their roots in the folk than any of the other governments we have had to endure." Ignoring the true needs of the folk, this "cosmopolitan liberalism" had only "enunciated political formulas, while promoting in the national economy that Manchesterian 'free development,' the end result of which spelled the destruction of the true essence of the folk." In opposition to this approach, Pernerstorfer called for giving political activity "a German content," and he promised that the nature of this content would become clear "when we allow German work and German art in their manifold forms to pass before our spiritual eye."[29] The publication of the *Deutsche Worte* thus complemented the Deutscher Klub's continuing task of formulating a systematic party program by making it possible to explain to the party membership at large the various ideas being considered for inclusion in the program.

29. *Deutsche Worte* (1 May 1881), pp. 1–2. This paper will henceforth be cited as *D.W.* Beginning in 1884 the newspaper became a monthly magazine; hence the different citation with volume number and consecutive pagination.

The final phase of the discussions leading to the promulgation of the Linz program took place in the committee which had issued the proclamation and established the newspaper, although one new member, Anton Langgassner, had now joined its deliberations. The discussions of the program were so lengthy and acrimonious that one by one the various members withdrew until only Schönerer, Pernerstorfer, and Langgassner remained.[30] Thereafter several meetings took place in Linz at which Schönerer was represented by Pernerstorfer. These meetings produced some further changes and then Langgassner organized the final program into thirty-six points (three of which were soon eliminated).

On 16 August and 1 September 1882, the completed Linz program appeared in the *Deutsche Worte* with the statement that it was "a systematic organization of all those demands which have already often been made in these pages and on public occasions by members of our party, particularly by Schönerer."[31] In addition to the demands already presented in Friedjung's program and the proclamation of the Deutschnationaler Verein, the Linz program included several new points. In addition to calling for Galician autonomy, the program demanded that Dalmatia, Bosnia, and Herzegovina be included in Hungary (point 2). The proposal that German be made the state language was supplemented with two points encouraging the use of German in linguistically mixed areas as well as in the bureaucracy (points 5 and 6). There was also a new demand calling for an energetic defense of Austria's interests in the Mediterranean (point 33). Important new issues were introduced in the social reform sections. In addition to demanding the nationalization of the railroads, the program called for nationalization of the insurance system and for the provision of old-age and accident insurance (point 23). Three points (28–30) providing for the protection of the peasantry were included. Also, the plank calling for factory reform was clarified considerably by detailed demands for a normal work day, restriction of child and female labor, and employer responsibility for accidents (point 26).[32]

The Deutscher Klub had planned to climax its work on the new program with a mass convention in Linz at which Schönerer would

30. Pichl, vol. 1, pp. 105, 109.
31. *D.W.* (16 Aug. 1882), p. 2.
32. Pichl, vol. 1, pp. 112–15.

present the program and develop it as a coherent whole. At the last minute, however, the authorities intervened to prevent the meeting, and it was never held. Nonetheless, Schönerer's speech—most of it apparently written by Pernerstorfer—did appear in print, and its final words (which seem to have been Schönerer's own) convey well the content and mood of the Linz program: "I close gentlemen, in exhorting you! Let us remain unbowed in joy and sorrow, in need and danger, and let us take up the struggle with the battle cry: *For genuine German nationalism and for social reform*!" Thus did Ritter Georg plan to lead his troops into battle.[33]

Although Ferdinand Bilger and a number of modern historians have credited Friedjung with a dominant role in formulating the nationalistic points of the Linz program, Bilger also noted that its most important domestic points were based on the idea of radical social reform, and suggested that Schönerer played the crucial role in shaping these planks. "Here," wrote Bilger, "he may assert the claim that he depended on himself."[34] To support this point, Bilger cited Schönerer's first parliamentary speech in which he called for representation of the working classes in Parliament, as well as speeches in 1877 and 1878 in which he regretted the workers' tax load. The evidence, however, does not support Bilger's claim. Since Schönerer delivered his first speech in 1873, and then waited for four years before again alluding briefly to the workers' problems, it hardly bespeaks a deep commitment to social reform at this point in his political career. Nor are Bilger's three citations merely chosen at random from many similar examples. Although Schönerer's biographer Pichl also tried to show Schönerer's consistent dedication to the workers, he was able to produce no evidence, beyond the offhand remark in 1873, until the 1880s. His discussion of Schönerer as a social reformer moves quickly from the 1873 speech to the preliminary discussions of the Linz program. After his first speech, none of Schönerer's speeches in the Reichsrath except the two delivered in 1877 and 1878 (which did no more than deplore the tax load of

33. The preliminary manuscript of the speech written in Pernerstorfer's hand and bearing his name, as well as a final printed copy, can be found in the Pichl Nachlass, carton 35, folder 2. The final words in the printed copy are in one of a number of sections of the speech not found in the manuscript. It seems highly probable that these sections were added by Schönerer.

34. Ferdinand Bilger, "Georg Schönerer," *Neue oesterreichische Biographie* (Vienna, 1928), vol. 5, pp. 80–81.

the lower classes) even mentioned the interests of the workers or social reform until the 1880s.[35]

Actually, Schönerer's position during the first years of his political career was simply that of a progressive nationalistic liberal. An election speech of 13 September 1875 is typical: he demanded the greatest possible political freedom for all citizens, he called for various anticlerical measures such as banning the Jesuits and admitting the Freemasons, he deplored waste and corruption, and he called for a conflict-of-interests law. The speech also betrayed a few indications of the German nationalist outlook common among progressive liberals.[36] As Paul Molisch has observed, it was not until 1878 that Schönerer began to move toward the radical German nationalism with which his name is associated.[37] Adam Wandruszka also places Schönerer's conversion to social consciousness in this period: "Schönerer, who in 1875 had delivered in Parliament a flaming avowal of individual and political freedom, then demanded in his principles of 1880 the reform of the industrial system and the factory laws as well as the strengthening of the 'corporative spirit' of peasants and workers."[38] Moreover, this period saw an important change in Schönerer's political style. As Bilger has noted, "the unprecedentedly disrespectful form of his later language enters his parliamentary activity as early as 1878."[39] Gustav Kolmer also dates the beginning of Schönerer's high-pitched (*scharfe Tonart*) political style from the March 1878 speech to the Reichsrath in which he called the delegates political eunuchs.[40]

What happened, then, to change Schönerer from the respectful liberal of 1875 to the extreme and venomous nationalist of 1878? The vague suggestion by Paul Molisch that Schönerer's association with the alumni (*alte Herren*) of certain student organizations might provide the answer to this question, deserves careful consideration, particularly considering the unusual way in which Schönerer came to be involved with the Leseverein der deutschen Studenten Wiens

35. Pichl, vol. 2, pp. 247–48; vol. 3, pp. 26–40.

36. The speech is summarized in Pichl, vol. 2, p. 388.

37. Paul Molisch, *Politische Geschichte der deutschen Hochschulen in Oesterreich von 1848 bis 1918* (Vienna, 1939), p. 98.

38. Wandruszka, *Oesterreichs politische Struktur,* p. 294.

39. Bilger, p. 78.

40. Gustav Kolmer, *Parlament und Verfassung in Oesterreich* (Vienna, 1903), vol. 2, p. 296.

and the Pernerstorfer circle.[41] The story of how this relationship developed was anonymously recounted in a magazine article many years later. The author identified himself only as a former member of the society who occasionally participated in the informal meetings of the Leseverein leaders with those of the affiliated fraternities.[42] It was at one such meeting that Anton Haider broached the idea that the Leseverein should attempt to secure for itself a representative in Parliament who would defend the interests of the student community. Haider had been president of the society for several years, and it was under his able leadership that the organization had achieved not only structural and financial solidity but also the desired position of influence among the university's students. Shortly before the end of the academic year 1875–76 he had resigned his official position, but even so he continued to advise and guide the society informally. It was in one such informal session that the author of the article arrived to find Haider discussing the unsatisfactory nature of the society's political connections:

> Haider said that we had no suitable parliamentary deputy who represented us, visited our meetings, taking from us here, enriching us in return. "Kopp is no longer what he was," he felt, "Sturm long since not. They are all of too muted a color [*gedämpft in der Farbe*] and don't really fit our views well. We need a deputy who is completely our man, whom we can joyously cheer, in whom we can trust, who can have confidence in us."

At this point another member of the society interrupted to observe that there was no such person, to which Haider replied that "someone could become one." When asked who this might be he replied, "*His name is Schönerer*. He is still little known; he is young, just recently elected and his direction [*Richtung*] is not yet so set, but I observe that he would fit together well with us—I believe we already agree with him, without his really knowing us. We should invite him here [and] speak with him. I believe he would be the right one." Haider's suggestion met with no objections, and Georg von Schönerer was invited,

41. Molisch, pp. 102–03.

42. "Erinnerungen (zwanglose Mitteilungen eines 'alten Herren')," *Mitteilungen des Verbandes alter Burschenschafter "Wartburg,"* vol. 7 (Dec. 1897), p. 1. The most important part of this article is reprinted in Pichl, *Schönerer,* vol. 3, p. viii. This article will henceforth be cited as *Wartburg*.

appeared, "became acquainted with our people [and] our ideas, and we understood one another magnificently." During the following academic year (1876–77) Schönerer joined the Leseverein as a supporting member, and on 3 November 1876 he was accorded the honor of being elected an external (*Auswärtige*) member of the society, a distinction only one step below that of honorary membership.[43] As the author of the article observed:

> Schönerer was our man. Ever after, the German nationalist students celebrated him as their champion. He was always there, he spoke at our parties and wherever he appeared he had a student guard. . . . That was the beginning of the relationship between the German nationalist students and Schönerer, which became so intimate, and which would yield such various fruits.[44]

Since the dramatic change in Schönerer's political outlook and style occurred during the two and one-half years between September 1875 and March 1878 (the dates of his two radically different speeches) this testimony strongly suggests that Schönerer's contact with the Leseverein accounts for that change. Although the author of the article describing the meeting does not give its date, he does say that Haider was no longer president of the society, which indicates that the meeting occurred after 9 May 1876, the date Haider resigned.[45] Since Schönerer joined the society as a supporting member during the following academic year and was honored by election to external membership on 3 November 1876, the initial contact must have been made during the period from 9 May to 3 November.[46] This date tallies roughly with one given in an 1886 political speech by Pernerstorfer in which he said of Schönerer that in 1875 and 1876 he and his fellow students had "raised him on their shield."[47]

Although later historians have almost completely ignored the relationship between the authors of the Linz program and the Leseverein, contemporaries involved in the deutschnational movement

43. *Jahresbericht* 1876–77, p. 11.
44. *Wartburg,* vol. 7 (Dec. 1897), p. 1.
45. Albert Hiller, "Der Leseverein der deutschen Studenten," p. 20.
46. *Jahresbericht,* 1876–77, p. 11.
47. *D.Z.* (3 July 1886), p. 2.

clearly recognized its importance. An article that appeared in the *Deutsche Worte*'s student section six weeks before the publication of the program declared "the existence and effect of the Reading Society of the German Students of Vienna is a fact of epoch-making significance for the history of the Germans in Austria. It must be repeated again and again that the entire German nationalist movement which . . . has grown up in recent years was called forth and is led by men who are either alumni of a fraternity (*Burschenshaft*) or of the Reading Society." To support his point, the author cited various movements and organizations including "the party of the *Deutsche Worte,* the true German People's Party [which] is recruited primarily from former members of the Leseverein or those who stood in some kind of intellectual relationship with it."[48]

Viewing the controversy over the origins of the Linz program in the light of Schönerer's intimate relationship with the student radicals of the Leseverein and the Pernerstorfer circle not only clarifies that controversy but also suggests some of the reasons why the evolution of this program exercised such a dramatic influence on subsequent political history. The Linz program was distinguished from numerous other programs promulgated at the same time by its union of German nationalist demands with demands for far-reaching social and political reform. This combination of nationalism and social concern was also the most striking political characteristic of the Leseverein, and more particularly of its intellectual leaders, the members of the Pernerstorfer circle. As members of the Socio-Political Society, Friedjung, Pernerstorfer, and Adler had endorsed expansion of the suffrage and state intervention to solve social problems as early as 1870, before most of them had even entered the university, and from that time forward the circle's espousal of social reform as well as German nationalism had grown progessively stronger and more effective in response to such successive crises of the liberal order as the crash of 1873, the Ofenheim scandal, and the formation of Taaffe's "Iron Ring" government. Since the movement represented by the *Deutscher Klub* had evolved and prospered largely in response to liberal failures, it is not surprising that it should offer effective political lessons to the various mass parties confronting the liberal order at a later stage in its decline, and as Wandruszka has

48. *D.W.* (16 July 1882), p. 1.

shown, all three of modern Austria's great mass movements relied heavily on the *Deutscher Klub*'s Linz program. It thus seems far more plausible to view this program as the product of a student movement which had struggled to confront Austria's national and socio-economic problems for over a decade, than to ascribe it primarily to Schönerer, who had shown only the mildest interest in these problems before his contact with the members of the Pernerstorfer circle and the Leseverein. The organization responsible for formulating the Linz program, the *Deutscher Klub*, owed its establishment to the Leseverein, and the Linz program was in every sense a continuation and a realization of the national and social concerns which had long characterized the outlook of this student society.

Georg von Schönerer, the Knight of Rosenau, was well suited to the leadership of this romantic political movement. As Carl Schorske has shown, he shared the feelings of generational revolt which had shaped the outlook of his student friends, and the indifference of his parliamentary colleagues during his brief period as a liberal may well have speeded his alienation from liberal ideals.[49] Once Schönerer accepted the proffered friendship of the Leseverein, he embraced its principles with enthusiasm, thereby tapping the boundless energies of youthful discontent and assuring himself a passionate and dedicated following. In the deliberations over the Linz program, Schönerer unquestionably played a major role, and if many of his convictions were rather recently acquired, he expressed them none the less forcefully. Undoubtedly he also contributed ideas which were much more fully his own, such as the proposals to improve the lot of the peasantry. Schönerer's educational and professional experience was in agriculture, and a concern for its problems marks his political activity from 1873 forward. Also, as Schorske has suggested, such proposals as the nationalization of the railroads certainly bespeak Schönerer's personal touch. Nonetheless, Schönerer's debt to his student followers was immense, for they had provided the intellectual and emotional forces which brought him to political prominence just as they had originally sought him out to establish this relationship "which would yield such various fruits."

49. Carl E. Schorske, "Politics in a New Key: An Austrian Triptych," *Journal of Modern History* 34 (Dec. 1967) : 346–52.

7. Pernerstorfer's Metapolitics

While the Linz program defined the long-range goals of the new deutschnational movement, the task of giving substance to these goals on a day-to-day basis fell primarily to Pernerstorfer in his dual capacities as chairman of the Deutschnationaler Verein and editor of the party organ. Through the *Deutsche Worte,* Pernerstorfer could shape the movement to fulfill the task he had enunciated in the first issue of his paper, the task of giving Austrian politics a "German content." In that issue, Pernerstorfer had promised that this would be accomplished "when we allow German work and German art in their manifold forms to pass before our spiritual eye," and in a later article he specifically declared that "the preparation of friendly relations between German art and German politics has been definitely, if not explicitly, taken into our program."[1] However unofficial its status, this aesthetic dimension of the movement's activity had a profound impact on the style and tactics of deutschnational politics, and ultimately it was responsible for political innovations as significant and influential as any of those proposed in the formal party program.

Just as the Linz program drew much of its substance from the outlook of the radical student movement of the late 1870s, so too did this unofficial commitment to an aesthetic politics owe much to the preparatory work of such student groups as the Pernerstorfer circle and the Leseverein. Since the Nietzschean-Wagnerian conception of a cultural community assumed the unity of art and politics, the members of the circle who had dedicated themselves to this ideal community in their letter to Nietzsche embarked on their political careers with a well-developed theoretical framework for bringing the power of art to bear on political reality. As early as 1877 this idea was explicitly advanced by another member of the circle, Heinrich Friedjung, whose *Ausgleich mit Ungarn* invoked the masculine spirit of art as a remedy for the impotent paralysis of liberal politics. Impatience with the restrained political style of progressive

1. *D.W.* (1 May 1881), pp. 1–2.

liberals such as Kopp and Sturm had also figured in the Leseverein's approach to Schönerer in the summer of 1876. As Anton Haider explained, these liberal politicians were too moderate, too muted in color; and in Schönerer the leaders of the Leseverein hoped to find a representative who would move beyond this moderation to give full expression to their passionate feelings. Schönerer more than fulfilled these expectations as the first practitioner of what later came to be known as the politics of the sharper key, and this new political style has been seen as a crucial ingredient of various twentieth-century mass movements.[2] Since both Gustav Kolmer and Richard Charmatz have dated Schönerer's shift to the sharper style at about 1878,[3] shortly after his first contact with student groups, the role of Schönerer's student supporters in shaping the new style deserves careful examination. A year before Schönerer's shift, Friedjung's *Ausgleich* had set the tone for the new political style with the observation that "Orpheus only dared to walk with his lyre among the powers of the underworld because he knew there lives in the obscure masses a feeling which will be awakened to thundering emotion by a full tone."[4] Informed by the spirit of Orpheus—or at least Wagner—Pernerstorfer, Schönerer, and the other contributors to the *Deutsche Worte* set out to develop a politics which did indeed awaken thundering emotion in the obscure masses.

One of the clearest statements of how the deutschnational movement expected to unite the forces of art and politics can be found in a brief article Pernerstorfer wrote for the *Deutsche Worte* in 1884. Entitled "Metapolitics," it concerned a dispute between a Professor Immanuel Hoffmann and the *Bayreuther Blätter* over the value of the plebiscite as a political tool. The *Bayreuther Blätter* disapproved of the idea, and Hoffmann had written them a letter defending it. The *Deutsche Worte* reprinted his letter, asking its readers to ignore the substantive issue of the plebiscite and "to direct their attention particularly to the suprapolitical [*überpolitischen*] perspectives which followed from regarding political life as a part of the total national life." Hoffmann took his suprapolitical viewpoint directly from

2. Schorske, "Politics in a New Key," *Journal of Modern History* 34 (Dec. 1967) : 345.

3. Kolmer, *Parlament und Verfassung in Oesterreich,* vol. 2, p. 296. Charmatz, *Lebensbilder aus der Geschichte Oesterreichs,* pp. 145–47.

4. Heinrich Friedjung, *Der Ausgleich mit Ungarn,* p. 1. This work will henceforth be cited as *Ausgleich.*

Wagner's works. In his letter he argued that "art and religion cannot lead an existence separate from politics. . . . As true art, according to the Master's words, can only thrive on the ground of true morality, so no people can have a true art or a true religion as long as its political life rests on lies." Hoffmann stressed the need for restoring a communitarian outlook: "We can only be saved *together*. . . . Bayreuth can only become Germany when the peaceful shoots, which—however parched and weak—have everywhere taken root among us, are strengthened. If one member [*Glied*] suffers, then all members join in suffering."

Here again one recognizes the concept of the cultural community which dominated the theories of Wagner and the early Nietzsche, and in speaking of this community in such organic terms, Hoffmann suggested a basic criticism which this outlook leveled against the scientific culture associated with liberalism: "The world-historical error which lies at the basis of our civilization and stamps it as a culture of lies is that of regarding the fragrance of the flower as better than the flower itself, of prizing the distilled perfume higher than the living essence, of believing the extract of the folk wiser than the folk itself." The *Deutsche Worte* subscribed fully to this viewpoint, describing it as "a significant manifestation of that direction of thought which is also completely our own. It wants a mighty *unity of life* through the destruction of all artificial appearance and through the revelation of inner 'truth.' "[5] Relying basically on the Schopenhauerian distinction between deceptive phenomenal appearance and nature's inner essence, this outlook associated liberal culture with the former and saw in the latter the binding force of their community, a binding force revealed in the spiritual realms of art and religion.

Since the unifying force of the cultural community manifested itself in a spiritual realm, the *Deutsche Worte* repeatedly stressed that it

5. *D.W.* 4 (1884) : 250–52. The title of the article "Metapolitics" was evidently taken from Constantin Frantz, "Oeffener Brief an Richard Wagner," *Bayreuther Blätter* (June 1878), p. 169. He wrote of politics, "Sie muss sich zur *Metapolitik* erheben, als welche sich zur gemeinen Schulpolitik ähnlich verhält, wie zur Physik die Metaphysik." Frantz believed that German politics and art should be united in the common cause of furthering the German spirit: "So wird die wahre deutsche Politik der deutschen Kunst auch erst die rechte Stätte bereiten, wie andererseits die Kunst die Politik beflügeln wird zu immer höherem Aufschwung." Frantz also approved of the Wagnerian union of nationalism and socialism on the purely practical level. Peter Viereck's *Metapolitics from the Romantics to Hitler* (New York, 1941), adopts Frantz's term as its title and explores the tempting similarities between Wagner's political outlook and Hitler's.

adhered "to the viewpoint of the solidarity of spiritual [*geistigen*] and material interests." In an 1882 article, Pernerstorfer denounced the "Manchesterian outlook" with its policy of "criminal laissez-faire," and while expressing some sympathy for the social-democratic movement, he also rejected its materialism. In explaining what the *Deutsche Worte* understood by the term "national solidarity" Pernerstorfer declared, *"The national idea . . . means to us the full and intimate physical and spiritual solidarity* [*Zusammengehörigkeit*] *of all fellow nationals."* Not only did this imply overcoming class and economic barriers to attain social cohesiveness, but it also demanded the participation of all in the national community's spiritual–intellectual concerns. In striving to attain its goal of a dignified human existence for all, the paper emphasized that such an existence did not merely involve the "enjoyment of material goods, but rather that these are only means to a higher goal. They should give every individual the opportunity of appropriating the spiritual heritage of his nation in order actually to be able to be . . . *at once a receiving and creating member in the great body of the German folk community*."[6] Pernerstorfer thus saw full participation in the spiritual realm of the cultural community as the ultimate goal of the national and social reforms proposed by his movement.

An article appearing in the *Deutsche Worte* in 1884 also emphasized the distinction between the individualistic outlook of liberalism and the aesthetic, communitarian approach of Pernerstorfer's movement. "Some declare that the riches, energy, and power of individuals provide the riches, energy, and power of the state." Others, however, believe that "forces produce an effect only when they are united. . . . It is the harmony of the forces which maintains the whole and makes it strong." For this reason, the author urged members of the folk to exert themselves to increase the "spiritual and moral powers of each individual" and to "recognize in all the other members of our nation, the parts of that great unity to which we belong and from which we have derived our essence."[7]

In the völkisch cultural community envisioned by the Wagnerites of the *Deutsche Worte*, political and aesthetic theory merged in an ideal unity of life to offer a coherent ideological alternative to the liberal credo, and the fact that the cultural community centered

6. *D.W.* (16 Sept. 1882), pp. 1–2. See also *D.W.* 4 (1884) : 297.
7. *D.W.* 4 (1884) : 76–77.

around theatrical art carried particularly important implications for political practice. This can be seen in the various tributes which the deutschnational movement offered to Richard Wagner after his death in February 1883. In his early works Nietzsche had seen Wagner's musical dramas as the focal point of the emerging community of the German nation, and in the months following the composer's death, the *Deutsche Worte* published a three-part article developing this idea at some length: "Richard Wagner's Significance for the German Nation." Although the *Deutsche Worte* did not give the author's name, it was probably Heinrich Hengster, later a frequent contributor of articles on Wagner and Wagneriana. The year before the articles appeared, Hengster had offered his services to the *Deutsche Worte* in a letter[8] which noted that "German art and German politics" should "never lightly be separated from each other." He went on to argue, "Only through faithful cultivation of noble German art can . . . the feeling for a great German community [*Gemeinwesen*]—and thus the longing desire and energetic striving for such—be awakened."

After an elaborate explication of the Wagnerian outlook's philosophical structure with its distinction between the worlds of appearance and essential reality, the article focused on the importance of drama as an art form which allowed man to transcend the world of mundane appearance and understand the basis of human existence. As Nietzsche had done in his *Birth of Tragedy,* the author saw the culture of ancient Greece as Wagner's model for this kind of dramatic art. "Wagner found the drama in its ideal purity and sublimity among the Greeks; here religion and art were joined in a bond which produced a community [*Gemeinwesen*] that after two thousand years seems to us today like a beautiful dream of humanity." According to the author Wagner believed that the Greek community (*Gemeinwesen*) rested on a strong sense of nationality; he assumed "that the Greeks felt themselves to be a nation and were capable of producing a national culture which in turn made it possible for the Hellenic folk spirit to recognize itself in national drama."[9]

While the Greek example may have provided the model for the drama-centered community (*Gemeinwesen*) Wagner hoped to create, the composer used new means to achieve the community feeling of

8. April 24, 1882, Adler Archiv.
9. *D.W.* (1 March 1883), p. 7.

the ancient tragedies. In contrast to the Greek model, the author of the article noted: "The music's center of gravity lies in the orchestra which takes the place of the chorus in ancient tragedy," and he saw this as an advantage "in that it makes possible its organic union with the singer's words through the thousand threads which interweave the entire drama and have the capacity of revealing to the soul of the listener all the moments of feeling in their most subtle ramifications and their deepest profundity. . . . Through the newly introduced principle of free and unlimited modulation, the music has profited enormously in specific dramatic expressiveness," and this expressiveness had the effect of drawing the members of the audience together in the common emotional flow of the drama.[10]

The tremendous political potential inherent in this artistic model can be seen in another of the events marking Wagner's demise, the elaborate wake held by the deutschnational university students in March 1883. The extent of Wagner's popularity among Vienna's students was indicated by one of the most prominent participants in the wake, the young Hermann Bahr, who exaggerated only slightly in his claim that "every young person was a Wagnerian then. He was one before he had even heard a single measure of his music."[11] By 1883, Count Taaffe's conservative pro-Slav policies had driven the vast majority of the German-speaking students into the deutschnational camp, and a certain sympathy for the cause had been expressed even by the Rector of the university, a man who shared the educational tradition which had earlier influenced so many of the movement's student leaders. At his inauguration as Rector, Anselm Ricker, "a member of the Benedictine monastery 'zu den Schotten,' amidst stormy exultation, recalled that exactly five hundred years earlier, a member of this Benedictine monastery, the Abbot Donaldus, had likewise been invested with the rectorate of the University of Vienna, and in this capacity had led the defense of the oldest German university, the University of Prague, against all the disturbers of its rights."[12] The Wagner wake thus came at a time when feeling for the German nationalist cause ran high, and the event

10. *D.W.* (1 April 1883), p. 3.

11. Hermann Bahr, *Selbstbildnis* (Berlin, 1923), p. 139.

12. Beurle, *Beiträge,* p. 55. Ricker was Rector in 1881–82. *Geschichte der Wiener Universität von 1848 bis 1898,* ed. Akademischen Senat der Wiener Universität (Vienna, 1898), p. 400.

produced dramatic results. As Karl Beurle, one of the participants, noted at the beginning of his account, "It will indeed be a picture of the time!" The wake took place on 5 March 1883 in Vienna's largest hall, the *Sofiensaal,* and it attracted some four thousand guests. According to Beurle, "the galeries and loges were filled with ladies from the best circles of society dressed completely in mourning."[13]

The decorations symbolized the loyalties of the crowd. Ostensibly in expectation of the German ambassador, one of the loges was "richly decorated and fitted out with the German imperial arms." While an immense flag of the German Empire dominated the room, the Austrian colors were nowhere to be seen. A bust of Wagner placed near the middle of the room and surrounded by palm leaves completed a setting in which religious, artistic, and political symbolism merged in the approved Wagnerian manner.[14] The first speaker, Richard Kann, struck the religious note suggested by the palm leaves: "Spring decorates Richard Wagner's grave and nature rustles her sweetest greetings to the one she loved so much; the seed ripens and from all districts festive crowds draw near Bayreuth, for there is a heritage to manage—one whose precious vessel must be the entire German nation." The next speaker spoke on Wagner's art as an expression of German nationalism, noting that his "magnificent *Emperor*'s *March* expresses the full rejoicing of the nation that the German once again has a fatherland." The audience greeted these words with shouts of approval and as the speaker closed amidst thunderous applause, the Academic Choir gave musical expression to the militant mood of the audience by performing the battle hymn from Wagner's *Rienzi*.[15]

After several more selections in honor of the composer, this first musical interlude ended on the reverential note with which the ceremony had begun: "The melancholy conclusion . . . put the assemblage into a serious, hallowed mood." Pernerstorfer then spoke on the prevailing corruption of the press and called upon youth to free itself from this pernicious influence. Karl Beurle noted the presence of certain professors and rejoiced that "the men of learning also have a heart capable of feeling with us." He discussed the various

13. Beurle, p. 56.
14. Pichl, *Schönerer,* vol. 2, pp. 340–41.
15. Beurle, p. 57.

ties that bound together the Germans of the Empire with those of Austria, and when he read a letter of sympathy from Field Marshall von Moltke, the audience responded by singing the "Watch on the Rhine." After yet another speech calling for close ties between Austria and Germany, the orchestra played selections from Wagner's *Tannhäuser*.[16]

The climax came in the third act. Throughout the evening the numerous emotional peaks had been celebrated by toasts, and excitement began to mount as the successive speakers delivered ever more fervent expressions of their devotion to the German Empire, expressions which many Austrians of the older generation regarded as treasonous. The police commissioner, who had been following the proceedings, began to warn the speakers that he would be forced to intervene if they persisted in such declarations. Then, in the final speech of the evening, the young Hermann Bahr spoke on Wagner as a political leader. Bahr had been chosen to speak at the last moment as a replacement for someone who had fallen ill, and in frantic preparation he had plunged for the first time into Wagner's prose writings, where he found "actually everything that mankind needed for regeneration; indeed, it was not just a powerful artist who spoke here; it was a prophet; here rushed all the springs of life." Relying heavily on citations from Wagner's earliest and most revolutionary political works, Bahr made his address a passionate appeal for liberty and for strong ties with Germany.[17] The high point of the speech came when Bahr spoke of realizing Wagner's dream "of the awakening of the enchained Kundry and her reunion with her sisters in the neighboring land." This allusion to pan-German hopes unleashed a storm of approval from the audience, and again brought a police warning. When their demands that Bahr moderate his tone served only to arouse the audience still more, the police forbade any further speeches. Although none had been planned, this declaration so enraged the crowd that they ignored the police and called for Schönerer to speak. Schönerer rushed to the podium and delivered a few passionate sentences before the police interrupted his final cries of "Long live our Bismarck!" After one last toast in honor of Wagner the crowd dispersed singing the "Watch on the Rhine."[18]

16. Ibid., pp. 57–59; Pichl, vol. 2, p. 341.
17. Bahr, *Selbstbildnis*, pp. 141–43.
18. Pichl, vol. 2, p. 341; Bahr, pp. 143–47. Bahr's speech made him so popular with his

Even without police assistance, the Wagner wake was a triumph of political stagecraft for the deutschnational movement. Managed with a sensitivity to crowd dynamics born of the Wagnerian theater, the event produced one of the movement's most effective demonstrations of political strength. As Wagner had worked for a synthesis of religion, art, and politics on the model of Greek tragedy, so his followers honored him in a setting redolent with the symbols of this synthesis. Just as Nietzsche had seen the Dionysian rites of Greek prototragedy as an expression of nature's eternal rebirth, and just as Wagner's musical drama *Parsifal* had celebrated the same faith in more Christian garb, so did Vienna's Wagnerites mark the Master's death with a dramatic presentation focusing on the theme of regeneration. Moreover, as the chanting chorus had directed the emotional development of the prototragedy toward that point where audience and chorus became a unified entity expressing the community of the celebrants, and as music—particularly that of the orchestra—had filled a similar function in Wagner's operas, so did both choir and orchestra provide emotional direction in arousing the audience of the Wagner wake to a unified outburst of political feeling. Throughout the wake, the music supported the dynamics of the program as a whole, now reinforcing militant feelings (as with the battle hymn of *Rienzi*), now transmuting the mood to one of deep seriousness (immediately before the second series of speeches) and finally it drew audiences and performers together in the choruses of the "Watch on the Rhine" with which the wake concluded.

Immersed in the theories of Nietzsche and Wagner, the party of the *Deutsche Worte* fully appreciated the relevance of the Dionysian and Apollonian art forces to a mastery of crowd psychology. As one of the paper's regular contributors later reported in an article on the Munich *Oktoberfest*, "Indeed, I saw masses, but nothing that would

---

fellow students that they held another meeting to mourn his expulsion from the university. This celebration was forbidden, but they held it anyway. When the police then dispersed it, they marched in a body to a tavern in the Josefstadt where they continued. The Josefstadt police then ejected them forcibly and they continued their party in the Alsergrund. As the evening wore on, the periodic encounters with the police grew ever more violent, and Bahr was on the point of impaling a policeman on his sword when Pernerstorfer picked him up and carried him struggling from the scene of battle. Still carrying Bahr, Pernerstorfer ran as far as the Votivkirche, where he put him down. After Bahr had recovered his senses, they sat there calculating the years in prison which that thrust of the sword might have cost.

have moved them in one sense; above all, Dionysian enthusiasm was completely lacking; it was a big, dull swarm of many individuals without any coherence."[19] As Wagnerites well understood, this coherence depended on the capacity of various form-giving dramatic elements to channel individual emotional reactions toward a common experience. In the Wagner wake the visual symbols as well as the speakers' words successfully served this purpose, while the music helped to intensify the emotions of the crowd.

As might be expected, this deutschnational spectacular received rather poor reviews in the liberal press. Karl Beurle wrote: "Probably never before has a nation tolerated with such equanimity the kind of sustained scolding and ridiculing of its academic youth by a tribe of journalists as the German nation of Austria did then."[20] The papers also demanded punishment for those responsible, and after assuring the public that only a small minority of its students were involved, the university expelled Hermann Bahr and Franz Dafert (the principal organizer of the wake). Although the authorities secured the removal of Schönerer's parliamentary immunity so that he could be prosecuted for his part in the proceedings, the case was eventually dropped for lack of evidence.[21] The intensity of this reaction to the ceremony measures the extent to which it threatened the most basic interests and ideals of the liberal order. Not only did it suggest that the nation's intellectual elite had collectively embraced a treasonous ideology with cultural values directly opposed to those of Austrian liberalism, but it also demonstrated the emotional power of their aesthetic politics, a politics which posed a dangerous threat to liberalism.

While liberals denounced this kind of agitation of political feeling, Pernerstorfer made it clear in the *Deutsche Worte* that the emotional aspect of the movement's political style represented a conscious departure from liberal practices. In an article published in April 1882 he noted that the German nationalist party was frequently criticized for its rashness but instead of denying the charge, he cheerfully accepted it: "It is indeed correct that with a political

19. *D.W.* 4 (1884) : 122. The author of the article was Heinrich Krzyzanowski, a man closely associated with the Pernerstorfer circle during the early 1880s (Mahler, *Briefe,* p. 472). Krzyzanowski was also a graduate of the Schottengymnasium (1873) Hübl, p. 300.

20. Beurle, p. 61.

21. Pichl, vol 2, p. 348.

party whose political creed is not least of all a matter of the heart, the inner fire sometimes stands out extraordinarily." Pernerstorfer thought it not surprising that this should bring a shudder to men whose coldness extended even into their hearts, and he indicated that the emotional style of his own political party was in large part a reaction to this. "Anyone who does not close his eyes will realize that just this enraging coldness is the principal reason that a passionate reaction often sets in against it."[22]

From the time of its establishment, the *Deutsche Worte* had repeatedly criticized the dispassionate style of liberal politics. In its sixth issue (16 July 1881 p. 2), it discussed the political climate of the previous decade: "Our popular leaders, insofar as they had preserved their German sentiment, concealed it behind all sorts of other words such as centralism, liberalism, culture, constitutional loyalty, nothing but words which, when heard by the people, left them cold even up to their hearts." At that time, idealism had appeared dead, and "stock market liberalism" was in complete control. Since then, however, the political tone of such places as Prague had changed and "the lukewarm and gray liberal, the cosmopolite dissolving in empty vapor and learned lies, had finally become an ordinary German again." According to the *Deutsche Worte,* then, the liberals practiced a politics which was too learned and unidealistic to stir the emotions. In an article of 1 September of that year (p. 2), Pernerstorfer specifically criticized Eduard Herbst (the liberal politician whom Friedjung had used to typify an overintellectual political style in his *Ausgleich mit Ungarn*) on these grounds. "We hear from him not the warming tone of national manliness, we hear nothing of great tasks which are presented to us." Pernerstorfer also ridiculed the scholarly political style of three other liberal leaders—Ernst von Plener, Dr. Emil Sax, and Czedik von Bründelsberg: "The three men will surely save Austria! Admittedly, one must let them do as they please in order that their sublime thoughts are not distorted by the thoughtless mob." Pernerstorfer gave the following description of their political style (16 October, p. 1): "Truths which are familiar to every schoolchild are expounded with great majesty, citations of famous authorities [are delivered] with scholarly mien, before a reverent public." The liberal opposition was thus constantly

22. *D.W.* (16 April 1882), p. 2.

characterized as ilntelectual, scholarly, learned, and unfeeling—traits presented as weaknesses to be overcome by an emotional nationalistic politics.

Conditioned by an electorate restricted to the aristocratic, the wealthy, and the educated, Austrian liberalism could afford to deemphasize the appeals to emotion so essential to mass politics. The composition of the electorate also made mass meetings unnecessary, and the principal arena of the logical, scholarly politics of liberalism was the political club, an organization closely resembling a debating society. The proliferation of societies—artistic and scientific as well as political—was one of the hallmarks of liberal culture. So important a facet of life did it become that the *Neue Freie Presse*, the voice of Austrian liberalism, devoted a regular column to reporting the news of the various organizations. The society seems to have expressed the political wish-fulfillment of the Austrian burgher. His desire for constitutional order and due process found expression in the elaborate constitutions and bylaws that provided for a vast array of officers. The liberal realized his political ideal of a free and strictly rational exchange of ideas in the pattern of scholarly lectures and discussions which made up the intellectual fare of the societies' meetings. The narrow, exclusive nature of the memberships also reflected the Austrian liberal's belief that only the upper classes were properly prepared for the exercise of political power. The society, then, was essentially a smaller and more perfect version of the Austrian Parliament—or perhaps more accurately the Parliament was the political society writ large.

None had embraced the spirit the of political society more enthusiastically than the members of the Pernerstorfer circle. Beginning with the literary Telyn society, they had participated in the Socio-Political Society, the Leseverein, the Deutscher Klub, the Schulverein, the Deutsch-nationaler Verein, and the Deutscher Verein. By 1883, however, Pernerstorfer seems to have realized the difficulty of transcending the political style of liberalism while retaining the archetype of liberal politics, the political society, as the basis of organization. Pernerstorfer's metapolitics, keyed to emotion as well as reason, to the masses as well as the classes, demanded a new organizational principle. In a *Deutsche Worte* article entitled "Toward Party Organization," he declared, "*We must give up the idea of being able to achieve an active national and political life through political societies.*"

These organizations, according to Pernerstorfer, were entirely unnecessary for the stimulation of nationalism, and he cited the case of Galicia to support his point. There the political society was unknown, but nonetheless the Poles displayed an enviable national and political life.[23]

In a continuation of the article in the next issue, Pernerstorfer stated his conviction that "national consciousness and striving *cannot be instructed,* cannot be taught by means of *conventional upbringing* and carried into the broad classes of the population." He added that because of this conviction, "we also do not think much of all *addresses* and *reports*, even if they are not delivered in the unsystematic and purposeless fashion which occurs in our political societies." Where the liberal penchant for openly discussing political questions in scholarly lectures assumed an electoral elite Pernerstorfer looked to the day of the mass movement, and such a movement, he believed, would require the leadership of a small, select group discussing their goals and tactics in private. "To understand the course of political events, to recognize what is necessary for our people, to find the path which we must take to reach our goals, all this knowledge *was* and will *always* be native only to *the few,* to the elect." Pernerstorfer agreed that "it is theoretically very nice, if our national interests are made clear by free discussion in open meetings, if all this takes place according to broad democratic principles," but he also believed that in actuality, this procedure yielded few results. For this reason, the party leadership should be allowed to speak with an authoritative, decisive voice, and the bulk of the party should put aside their individual opinions and turn to the important task of agitation. As Pernerstorfer had observed earlier in the *Deutsche Worte* (1 October 1883), the problem with *Vereinsmeierei* (exclusive interest in local club life) was that it ignored "the effect and *success* of political agitation, and that is, after all, always the main thing."

After setting out these general principles to be observed in the development of an effective party organization, Pernerstorfer suggested specific organizational forms and techniques (16 October). Nothing reveals more clearly the distance Pernerstorfer had traveled from nineteenth- to twentieth-century politics than this list of pro-

23. *D.W.* (1 Oct. 1883), p. 3. The article is signed "r" (Redacteur, or Editor). Pernerstorfer was the sole editor of the paper.

posals. The centralized party leadership would be in the hands of a committee of trustees (*Vertrauensmänner*) each of whom would be in contact with the party leadership of a specific local area. Apparently, membership in the local party cells was to be secret, for one of the proposals was that party comrades (*Parteigenossen*) would be united only by the mutual knowledge that they were members of the party. They would maintain contact on a personal and social level. All comrades would receive the party paper and its availability in local coffeehouses and libraries would be ensured; they would also pay regular dues. Party members were to spread their ideas in private circles and in their families. "In particular, wives, young women, and the youth . . . must be won over to the nationalist outlook."

The article suggested that the local party groups should attempt "as far as possible to fill *influential positions* with party comrades." This applied not only to municipal and provincial government but also to various local clubs and societies. Furthermore, the article cautioned against undermining the value of infiltration; party members whose situations hindered them from making public their allegiance to the party should not be forced to do so: "They have enough to do on the inside, and in this way, their power and influence remains secure and preserved." The article also stressed the importance of having an exact knowledge of the social power factors of a locality. These must be intelligently taken into consideration and used, "for among the masses you just cannot succeed with abstract principles." Stressing the importance of working among all classes, the article demanded that party members be prepared to accept new ideas encountered in this way. Different opinions could not simply be dismissed with a genteel smile as thoughtless. "Often, then, thoughtlessness [*Gedankenlosigkeit*] is on our side." Pernerstorfer cautioned against an inflexible adherence to certain words and phrases, noting that many people mentally crossed themselves when they heard the word *deutschnational*. For this reason, he advised the party member to call himself a *deutschliberal*. After he had explained his position and won the sympathy of a prospective convert, he could then call himself a deutschnational if he wished.

In this article Pernerstorfer rightly claimed that "the German nationalist party is walking on paths previously *completely untrodden* and *unknown* to the Germans in Austria," and he warned that "the revolution in the views and conceptions of an *entire* nation cannot be accomplished . . . with a wave of the hand." Pernerstorfer made it clear that his movement considered itself an expression of a generational reaction against the older, liberal order: "We must declare that we are striving for an organization of the 'young,' i.e. the young in outlook, but in most cases also the young in age. . . . We will not win over our old and elderly politicians." According to Pernerstorfer this party of youth totally rejected the outlook of its liberal elders: "We are fire and water. The *only* necessity is to determine which will become *stronger*. Our worst enemies, the greatest misfortune of the Germans of Austria, are the liberal Germans." Where liberal politicians liked to pride themselves on a logical, learned presentation of their ideas, Pernerstorfer and his fellow party members moved beyond this to a politics of reason and feeling, to a metapolitics based on the Wagnerian ideal of a "mighty unity of life." Reason had presumably been satisfied by the detailed proposals of the Linz program, so in the article on organization, Pernerstorfer concentrated on making emotion serve the party's ends by developing a party structure that could carry out political agitation on a mass scale.

These ideas were enunciated in the wake of a serious split within the ranks of the deutschnational movement. Pernerstorfer and Schönerer had been in disagreement on certain issues for some time, but in the interest of maintaining party unity, an open conflict had been avoided. Finally in June 1883 the break occurred, and the *Deutsche Worte* published a series of acrimonious letters in which matters of both personality and principle played important roles. Pernerstorfer deeply resented Schönerer's dictatorial manner and when ordered to print one of Schönerer's speeches even though he disagreed with it, he became permanently alienated.[24]

However abrasive Schönerer's personality, the basic cause of the split concerned his espousal of racial anti-Semitism within the deutschnational movement, a development that radically altered the political course pursued by the Pernerstorfer circle. Even though several members of the circle were Jewish, they had long accepted a form of cultural anti-Semitism as part of their völkisch reaction against the bourgeois liberalism of their parents (a phenomenon George Mosse illuminated in his article, "The Influence of the

24. *D.W.* (16 June 1883), p. 2.

völkisch Idea on German Jewry"). Mosse notes: "Starting in the last decades of the nineteenth century, the völkisch movement became linked to a revolt by the youth of the bourgeois classes, which took the form of a deepened feeling by its initiators toward the Volk of which they felt themselves a part." Since they saw themselves as members of the German Volk, even the Jewish members of the Pernerstorfer circle felt it essential to reject what they regarded as Semitic cultural traits. As Mosse observes, the Jew was seen in stereotype as being intellectual and artificial, rootless and alienated from nature, and also particularly devoted to capitalism and urban life. Moreover, "Many Jews felt this image of their own people to be appropriate, and many of the young, especially, thought they saw it exemplified by their parents."[25]

While the members of the Pernerstorfer circle fully shared this outlook, they did so on the assumption that membership in the German nation rested on a cultural rather than a racial definition of the Volk. All the important influences in their development of a völkisch ideology pointed in this direction. The history of the Schotten Monastery exemplified this principle, and the cultural mission espoused by Nietzsche and Wagner in the early 1870s also ignored racial questions in invoking art as the unifying force within the German Volk. (Only later did Wagner make race an important ingredient of his German nationalism.) Nonetheless, as a result of their beliefs, those Jewish members of the Pernerstorfer circle who were deeply involved in formulating the nationalistic demands of the Linz program—Friedjung, Adler, and Bondi—found themselves in a highly vulnerable position. Possessing an almost religious faith in the educational mission of German culture, their political plans tended to assume that Austria's other non-German nationalities would learn to share that faith—an assumption which political reality failed to justify.[26] At the same time, the circle's conception

25. George Mosse, "The Influence of the völkisch Idea on German Jewry," *Studies of the Leo Baeck Institute,* 1967, pp. 84–87.

26. As A. J. P. Taylor has observed, "Friedjung regarded himself as a German, but he was only a German by adoption: he had become a German, because he valued German culture, and the process was no less deliberate for being subconscious. He therefore tended to expect a similar subconscious recognition of German superiority from the other races and he could not understand the reluctance of the Czechs, the Slovaks, or the Croats to follow his example." Friedjung, *The Struggle for Supremacy in Germany,* trans. A. J. P. Taylor and W. L. McElwee, p. iv.

of the German Volk as a cultural rather than a racial entity led them to underrate the strength of racial anti-Semitism as a political force. When Schönerer enthusiastically embraced this cause in the early 1880s he threatened the basic cultural identity of the circle's Jewish members and forced the circle as a whole to reappraise its fundamental political and cultural assumptions. When Pernerstorfer proved unwilling to abandon his Jewish friends the break with Schönerer became inevitable, and in June 1883 Pernerstorfer resigned as chairman of the Deutschnational Society.[27] At the same time he refused to give up the editorship of the *Deutsche Worte*, and this forced Schönerer and his followers to establish a new party organ, the *Unverfälschte Deutsche Worte* (*Unadulterated German Words*).

The break with Schönerer represented a serious setback for the political hopes of the Pernerstorfer circle, producing an important shift in both the content and style of its political activities. Even in their earliest political discussions—carried on within the Socio-Political Society in 1870 and 1871—the members of the circle had held somewhat different views on questions of social and political reform. While Pernerstorfer and Adler usually stood on socialistic principles, Friedjung leaned to the left-liberal position of social reform within the existing socioeconomic framework. These differences had never led to serious disagreements in terms of political action, but they did dispose the circle's members to somewhat different expectations with regard to establishing a political base for their movement. Where Friedjung hoped it would be possible to convert the existing left-liberal groups to a more militant position on nationalism and social reform, Pernerstorfer and Adler looked to the creation of an essentially new political movement appealing to those elements of society previously excluded from political life, such as the artisan and working classes. With the failure of Friedjung's efforts to interest the left-liberals in his proposed Deutsche Volkspartei in 1880, he and the other members of the circle had then followed Pernerstorfer's lead in attempting to build a new and more radical movement with the aid of Schönerer and his associates. The Linz program, oriented toward the grievances of the peasants, the workers, and the members of the lower-middle classes, attempted to attract these divergent groups by appealing to a common feeling

27. *D.W.* (16 June 1883), p. 2.

of national pride. However, when the desire for a mass following led Schönerer to translate national pride into antisemitic hatred, the circle broke with him and once again reverted to Friedjung's tactic of attempting to convert the liberal left. By this time the Taaffe government's pro-Czech policies had begun to stimulate increased national feeling among the German liberals and this development allowed the circle to hope for better results than those of the 1880 approach.

In pursuit of their new goal, the members of the circle set about transforming Dr. Kopp's Deutscher Verein into the nucleus for their new party. This left-liberal society, established in 1867, had been close to the Leseverein during the 1870s. There was a significant interchange of membership between the two groups, as well as a common interest in stimulating German nationalism. After the dissolution of the Leseverein, the former members of the student group who participated in establishing the Deutscher Klub (the organization in which the Linz program was drafted) also joined the Deutscher Verein. Kopp's older and more conservative faction, which retained control of the society until 1885, agreed with many of the nationalistic demands of the younger members, but on questions of economic and social reform it stood much closer to the traditional liberal position of laissez-faire. During the early 1880s the younger faction "formed the left wing of the Deutscher Verein" and, as Pernerstorfer indicates, even though there remained substantial differences on political and socioeconomic questions within it, "there still went through this young German movement a strong democratic strain which manifested itself among other ways in the demand for the universal, equal, and direct right to vote. Gradually, we gained control of the Deutscher Verein."[28]

In January 1885, as the Deutscher Verein began its preparations for the elections scheduled for the summer of that year, the society's left wing made its successful bid for leadership. Under the expanded franchise established by the Taaffe government in 1882, all those who paid at least five gulden in direct taxes received the right to vote and, since this step toward increased democratization of political life seemed to call for a new approach on the part of the society, Kopp and his associates were persuaded to yield control to the

28. Pernerstorfer, "Von Schönerer bis Wolf," *Der Kampf* 4 (Oct. 1910–Sept. 1911); 390.

younger and more radical faction. According to the *Deutsche Zeitung*, Vienna's progovernment newspapers nervously anticipated the change by expressing concern that "the 'radical elements' now appearing on the scene will find favor with the Viennese population and by lamenting that they want to draw the latter into the 'nationalistic deluge.'" Among the members newly elected to the leadership of the society were Otto Steinwender and Serafin Bondi, both drafters of the Linz program and frequent contributors to the *Deutsche Worte*; Dr. Gustav Gross, a close political associate of Pernerstorfer; and Dr. Karl Ausserer, a member of the Styrian provincial legislature (*Landtag*).[29]

The meeting at which the "radicals" assumed control of the society took place on 7 January, and during the following weeks the society met frequently to work out the program on which it would contest the June elections. As could be expected from the nature of the group, their platform relied heavily on the proposals of the Linz program. On 24 January Steinwender delivered an address to the society outlining what he saw as its principal task: the stimulation of German national feeling. Noting the recent progress of the German nationalist cause in Bohemia, Steinwender suggested that the aristocratic conservatives who still supported the pro-Czech Taaffe government would soon find themselves isolated: "The sharper the opposition in which they place themselves to a cultural nation [*Kulturvolk*] and its irrefutable demands, the nearer the day which will mark a final end to their privileges and conceits." After assessing the prospects for the nationalist cause among various segments of the population, Steinwender went on to detail specific demands for the defense of German interests within the Habsburg Empire, and all these points (autonomy for Galicia, unity of the Austrian half of the Empire and its separation from Hungary, economic union, and a close alliance with Germany) were drawn directly from the Linz program. At the end of his speech Steinwender turned briefly to the issue of social reform: *"A genuine and just national feeling is also absolutely indispensible for carrying out the difficult mission of social reform."* Noting that the national wealth was produced by workers—many of them children—whose lives were crippled and hopeless, he called for bringing these classes back into the nation and removing the age-old in-

29. *D.Z.* (5 Jan. 1885), p. 1; (8 Jan. 1885), p. 4.

justices. He specifically called for an expansion of the franchise to include the workers, but beyond this he made no specific proposals for redressing social ills.[30]

On reason for this rather cautious attitude was the diversity of viewpoints existing within the Deutscher Verein on questions of social and economic reform. A fundamental lack of unity on these questions became clear at a meeting two weeks later when Dr. Gross discussed "The Socio-Political Problems of Our Time." While calling for social reform, Gross concluded that the task of making the worker a nationalist must be completed before the social problem could be dealt with successfully, and this position generated an extensive debate on the problem.[31] A report in the *Deutsche Wochenschrift* noted that "more radical ideas were represented in particular by E. Pernerstorfer, who put himself completely on the collectivist standpoint, and by Dr. Victor Adler." Otto Steinwender was one of those who felt that social reform could be accomplished within the existing economic order. The article expressed doubt that the society would move in the direction desired by Pernerstorfer but noted with interest that socialistic ideas were represented.[32] Thus, even though their program retained a somewhat vague call for social reform, the members of the new party, the "men of the sharper key," (*schärfere Tonart*)," as they soon came to be known, placed the strongest emphasis on German nationalism, a subject on which they were in much greater agreement.

Lacking unity on substantive political issues, it was highly appropriate that this new party should come to bear a name reflecting its style rather than its program. The term sharper key derived from one of the first policy statements issued by the new leadership of the Deutscher Verein, a statement arguing that national questions could "only be dealt with in a sharper key [*schärferen Tonart*] than was necessary at a time when the Germans did not have to defend themselves against a hostile coalition storming in on them from all sides."[33] In practice, however, the sharper key politics, attuned to the emotional power of German nationalism, differed only in degree from Pernerstorfer's earlier ideal of a metapolitics or from the still earlier

30. The speech is printed in *D.W.* 5 (1885) : 1–13.
31. *D.Z.* (15 Feb. 1885), p. 23.
32. *Deutsche Wochenschrift* (22 Feb. 1885), p. 5.
33. *D.Z.* (5 Jan. 1885), p. 1.

notion of a poetic politics which Friedjung had broached in his *Ausgleich mit Ungarn*.

In large part, the task of explaining the meaning of the sharper-key politics fell to the *Deutsche Wochenschrift,* a weekly newspaper which Friedjung had established in 1883, after the Pernerstorfer circle's break with Schönerer. Shortly after the radical faction had taken control of the Deutscher Verein, the *Deutsche Wochenschrift* printed (18 January 1885, pp. 3–5) an extensive summary of a speech by Dr. Karl Ausserer, describing it as an "exact expression of the 'sharper key' which, as the recent changes in the Deutscher Verein in Vienna have shown, will be decisive in the next election." The faith in political emotion characteristic of Pernerstorfer's metapolitics also inspired Ausserer's outlook, and it moved him to criticize those parliamentary deputies who "had used their influence to dampen once again the flame of national inspiration flaring up in the people." But Ausserer also warned that "*the greatest danger to our national rebirth* [is] that the passion and the fire which belong fully and wholly to our people will be led astray from the principal goal, from the national question." The danger Ausserer probably had in mind was Schönerer's antisemitism, for the antisemitic cause had already gained considerable support among members of the lower-middle class, many of whom would be voting for the first time in 1885. In the remainder of his speech, Ausserer outlined the national and social objectives of the party (permanent alliance with Germany, autonomy for Galicia, creation of a unified "Austrian" political entity free from Hungarian influence, etc.), and he concluded with a stirring appeal to pan-German feeling. Directing the attention of his audience to "our brothers in the Empire," Ausserer conjured up a picture of the "hoary hero Emperor" who, with "the mighty Chancellor at his side directs the fate of Europe—nay of the world—for the welfare, peace and prosperity of all." Ausserer expressed the pride and joy with which Austria's Germans observed "how the German spirit bursts its narrow boundaries, how its power expands, . . . how it works actively within itself for the welfare of the oppressed, *for we are of One blood and of One tribe, the children of the One mother Germania.*"

The similarity of Ausserer's rhetoric, with its images of the heroic brotherhood of the medieval German tribes, to that of Richard Wagner and his followers was no coincidence, for like the members of the Pernerstorfer circle, Ausserer believed that art (and most particularly Wagner's art) would lead the way in the political regeneration of the German Volk. In an 1884 article in the *Deutsche Wochenschrift* (16 March) Ausserer had discussed the process of völkisch renewal, using the same terminology of nature mysticism which had characterized the speeches of the Wagner wake: "Even during the cold storms the careful observer has long since seen the approaching spring, the awakening nature. . . . An invisible elementary force works and creates deep in the interior of the earth. Everything germinates, sprouts, swells with sap and breathes with life." The reactionary period of the 1850s had not been able "to repress our national life completely. Below in the earth, in the folk, this life stirs and the careful observer can follow it in all the branches of its activity." Ausserer saw the first signs of spring in poems "which extolled freedom and solidarity," and these had been followed by "the magnificent sounds of those men who like Victor Scheffel and Julius Wolff, relying on our middle-high German poets, lead before us characters who are quintessentially German in manner and matter." Ausserer spoke of following these figures "back to that time when the valorous figures of our ancestors, when the Ottos and the Hohenstaufens, when a powerful German Empire earned honor and respect for the German name and German arms." These artistic images of medieval Germanic greatness had served to awaken the spirit slumbering in the German Volk: "These poets touched the strings of our hearts; as a result their song forced its way into the folk. . . . The melody soon found its way to the song. More rapidly than in any other branch of the life of the spirit, that overpowering, almost uncanny genius, Richard Wagner, led us, as in an assault, to the zenith of a national development in the kingdom of sound."

What Wagner had done for music, the men of the schärfere Tonart hoped to accomplish in politics, and in their efforts they profited greatly from the psychological theories of the Wagnerian theater. Just as Wagner's operas had attempted to direct and focus the general emotions which music aroused by making the music articulate the precise emotional response appropriate to the words and actions of the drama; so the speeches of the schärfere Tonart attempted not only to stimulate emotion, but also to focus it on the specific aims of the party program. Neither Wagner nor the men of the sharper key believed in arousing undefined, undirected emotion.

Although it employed essentially the same aesthetic psychology developed in Pernerstorfer's metapolitics, the political style of the sharper key reflected the impact of the break with Schönerer in a far greater sensitivity to the possible dangers of political emotion. As Friedjung explained in the *Deutsche Wochenschrift* (10 May 1885), "This is what is meant by sharper key: the previous hesitation will be replaced by national energy—but in no way by political narrow-mindedness or recklessness." He declared (31 May 1885) that "feeling and emotion have their proper place in politics, and without this strong support in the better parts of human nature, the life of the state degenerates only too easily into a game of ambition and a contest of intrigue." He went on to caution, "just no excess of soft, sloppy overflowing of the heart, just no enjoyment of iridescent, empty slogans!"

Friedjung's attempt to develop a political style that carefully balanced emotional appeals with reasoned principles reflected his overall strategy of creating a new party standing between the liberals and the more radical pan-Germans around Schönerer, a party drawing together the left-liberal groups with those former radicals who had become disillusioned with Schönerer's demagoguery. Such a party, appealing to German nationalist feelings without the excesses of Schönerer's anti-Semitism, might hope to win the support of many of those new lower-middle class voters who regarded liberalism with indifference while shrinking from the extremes of Schönerer's racism. As Friedjung explained later (*Wochenschrift,* 27 September, 1885) in justification of the new party, which became known as the Deutscher Klub, "One should realize . . . that the establishment of the Deutscher Klub was the sole means of opposing the constantly spreading Schönererian agitation." Friedjung argued that if the party had not come into being "this would have been the signal for a massive defection of voters to Schönerer"; however, there could be no return to the scholarly debating-club politics of the past. He argued that the party's leaders "should look deeper and candidly concede that the greatest oratorical gifts and the most exact knowledge of questions of finance and railroads are incapable of protecting the people from the thoughtlessness of the extremes in excited times." He concluded that in dealing with the Volk, "one must certainly speak its own language and must be the interpreter [*Dolmetsch*] of its lively and proper feelings for German nationalism." In style, then, the politics in a sharper key was pitched to the emotional tone of the masses, but, in Friedjung's view, the politician also had an obligation to translate the emotion of the mass into a reasoned program.

The new party did quite well in the elections of June 1885, and when the Parliament assembled in the fall, the Deutscher Klub counted some forty-seven members.[34] Among those newly elected were Ausserer, Pernerstorfer, and Steinwender. Pernerstorfer's victory (achieved with Victor Adler's financial backing) came in a district including Wiener Neustadt and it marked the beginning of a parliamentary career which lasted, with one brief interruption, for the rest of his life. Although Friedjung did not run for Parliament, he soon gained one of the most influential positions within the new party when he was chosen to become editor of the party organ. He gave up the editorship of his *Deutsche Wochenschrift* to assume that of the *Deutsche Zeitung*, a well-established daily newspaper purchased by the Deutscher Klub early in 1886.

Although Friedjung's editorship of the *Deutsche Zeitung* was quite successful in terms of increased circulation and income, he soon began to encounter serious difficulties as a result of the internal divisions within the party. The unity of rhetoric or style provided by the sharper key politics sufficed for the heat of the election campaign, but it did little to diminish substantial ideological differences on such issues as social reform. Moreover, Schönerer's continued anti-Semitic agitation posed a serious threat to the unity of the party, for some of the more radical nationalists within the Deutscher Klub continued to flirt with the use of racial anti-Semitism as a means of currying favor with the new electorate. Both of these factors played a role in the campaign against Friedjung led by Otto Steinwender and his faction of the party. While Steinwender refused to acknowledge that anti-Semitism represented the primary complaint against Friedjung, he did suggest that it was inappropriate for a German nationalist party to have a Jew as its chief spokesman. In an effort to still the conflict, Friedjung attempted to persuade Steinwender that his support within the party was far too small for him to succeed in replacing Friedjung with a man of his own views. According to Friedjung, Steinwender's response was clear and straightforward: "He had no answer to my arguments that he couldn't possibly

34. Gustav Kolmer, *Parlament und Verfassung in Oesterreich* (Vienna, 1907), vol. 4, p. 13. See also Richard Charmatz, *Deutsch-Oesterreichische Politik* (Leipzig, 1907), pp. 174–76.

achieve a change in his sense; but he did add 'One always has the power to destroy!'"[35] Both Friedjung and Steinwender proved to be correct. When the conflict came to a head in February 1887, the majority of the party (consisting primarily of the left-liberal element) backed Friedjung by passing a resolution declaring that "the Deutscher Klub rejects any common cause with endeavours and factions which elevate class or racial hatred to a principle." Nonetheless, Steinwender accomplished his purpose, for the conflict generated such bitter feelings that in the ensuing party split almost all of the more radical faction resigned, even including many who completely disagreed with Steinwender's anti-Semitism. The inherently unstable union of left-liberal and radical groups within the Deutscher Klub simply dissolved under the disruptive impact of the anti-Semitic attack. The collapse of Friedjung's hopes for a new party also entailed the loss of his job as editor of the *Deutsche Zeitung,* for the controversy so alarmed some of the financial backers of the paper that they decided to withdraw their support and thus forced the sale of the paper.[36]

Having earlier sacrificed his own paper, the *Deutsche Wochenschrift,* to assume the editorship of the *Deutsche Zeitung,* Friedjung now found himself without any forum for the expression of his views. These events left Friedjung's political career completely shattered. His attempts to create a new moderate German nationalist party had failed. He had suffered deeply from the anti-Semitic attacks leveled against him in the name of the German culture with which he identified so closely. He had been deprived of his position as editor at a time when his efforts were beginning to produce good results in terms of increasing circulation and income. It is scarcely surprising that in the face of this bitter frustration of his political hopes, Friedjung should decide to abandon politics and return to his former profession. It was in the years immediately following this political defeat that Friedjung wrote the work on which his reputation as a great historian primarily depends, *The Struggle for Supremacy in Germany.* Disappointed by his exclusion from the German nationalist cause, Friedjung's energies found an appropriate substitute in tracing what he saw as the historical tragedy of Austria's exclusion from the Germanic homeland.

35. Heinrich Friedjung, *Ein Stück Zeitungsgeschichte* (Vienna, 1887), p. 7.
36. Pichl, vol. 1, pp. 257–62.

Although the collapse of the Deutscher Klub also deprived Pernerstorfer of his political base, he suffered far less than Friedjung. He continued to edit the *Deutsche Worte,* and in Parliament he assumed the status of an independent and managed to be reelected on that basis. In contrast to Friedjung whose political defeat pushed him back into a passive liberalism, Pernerstorfer once again began to look beyond the limits of the existing electorate to the members of the working classes whom Victor Adler had meanwhile begun to organize into a political force. While the initial attempts at tapping the emotional power of the masses, represented by Pernerstorfer's metapolitics and Friedjung's schärfere Tonart, had ended in failure, these experiences carried valuable lessons for the members of the circle who remained active in politics. The search for a poetic politics had demonstrated beyond any doubt the power of political emotion latent in the masses, but Schönerer's anti-Semitic agitation had also shown how destructive such a force could be when cut loose from the control of reason and principle. It remained for Victor Adler to show that emotional energies could become an equally potent force for constructive political action when subjected to such rational control.

8. Victor Adler: The Politician as Artist and Psychologist

"Der Doktor," as he was called, chose his words carefully as he addressed his audience: "The brain is an organ of repression and therein lies its majesty. But when the brain engages in nothing but repression, then it does so at the cost of being able to activate its motive centers."[1] In this case it was the body politic which most concerned the doctor, and the paralysis he feared was one he thought could result from imposing too strict an ideological framework on the vital reality of a political movement. In speaking these words at the socialist party convention of 1901 Dr. Victor Adler gave expression to a settled view on the proper political and psychological balance between the vital activism inherent in a popular movement and the ideological control to be exercised by party doctrine. Both as metaphor and in its substance, Adler's statement suggests that even as the leader of the Austrian Socialists his thoughts and policies continued to be guided by that intimate coherence of politics and psychology so characteristic of deutschnational aesthetic politics.

Despite Adler's deep involvement in the deutschnational movement and its Wagnerian ideology, most historians have neglected to emphasize the importance of this involvement to his subsequent career as the leader of Austria's Social Democrats. For many years the inacessibility of documents from the early period of Adler's life prevented close examination of this involvement, and in addition some historians have been reluctant to stress Adler's ties to an antagonistic political movement closely associated with the rise of anti-Semitism. One contemporary socialist leader who was well aware of these ties and was ideologically troubled by them was Karl Kautsky, and he nonetheless acknowledged that in certain respects Adler had profited from his deutschnational experience.

1. Victor Adler, *Aufsätze, Reden und Briefe,* ed. Friedrich Adler, Michael Schacherl and Gustav Pollatschek (Vienna, 1922–29), p. 351. This collection will henceforth be cited as *Aufsätze.*

"He received in it a political schooling, a familiarity with relationships and people, which the other leaders of Austrian Social Democracy . . . had lacked until then. With Adler's entry into their ranks, the dominance of political naiveté came to an end."[2] Although Kautsky does not specify further what qualities of Adler's leadership he thought could be traced to this earlier political schooling, he clearly did believe that it contributed to the success of that leadership.

Undoubtedly the clearest and most convincing treatment of Adler's movement from the deutschnational to the socialist camp during the 1880s is that provided by Hans Mommsen in his study of Austrian social democracy and the nationality question. In contrast to earlier interpreters of Adler, Mommsen fully appreciates and rightly emphasizes the importance of his youthful political activity to his outlook as leader of the Social Democrats, and in explaining his conversion to the socialist cause Mommsen sees a high degree of continuity in Adler's commitment to democratic radicalism from the time of his early interest in Lassalle to his later encounter with the outlook of Marx and Engels. During the 1880s, when the growth of racial anti-Semitism within the deutschnational movement was beginning to threaten the coherence and integrity of the nationalist cause, Adler established increasingly close contacts both with the local leaders of the workers' movement in Austria and the more Marxist oriented leaders of the socialist movement in Germany. Despite the distrust which his German nationalist past aroused in such ideologues as Kautsky, Adler's standing as a socialist was greatly strengthened by the close personal relationship he was able to establish with Engels, whom he met on a trip to London in 1883. Adler found that the shared with Engels a practical, nondogmatic approach to socialist theory as well as a high degree of sensitivity to questions of political tactics. Moreover, as Mommsen has shown, Adler also saw a certain *Grossdeutsch* (Great German) element in Marx and Engels, so here too he was able to find a degree of consensus between the moderate nationalism of his outlook in the 1880s and the viewpoint of the leaders of international socialism. Mommsen notes that "at that time Adler represented, no less than Engels, Bebel and Liebknecht, a moderate Grossdeutsch stand-

2. Quoted in *Victor Adler, Briefwechsel mit August Bebel und Karl Kautsky*, ed. Friedrich Adler (Vienna, 1954), p. 48. This book will henceforth be cited as *Briefwechsel*.

point, but was fully aware that a union of the German region of Austria with the Empire was completely impossible politically even if desirable in the long run." While there are undoubtedly a number of such elements of continuity which have been overlooked or underemphasized in dealing with Adler's shift from deutschnational to socialist politics, the only one which can be pursued adequately within the framework of this study involves his continued exploitation of the artistic dimension of politics so basic to the Wagnerian outlook. Adler's biographer, Max Ermers, alludes to this when, in his discussion of Adler's tactics he remarks that "music and tone [*Tonart*] play a large role in politics." While Ermers does not elaborate on this aside, viewing Adler's later career in the light of his Wagnerian background reveals that even within the context of socialist, working-class politics, Adler's attitudes and actions continued to be influenced by his youthful enthusiasm for the cultural theories of Wagner and Nietzsche.[3]

Shortly after Heinrich Friedjung's first political pamphlet had appeared in 1877, Victor Adler wrote his friend a letter of praise and congratulation in which he went on to speak of devoting himself with renewed energy to "*my* work, to *my* discipline . . . I believe I can be of more use to my people as a thorough doctor and psychiatrist than as a superficial politician."[4] Ultimately Adler learned how to combine his two interests far better than Friedjung, whose career as a poetic politician proved so disastrous, but in the various political activities carried on by the Pernerstorfer circle in the late 1870s and early 1880s Adler usually played a less significant role than either Friedjung or Pernerstorfer. During these years Adler devoted most of his time and energy to his professional medical duties.

While Adler's day-to-day activities as a doctor diverted much of his energy from the political and philosophical theorizing which had absorbed him as a student, it would be a mistake to regard these activities as in any way disjoined from the theories of his student

3. Hans Mommsen, *Die Sozialdemokratie und die Nationalitätenfrage im habsburgischen Vielvölkerstaat* (Vienna, 1963), pp. 101–27; Ermers, *Victor Adler*, p. 265. Although Ermers' work has been supplanted in many respects by subsequent studies, it retains considerable value for its sensitive insights into Adler's character and work. Braunthal's *Victor und Friedreich Adler* incorporates the new material available in the Adler Archiv into an excellent and fascinating study of father and son. Although brief, Richard Charmatz' essay on Adler in his *Lebensbilder aus der Geschichte Oesterreichs*, pp. 178–202, offers a well-balanced and sensitive appraisal of Adler's personality and historical significance. This work will henceforth be cited as *Lebensbilder*.

4. Adler to Friedjung, Berlin, 12 Dec. 1877, Adler Archiv.

days. Indeed, Adler's letter to Friedjung was written less than two months after he had signed the collective letter to Nietzsche in which he and the other members of the circle pledged to make the philosopher's *Schopenhauer as Educator* their guide in life. Nietzsche constantly emphasized the sterility of all theory that remained detached from life, and Adler's letter to Friedjung can be seen as an expresson of his determination to give his philosophical and political ideals immediate, practical expression. To a surprising degree Adler's medical career allowed him to realize this intention. As the letter to Friedjung indicates, Adler specialized in psychiatry and in this connection he worked closely with Professor Theodor Meynert. Since Meynert's psychiatry relied heavily on the work of Schopenhauer, Adler's professional training complemented and extended the Wagnerian-Nietzschean-Schopenhauerian outlook developed within the Pernerstorfer circle. As a doctor, Adler devoted himself to serving the medical needs of the poor, and in his treatment of such problems as alcoholism, his psychiatric training served him well. During this period Adler also became deeply involved with the problems of factory working conditions and their effect on the health of the poor. His political activity within the deutschnational movement, where he argued for radical social reform, thus reflected not only his long-standing commitment to this goal on theoretical grounds but also his more recent day-to-day contact with the various ills of the working class. As a doctor of the poor he gained firsthand evidence to reinforce the argument that the "social question" called for immediate action.

While still deeply involved in the deutschnational movement, Adler also began to establish contact with various socialist intellectuals and political leaders. One of them, Karl Kautsky, became closely acquainted with Adler in 1882, and in his memoirs Kautsky recalled the deep impression made on him by Adler's circle of friends: "Around him was assembled a corona of intellectuals—doctors, lawyers, musicians, journalists. . . . All who belonged to it were interested in socialism, many were almost socialists. Only one thing divided me from all of them: their outspoken, intense German nationalism." Kautsky noted that many of the circle's members were Jewish, but that even so, "they were inspired nationalists, many of them outright chauvinists. . . . While wanting to have nothing to do with the Habsburgs, they were all the more enthusiastic about the Hohenzollerns. The Jews of Austria were at that time the most passionate advocates of the *Anschluss* which Bismarck decisively rejected."[5]

For many years afterward, Kautsky continued to suspect the sincerity of Adler's and Pernerstorfer's socialism on the grounds that this kind of militant nationalism contradicted Marxist theory, but to the members of the circle, accustomed to viewing the matter in a Wagnerian context, nationalism and socialism were but two dimensions of the same faith. In his early writings Wagner had even gone so far as to call himself a communist, and in 1872 the composer explained that his earlier espousal of "communism" would not have been so enthusiastic "if I had not also seen in this concept the principle of a social-political ideal according to which I conceived of the Volk in the sense of the incomparable productiveness of the prehistorical community of property [*Urgemeinschaftlichkeit*]."[6] One of Adler's efforts at calming Kautsky's fears clearly reflects this Wagnerian conception of the community of the folk. In a letter to Kautsky written in August 1886, Adler declared, "I have never doubted that one . . . can be a good nationalist in addition to an international Social Democrat. Yes, I might say further, that he who is seriously a nationalist must consequently become a communist (a train of thought which causes gooseflesh to rise on the backs of our national Philistines when Pernerstorfer presents it in detail at electoral meetings)."[7] This use of the word communist seems far closer to Wagner than to Marx.

While Pernerstorfer and Adler continued to see nationalism and socialism as consistent ideals, the rise of racial anti-Semitism in the 1880s brought about a major shift of emphasis from the former to the latter. In tracing his own political development in a *Deutsche Worte* article written in 1892, Pernerstorfer explained the nature of his earlier commitment to the cause of German nationalism: "Raised in a time of great national excitement and exaltation, while at the same time preoccupied from my youth on with democratic, indeed socialistic thought, I imagined that the German nationalist movement, like the other national movements and like the national movement of the Napoleonic wars of liberation . . . would be of an essentially democratic nature." Pernerstorfer noted that the man who

5. Karl Kautsky, *Erinnerungen und Erörterungen,* ed. Benedikt Kautsky (The Hague, 1960), p. 530.

6. Wagner, *Schriften,* vol. 3, p. 5. This is in the 1872 introduction to *Die Kunst und die Revolution* (1849).

7. Adler, *Briefwechsel,* p. 12.

brought the deutschnational cause into the Austrian Parliament, Georg von Schönerer, had begun his career in the 1870s as a democrat and that "only in 1882 did Schönerer's decisive turn toward an ever more exclusive anti-Semitism take place. . . . Schönerer abandoned the cause of democracy at the same rate at which he developed anti-Semitism into a political system." Pernerstorfer went on to say that in his subsequent efforts to uphold the "peoples' cause" within the parliamentary Deutscher Klub, he eventually found himself isolated and thereupon decided to become an independent. He concluded by stressing that the emphasis on sociopolitical problems which had characterized the *Deutsche Worte* from the mid 1880s onward would henceforth be increased still more to show "that at the present time the social factor determines everything and that in the near future it will be even more dominant. Since life is a unity, . . . politics, literature, and art can only be understood in conjunction with the greatest movement of the present."[8] Within the traditional Wagnerian framework based on a unified view of culture, Pernerstorfer thus shifted the primary political focus from national to social cohesion and, as his article suggests, the development of racial anti-Semitism played a major role in the shift.

Adler's commitment to German nationalism also underwent a similar modification during the 1880s. Where Karl Kautsky found Adler and his friends passionately devoted to pan-German nationalism and resolutely opposed to the Habsburg state in 1882, Adler expressed a markedly different attitude in an August 1886 letter to Kautsky. Referring to his earlier nationalism, he declared that he "had also gone through a development in this respect—that earlier the national struggle stood much more in the foreground of my interests and I regarded it as more promising than today—that with more insight into national relationships I also learned to recognize in them the influence of economic forces." However, as was the case with Pernerstorfer, Adler's diminished interest in nationalistic politics did nothing to reduce his deep faith in German culture. In the same 1886 letter to Kautsky, Adler declared, "To be sure, I regard the maintenance of the German national character [*Volksindividualität*] as something 'having value in itself,' and I regard the Slovenization or Czechification of German children as a damaging injustice to them, as a diminution of their intellectual

8. *D.W.* 12 (1892) : 1–2.

standard of living."[9] Moreover, Adler continued to maintain his regard for the cultural heroes of the Wagnerian movement, including Wagner himself. In his description of the intellectual life of Adler's house in the Berggasse, Max Ermers notes that "Goethe, Jean Paul, Richard Wagner and Beethoven were the invisible gods of the Berggasse. . . . At certain times there was no performance of the Beethoven *Ninth* or of *Tristan und Isolde* which Adler—and with him Wilhelm Ellenbogen—would have missed."[10]

Adler also retained his faith in the power of music to generate a feeling of community, and he expressed this faith in his tributes to Josef Scheu, the composer of *Das Lied der Arbeit.* A celebration of this composition glorifying the working man was held in October 1898, and at it Adler declared, "It is, moreover, the power of music . . . which leads us to the highest peak of feeling, where all particulars disappear, and only the great, the sublime, meets our gaze. The highest expression of our solidarity, the inspiration for the holy cause around which the masses assemble as brothers—. . . one cannot *speak* of that, one must sing it." As in the Wagnerian cultural community, art, religion, and politics coalesced in Adler's vision of a music capable of revealing the ties which united all mankind. In a later (1907) tribute to Scheu, Adler again praised the composer for fulfilling the cultural mission of art: "He has taught the proletariat to experience art." Scheu had succeeded in placing "holy art in the service of the holy cause of freedom."[11]

The ideas which Adler and Pernerstorfer expressed on art and culture after their successive migrations from the deutschnational to the socialist camp, show that both men continued to view cultural issues within the context of the old *Deutsche Worte* policy of establishing friendly relations between art and politics. To what extent, then, were they active in giving this policy effective expression within the socialist movement? In an 1887 article in *Gleichheit,* Adler saw two sides to the coming world revolution: "In a purely mechanical fashion the economic revolution goes its inexorable way . . . but a revolution in the consciousness of mankind goes forward at the same time. . . . The revolutionizing of the brain is the real assignment, the immediate goal, of the proletarian parties of Social De-

9. Adler to Kautsky, Vienna, 21 Aug. 1886; Adler, *Briefwechsel,* pp. 13, 12.
10. Ermers, p. 236.
11. Adler, *Aufsätze,* vol. 11, pp. 27, 29.

mocracy."[12] As the historian Richard Charmatz has observed, the socialist party went far toward the realization of this goal under Adler's leadership: "The social-democratic agitators became missionaries who first had to save humans and humanity; the great cultural labor which they accomplished is even acknowledged freely by the middle class." According to Charmatz, Adler proved himself "to be an incomparable educator [who] constantly worked to elevate the working class morally and culturally. . . . What was accomplished in this area is all too often overlooked."[13] In his history of European socialist thought, G.D.H. Cole agrees that in comparison with other movements the Viennese socialists distinguished themselves above all in the success of their cultural work. "The Austrian, or at any rate the Viennese, Socialists became the most highly cultured and instructed body of proletarians in the entire world."[14] In this passage Cole refers to the state of the Viennese workers in the period just before World War I and, as Charmatz emphasized, this situation stood in marked contrast to the plight of the workers of an earlier period. He recalled "the proletarian of the 1870s and 1880s who not infrequently sought his pleasure in life through alcohol, who had no contact with the achievements of culture, who . . . quite frequently fell prey to a pathetic feeling of inferiority." In contrast, Charmatz pointed to "what had gradually become of this class, what a world of beauty had slowly begun to open up to it, what self-confidence has come over it."[15]

Within the socialist movement, Pernerstorfer played a particularly important role in opening up this world of beauty and culture to the appreciation of the worker. When he addressed the socialist party congress in 1894 (two years before formally joining the party), he stressed the party's cultural mission: "Everything which forms the cultural content of the present and the past, everything which is noble, great, and beautiful, has become concentrated in you."[16] After 1897 he served as the theater critic and feuilleton editor of the

12. Ibid., vol 6, pp. 27–28.

13. Charmatz, *Deutsch-oesterreichische Politik,* p. 301. *Lebensbilder* p. 183.

14. G. D. H. Cole, *The Second International 1889–1914, A History of Socialist Thought,* vol. 3, part 2 (London, 1956), p. 592.

15. Charmatz, *Lebensbilder,* pp. 183–84.

16. *Verhandlungen des vierten oesterreichischen sozialdemokratischen Parteitages abgehalten in Wien vom. 25. bis einschliesslich 31. März 1894 in Schwenders Kolosseum (Amorsaal)* (Vienna, 1894), p. 93.

party paper, the *Arbeiter Zeitung*.[17] At the height of his political career, Pernerstorfer continued to work toward realization of the ideal of a cultural community by helping launch a major effort to develop a theater for the Viennese working classes.[18] Pernerstorfer had been interested in this idea since the 1890s and in 1906, when Stefan Grossmann, a fellow critic of the *Arbeiter Zeitung*, proposed the establishment of the *Wiener Freie Volksbühne*, Pernerstorfer readily agreed to help.[19] As Eduard Castle indicates, their efforts met with considerable success: "The excellent organization of the Marxist working class was to be put in the service of the aesthetic education of the proletariat, to carry art to the folk. In fact, it proved possible to create a social-democratic party theater without difficulty," and support for the theater was particularly strong among the better-paid metal workers, printers and office clerks.[20]

Although the *Wiener Freie Volksbühne* rented various theaters for its productions during the first years of its existence, its organizers hoped to obtain their own house eventually. In 1911, to gain additional support for this project, the *Freie Volksbühne* decided to publish a magazine devoted to explaining the importance of the theater to the working class. Even though Pernerstorfer was chairman of the Social Democrats' parliamentary delegation (then the largest party in the Parliament) and vice president of the lower house, he nonetheless found time to assume the editorship of the new magazine.

The first issue of *Der Strom* began with an article entitled "Theater and Democracy," in which Pernerstorfer attempted to develop the historical and cultural framework necessary to understand the relevance of theater to democracy. His argument closely followed the theories of Nietzsche and Wagner, with a final Marxian twist. He began by tracing the intimate relationship between myth and religion in primitive cultures. Referring to their religious practices, he notes,

> These have a thoroughly artistic character, yes, from the very start a certain artistic, dramatic character: song, dance, procession, symbolic presentations. . . . Drama thus has a religious origin: that is to say it is an affair of the community, it is an expression of the community. For the folk, high and low, feels

17. Arthaber, "Engelbert Pernerstorfer," p. 108.
18. Castle, *Geschichte der deutschen Literatur*, p. 1555.
19. Stefan Grossmann, *Ich war begeistert: Eine Lebensgeschichte* (Berlin, 1930), p. 171.
20. Castle, p. 2042.

> itself one in relationship to the omnipotence of the Gods! . . . Even with the Greeks and Romans the old dogmatic religious performances were not fully retained; separated from religious practices the drama became secular, but it remained, particularly in Greece, a communal affair."

Medieval Catholicism perpetuated the union of religion and theater, but in the modern period "with growing industrialization, the theater finally becomes an affair of the middle class." With this development in the nineteenth century, the theater became merely a subject and a scene for trivial conversation. "The great mass of the nation is effectively excluded from the theater as from art generally. The drama, intimately tied to the collective whole of the nation through its religious origin and development, became the affair of narrow privileged circles." Now that the proletariat had begun to assert its political power and had set for itself the goal of a "complete reordering of society," Pernerstorfer believed the time had come for it to reclaim the theater and return it to its original role as an affair of the community as a whole. "Once nation and theater belonged closely together. They will only grow together completely again when the new life forms of a great future—in which the nation will again become unified on a higher cultural level—will perhaps create a new dramatic art which will not be inferior to the greatest creations of ancient art."[21] Although now in a socialist rather than a nationalist context, Pernerstorfer's vision of a higher cultural community differed little from that espoused by himself and other members of his circle first in their 1877 letter to Nietzsche and then in their political activities of the early 1880s.

Another article in the first issue of *Der Strom* specifically discussed Wagner's importance to the conception of "popular" art. The author, David Joseph Bach, was the music critic of the *Arbeiter Zeitung* and the organizer of the highly successful Workers' Symphony Concerts, which were held from 1905 on.[22] Bach wrote, "To bring art to the entire nation, to bring the entire nation to art, is the dream of every artist even if he is not as aware of the laws of artistic creation and development as a Richard Wagner." In

21. Engelbert Pernerstorfer, "Theater und Demokratie," *Der Strom* (April 1911) : 1–3.

22. Castle, p. 1556. In discussing Adler's interest in Wagner, Max Ermers notes, "Das Bayreuther Mysterium des sozialistischen Zukunftsmusikers war lange Zeit für Adler ein Stück vorweggenommener Sonne des Zukunftsstaats. Aus dieser geistigen Einstellung heraus bejahte er den jungen Arbeitersang und die Arbeiter-Symphonienkonzerte, die in Oesterreich, namenlich in Wien, rasch Verbreitung fand." (p. 236).

discussing which art forms were most appropriate to the achievement of this ideal, Bach focused attention on the folk song, "the unquenchable spring out of which all the great masters have created. . . . The masters of the German art song always knew the way back to the land of childhood. Back? It had a profound meaning when Nietzsche once called the land of childhood our future." Bach's suggestion that the future pointed back toward the lost unity and childlike simplicity of the folk corresponded to the longing for the innocence of childhood so characteristic of such Wagnerites as Lipiner and Mahler. Bach explained the nature of this truly communal theater by examining the relationship between the work of art and the audience. Wagner's great musical dramas appealed not to an unreceptive social fragment, but "to the great commonality. Also in that there lurks a bit of Wagner's revolutionary essence, and an intuitive feeling allows every popular audience to experience this directly with each of Wagner's works. Wagner has the greatest effect on the folk."[23]

In a later article on Wagner, Pernerstorfer specifically linked the aims of socialism with those of the composer. "Socialism will be the first to create a condition consciously, in which no one will be prevented by restrictive social forms from becoming a *whole* man." Only when this had been accomplished, "only then will Richard Wagner's dream of the majesty of the work of art become true."[24]

It is clear, then, that the men who articulated the cultural outlook of the socialist movement in the *Arbeiter Zeitung* and *Der Strom* relied explicitly on the Wagnerian tradition of the democratic communitarian theater in explaining their highly successful efforts to bring culture to the proletariat. In accounting for that success, it seems probable that the emphasis on community through art expressed in their various activities contributed significantly to the high degree of cultural cohesiveness which Cole describes as characteristic of the Vienna workers:

> Even more than in Germany, Socialism became, above all in Vienna, a way of life and developed its own cultural institutions in both the intellectual and the artistic fields. It had its own music . . . It had its own educational services, extending over a wide field.[25]

23. D. J. Bach, "Volkstümliche Musikpflege," *Der Strom* (April 1911):13–14.
24. Pernerstorfer, "Theater und Demokratie," *Der Strom* (April 1911):390.
25. Cole, *Socialist Thought*, p. 542.

Cole points out that the Vienna socialists also "managed, on the whole, to make their intellectualism and their culture means to solidarity rather than sources of disruptive sectarianism." Here then, among the workers of Vienna, Adler and Pernerstorfer had helped to build a cultural community which realized in large measure the idealistic expectations of their youth.

Although the kind of cultural theory and activity represented in *Der Strom* had been an important element of the aesthetic politics of the deutschnational movement in the 1880s, an even more important element was the propagation of an essentially aesthetic conception of political style and tactics. In the Wagner wake of 1883 the dramatic techniques of the Wagnerian theater fostered and directed an outpouring of political emotion, just as the *Deutsche Worte* pursued its metapolitical ideal by proposing an increased emphasis on political agitation rather than intellectual exchange. To what extent did Adler also profit from this aspect of the aesthetic political tradition as leader of the Austrian Social Democrats? On the issue of oratorical style it seems clear that Adler owed little to the aesthetic political tradition, for his speeches bore scant resemblance either to those of the Wagner wake or to those of such practitioners of the sharper-key politics as Georg Schönerer or Karl Lueger.[26] Above all Adler was known for the clarity and logic of his speeches. Yet in other ways Adler's youthful immersion in völkisch art and politics did contribute to his leadership of the Social Democrats and did help lend to his leadership a distinctive quality that set it off from that of other European socialist movements.

In attempting to isolate and identify this quality it is necessary to begin by examining Adler's relationships with the leaders of other European parties and their perceptions of him and his party. Cole has observed of Adler: "In the Second International he was a great figure alongside Bebel, Vandervelde and Jaurès; and his voice was always that of a conciliator, urging the need for unity and citing his own party as an example of it in a state in which international unity was particularly difficult to maintain."[27] The reformist leader of the Belgian party, Emile Vandervelde, expressed a similar view shortly after Adler's death:

26. Schorske, "Politics in a New Key: An Austrian Triptych," *Journal of Modern History* 39 (Dec. 1967) : 343–86.
27. Cole, p. 545.

> I have never known anyone—I repeat anyone—who so combined in his own person all those qualities of character and understanding that go to make up the great party leader. He valued ideals without being blind to reality; he had a thorough grasp of doctrine and also of facts, a wonderful balance of mind and heart, a magnetic power which made him capable of moving the people with composure enough to restrain them in the hour of indignation.[28]

If one focuses on Adler's conciliatory approach and his "balance of mind and heart" it is clear that other socialist leaders of the time were in agreement that Adler possessed these qualities although some of them were much less enthusiastic about them than Vandervelde. Even though Adler always remained close to the leaders of the German party they were often exasperated by his penchant for compromise, and at one point Karl Kautsky was driven to conclude in comparing Adler to August Bebel that Bebel's only advantage over Adler was "that as a non-Austrian he was not condemned to expending the better part of his strength in mediation, and as a result that he did not become accustomed to wanting to settle all differences by mediation."[29] This mediatorial disposition was intimately bound up with Adler's most basic views on the nature of political leadership, and on a number of occasions he drew attention to what he regarded as the advantage of his approach over that of the German socialists under Bebel's leadership. In an 1893 letter to Engels, Adler declared, "To be frank, I have often wondered that August Bebel knows so little about the psychology of the masses, and I now suspect that the mistakes which the German party leadership occasionally commits stem for the most part from this lack of knowledge. I suspect that they are very naive—I almost said too honorable."[30]

Adler's criticism of Bebel was inspired by a well-meant but damaging attempt by the German leader to intervene in the affairs of the Austrian socialists during a political crisis in 1893. In an article in the *Arbeiter Zeitung* Adler argued that such outside advice was completely inappropriate "because developments within

28. Quoted in Julius Braunthal, *History of the International,* trans. Henry Collings and Kenneth Mitchell (New York, 1967), vol. 1., p. 216.

29. Adler, *Briefwechsel,* p. 434.

30. Adler to Engels, 26 Nov. 1893; *Aufsätze,* vol. 1, p. 86.

the masses of the working class—its moods and the expressions of its will—are very difficult for an outsider to judge."[31] Julius Braunthal observed, in distinguishing Adler's techniques of leadership from Bebel's more orthodox and theoretical approach, "Adler had a disinclination for the hypothetical, the abstract, the construed. . . . For him politics was the art of action, the art of doing what was necessary to the moment."[32] For Adler, politics was an art in the most literal sense, and Karl Kautsky seems to have recognized this in a 1904 letter to Adler concerning their different attitudes toward the French socialist leader, Jean Jaurès. Kautsky explained his opposition to Jaurès in detail, but then declared that he had no hope of convincing Adler, for "in your politics the aesthetic always plays a certain role next to that of theory, and if Jaurès arouses so much sympathy, that can be traced back more to aesthetic feelings—which I must recognize and cannot overcome—than to political considerations. . . . Adler the politician has indeed opposed Jaurès sharply enough, but Adler the aesthete cannot make up his mind to open the trapdoor under such a magnificent phenomenon."[33]

As Kautsky's image of the trapdoor suggests, his differences with Adler involved the issue of Jaurès's theatricality, which Adler fully recognized when, after one of the French leader's most powerful speeches at the 1896 meeting of the International, he remarked, "Sarah Bernhardt ought to go to Jaurès for lessons."[34] Another exchange of letters shows that Kautsky's essential argument with Adler came down to the latter's higher valuation of what he called Jaurès's "intoxicating talents." Adler observed: "I in no sense regard him as the scoundrel you do, but he could be of a completely different value if he had somehow grown into a more rational, clear-headed man. But in comparison with his intoxicating talents, everything that one hears from the opposing side appears . . . deplorably petty."[35] Adler and Kautsky both disapproved of the use of these talents to discourage clear thought, but Adler the artist, with his higher regard for feeling, inspiration, and mass psychology. could not agree to open the trapdoor under such a magnificent phenomenon.

31. Ibid., vol. 10, p. 134.
32. Braunthal, *Adler,* p. 272.
33. Adler, *Briefwechsel,* p. 434.
34. M. Beer, *Fifty Years of International Socialism* (London, 1935), p. 92.
35. Adler, *Briefwechsel,* p. 408.

In Vandervelde's portrait of Adler as a man with "a magnetic power which made him capable of moving the people with composure enough to restrain them in the hour of indignation," as well as in Kautsky's perception of Adler the aesthete, there is a common element centering on a conscious appreciation of the theatrical dimension of politics. More specifically I would argue that a close examination of Adler's techniques of political leadership reveal that he was in every sense a master of political symbolism, and that it was in this that he was most noticeably in debt to his Wagnerian background. The power inherent in a symbol as a focal point of communal thoughts and feelings was as apparent to Adler as to his friend Gustav Mahler, and in the socialist leader's campaign to establish May Day as an international worker's holiday it is possible to study his efforts to employ this power in the interests of the working class. The first May Day celebrations from 1890 to 1892 were tied specifically to a campaign for the eight-hour day, but in attempting to persuade the reluctant leaders of the German party to go along with this international day of work stoppage, what Adler emphasized was not the issue of working hours but rather the idea of May Day as a symbol with the power to unite at a single moment the thoughts and aspirations of the working class as a whole: "The knowledge that at a given hour, on the same day wherever the capitalist order prevails, the workers are all filled with *one* idea, is a much deeper and much more revolutionary thought than one devoted only to labor legislation."[36] Considered as a political symbol, then, May Day effectively bound together the consciously formulated goal of the eight-hour day and the revolutionary fervor generated by the sense of oneness of the mass of the workers.

May Day did in fact prove to be a powerful symbolic tool in spreading the workers' movement in Austria. Looking back later to the first May Day in 1890, when the Austrian party was only a year old, Adler recalled, "It was a time of awakening, of urgency . . . The working class was about to awaken; it needed only the call, the appeal, to raise itself up and feel itself whole, as a struggling body and a unity, as a class against other classes, and thereby throw off the debilitating dream of its impotence. For us in Austria the May Day celebration was this waking call [*Weckruf*]." Just as Mahler

36. Adler, *Aufsätze,* vol. 6, p. 191. Adler addressed the German party conference of 1892 on this issue.

began his *Third Symphony* with a musical symbol (der Weckruf) which would awaken the dormant life force to a willful consciousness of its nature, so Adler sought to launch the fledgling socialist movement in Austria with the help of his own Weckruf, a political symbol aimed at arousing the slumbering working class to a willful consciousness of its power. However much these musical and political symbols differed in their form of expression they were employed by their creators in a remarkably similar fashion. Moreover, Adler's use of symbolism also resembles that of Mahler in that both operated within an essentially religious framework. Where Mahler imitated the structure of the religious prototragedy of ancient Greece in his symphony, Adler made effective use of a pagan religious rite to spur his political campaign. Adler stressed the point that the first of May was not the day of the world strike but rather an "international workers' holiday"; and the *Arbeiter Zeitung* declared, "The day should be *holy,* and it becomes holy by being dedicated to the highest interests of mankind."[37]

It seems probable that many of the similarities between Adler's May Day and Mahler's Third have to do primarily with the fact that both men were working with the same sort of pagan fertility rite that Nietzsche had illuminated in his *Birth of Tragedy*. The important point then is not so much that these similarities existed but rather that Adler was so well aware of how to use the religious and artistic elements of May Day to serve the cause of international socialism. Instead of trying to diminish or repress the religious elements in the interests of Marxist secularism, Adler chose to play them up and use the symbolism of the event to direct the feelings and thoughts of the workers to their membership in the working class as a whole. The consciousness of Adler's appeal to both the head and the heart can be seen in his speeches to the German Social Democratic Party Congress of 1892 where he attempted to persuade the Germans to follow the Austrian example in celebrating May Day. After referring to that unity of the workers in "*one* idea" which gives "a much deeper and much more revolutionary" character to the occasion, Adler argued that "we dare not overlook the religious impetus [*Moment*] that lies in this, and in that regard I would like to ask you

37. *Grosse Gestalten des Sozialismus, Victor Adler aus seinen Reden und Schriften,* ed. Anton Tesarek (Vienna, 1947) "Mein erster Mai," p. 84. The original article was first published in 1909.

to observe our opponents. They certainly do not underestimate these matters of feeling [*Gefühlsdinge*]. . . . They know how these momenta of feeling affect the masses, and they make use of them. We would do well to incorporate this sort of momentum of enthusiasm into our movement." In arguing his case, Adler relied directly on the firsthand experience of the Austrian party: "We have derived from May Day a power of inspiration which has had an effect like that of plowing virgin land; there where we had long been unable to make headway with our programs, with our very best speeches, the May Day celebration has taken such firm root in the heart of the proletariat that it will never again be able to be uprooted."[38] Adler thus saw May Day as a vehicle for communicating with the feelings of workers who could not be reached by rational appeal, and in this approach he could clearly draw on many years of experience with völkisch art and politics.

In addition to teaching him how art could tap the emotional forces essential to creating a community feeling among the masses, Adler's deutschnational experience had taught him how dangerous these forces could be when used recklessly or irresponsibly, as in Schönerer's anti-Semitism. In Adler's own aesthetic politics the psychological dimension always served strictly rational ends, and he himself emphasized this point at the Zürich meeting of the International in 1893 where he made yet another attempt to change the position of the Germans. Speaking in the name of the Austrian party, Adler gave his clearest statement of the bases of his party's position:

> We Austrians are no dreamers. If we have recognized the May Day celebration as an excellent means of agitation, that springs not from fantasy but from reality. The head is certainly an important matter but the feeling of international solidarity that the May Day celebration awakens in every last proletarian, this momentum of feeling [*Gefühlmoment*] is also a reality. We would be just as poor politicians for wanting to neglect the heart as the head.[39]

As Vandevelde indicated, one of the outstanding qualities of Adler's leadership was his balance of head and heart, and the May Day issue reveals just how closely that balance resembled the concept of

38. Adler, *Aufsätze,* vol. 6, p. 191.
39. Ibid., p. 194.

political "wholeness" which the *Deutsche Worte* had elaborated in the 1880s.

This balance of head and heart was also evident in Adler's sense of political tactics. At the party convention of 1903 one of the delegates voiced fears that the movement for universal manhood suffrage had stalled, and when he demanded a more inflammatory tactic, Adler replied, "You cannot expect to maintain any kind of movement at a high point for a longer time than the passion has a corresponding capacity to develop. That is psychologically impossible, even in mass psychology." Adler argued that the party had to keep alive "the consciousness of the wretchedness of our voting privileges" but that it was "impossible to maintain the struggle continuously at that boiling heat, at that apex, to which it could be escalated only at certain times under favorable circumstances."[40] Thus political consciousness was one thing, political passion another, and the degree of emphasis on one or the other depended on the particular political conditions prevailing at the time.

Adler's comments on tactics represented a well-considered position, and here, as in his use of political symbolism, it is possible to see the imprint of the psychological outlook he had learned as a student. In a letter to Engels (28 August 1892), Adler mentioned that he was thinking of writing a pamphlet on tactics, and then went on to say, "The critics of tactics always believe they are or can be a straight line, while they must be a wavy line [*Wellenlinie*], just like world history." Adler's reference to a wavy line was by no means simply a fuzzy image for the Marxist dialectic, but was something quite different. Although Adler never wrote the intended pamphlet, he did make clear his basic conception of tactics at the Socialist Party Congress of 1904. As in the previous year, the immediate topic concerned the decline in agitational activity carried out by the party, and in explanation Adler declared,[41]

> All psychological things—even politics is actually in the first instance a result of the brain—are accomplished in wavy lines [*Wellenlinien*]. There are wave peaks; but every high-water mark of a movement is followed with mechanical necessity by a retreat, a decline, which not only is a time of rest but again

40. Ibid., vol. 10, p. 220.
41. Ibid., vol. 1, p. 43; vol. 8, p. 236.

makes possible an escalation of agitation. A psychological agitation which is continuously at climax or which could be maintained for years at a high point, does not exist.

Adler naturally based his political tactics on the laws of human psychology as he understood them and, as has been seen, that understanding rested on his professional training in psychiatry as well as his extracurricular involvement in the Wagnerian philosophy of the deutschnational movement. In both instances the basic psychological model derived from the same source: Schopenhauer's conception of the striving will-to-live. Although lacking the philosopher's pessimistic connotations, Adler's description of the basic wave-like motion of human psychology clearly corresponds to Schopenhauer's model, in which each climactic expression of the will's passion was followed by relaxation and then by reassertion. Adler's tactics reflected the assumption that the working-class movement expressed this will-to-live on a mass scale. In commenting on the results of the 1907 elections, Adler declared, "The proletariat of all the nations which live in Austria . . . are filled with a strong will-to-live and are determined to transform this state . . . into an instrument for their development."[42] Politically, the will-to-live translated directly into the will-to-power.

In the case of the Austrian socialists their will expressed itself primarily in the long campaign for universal manhood suffrage, and by examining Victor Adler's part in the success of that campaign it is possible to see how important were his tactical skill and his sensitivity to political symbolism. These qualities helped him maintain control over a complex and explosive political situation while using that situation to realize the aims of his movement. In the final stages of the campaign for the right to vote, Victor Adler's abilities as psychologist and artist can be seen at their best.

It is unclear how long Adler could have continued to restrain the party firebrands with the argument that political and psychological conditions were not ripe for militant action, but in 1905 those conditions changed in a way that allowed him to demonstrate the efficacy of his psychological sense of tactics. The outbreak of the Russian Revolution in January of that year aroused the Austrian working classes from their apathy and kindled the hope that they too

42. Ibid., vol. 10, p. 491.

might secure such political reforms as the right to vote. Then on 9 September, as a result of a power struggle between Franz Josef and the politically dominant Hungarian gentry, the Hungarian Prime Minister Fejérvary announced that the government intended to introduce universal manhood suffrage within the Hungarian half of the Empire, a move which presumably would have undermined the position of the gentry and broken their resistance. The news of this dramatic proposal had an immediate impact within Austria. While those in favor of giving Austrian workers the right to vote hailed it as an indication that their cause could no longer be resisted, conservative circles attempted to forestall it. The Austrian Prime Minister Gautsch, who had described universal suffrage as a social danger and who had not been consulted on the Hungarian move, immediately tried to persuade the Emperor to withdraw the decision.[43]

When Gautsch's action became known several days later, the calls for violent action within the socialist movement increased, but since Adler continued to reject such demands, Vienna remained calm. As Julius Braunthal noted, "Adler . . . hesitated to embark on militant action before he had carefully tested the field of battle, explored the ripeness of the mass-psychological conditions and weighed the prospects for the outcome." On 22 September a conference of the socialist party leadership issued a manifesto denouncing Gautsch as an "enemy of the people" while in Parliament Pernerstorfer bluntly declared, "The government and the dynasty should take care lest through the denial of the people's rights they cause the revolutionary conflagration now raging in Russia to spread to Austria. It could happen that as a result of government policy the cry will be heard among the populace: 'Down with the Habsburg dynasty!' " During the month following the socialists' denunciation of Gautsch, the Czech branch of the party embarked on an ambitious action program including a mass demonstration in Prague and a one-day general strike, while in Vienna, under Adler's direction, the socialists continued to confine themselves largely to verbal assaults on the government.[44]

In the belief that Adler would need a parliamentary seat to direct

43. William A. Jenks' *The Austrian Electoral Reform of 1907* (New York, 1950), offers a careful analysis of the campaign for universal manhood suffrage.

44. Braunthal, *Adler,* pp. 151–53.

the campaign for universal suffrage, the socialist party leadership had meanwhile arranged for his election from a safe Social-Democratic district in northern Bohemia. Adler won the by-election on 16 October, a month and a half before the lower house was to reassemble to consider electoral reform. Within the socialist party, however, Adler's restrained tactics came under increasing criticism when the annual party congress convened on 29 October. The Czechs complained bitterly that while they had acted, the Viennese had done nothing; and they were particularly critical of Adler's negative attitude toward the idea of a general strike. Although Adler continued to maintain that the conditions for such drastic action were not yet ripe, many of the Czech leaders feared that Adler's caution would never allow him to seize the proper moment. The acrimonious debate over this issue would probably have become even more intense and divisive but for the intervention of outside events. During a speech by Wilhelm Ellenbogen, a telegram arrived announcing that the Russian Czar had yielded to demands for constitutional government, and when Ellenbogen interrupted his talk to announce the dramatic news, the convention dissolved in jubilation.[45]

When the delegates reassembled and resumed debate on the issue of the general strike, Adler's attitude had been substantially modified by the course of events. Sensing the revolutionary mood of the workers and the delegates, Adler delivered one of his most radical speeches. Declaring that the time had come to consider using the mass strike, he urged the workers to prepare themselves and warned the government of the heavy responsibility it took upon itself in opposing universal suffrage. The convention then passed a resolution declaring its intention to employ the mass strike should that be necessary in the struggle for the right to vote, and it entrusted the party's trustees (*Vertrauensmänner*) with the duty to decide at what point it should be used.[46]

With the news from Russia, the revolutionary mood of the workers in Prague and Vienna intensified greatly, and in the first days of

45. Ibid., p. 154.

46. For Adler's speech and the resolution see *Protokoll über die Verhandlungen des Gesamtparteitages der sozialdemokratischen Arbeiterpartei in Oesterreich* (Vienna, 1905), pp. 125–32, 68 (henceforth cited as *Protokoll*). For a detailed discussion of the party's internal debate over tactics and the role of nationalistic tensions in this debate see Mommsen, *Die Sozialdemokratie,* pp. 364–72.

November, disorders occurred in both cities. In Prague, barricades began to appear in the streets and a strike by rail workers paralyzed transportation throughout Austria. Meanwhile, Adler had reacted to news of the first disorders by deciding on an unusual step. Fearing that serious trouble might soon erupt and that the government would call in troops, he secretly sought out two members of the cabinet to explain the serious nature of the situation and to urge immediate action. At the same time, the party made preparations to give visible evidence of its strength by scheduling massive demonstrations throughout Austria for 28 November, the day Parliament was scheduled to reconvene.[47]

On the day appointed for the demonstration, the situation from the socialist point of view was still tense but considerably more optimistic than earlier in the month. The day after Adler's secret appeal to the government, the Emperor had summoned Minister-President Gautsch and informed him that he intended to introduce universal suffrage in Austria as well as Hungary.[48] Although this put Gautsch in the awkward position of having to do a complete about-face on the issue, he dutifully prepared to follow the wishes of his sovereign. The full extent of this reversal became public knowledge only when Gautsch addressed Parliament on 28 November, but the government had meanwhile given indications that it was reconsidering its position.

The idea for a work stoppage to mark the reopening of Parliament had first been revealed publicly on the first of November when at the conclusion of the debate on the mass strike, Victor Adler reported that, at a meeting the day before, the "trustees of the Vienna organization resolved that on the day the Parliament convenes work will cease in all Vienna." This announcement brought enthusiastic applause, and a few moments later the delegates unanimously adopted the strike resolution.[49] Nevertheless, just as Adler had earlier insisted on calling the first May Day celebration an international workers' holiday rather than a world strike, so in the planning of the suffrage demonstration the party leadership also avoided using the inflammatory and revolutionary term general

47. Braunthal, *Adler,* p. 158.
48. Apparently the Emperor took this action in response to Adler's appeal. See Braunthal, *Adler,* p. 159.
49. *Protokoll,* p. 137.

strike or even the more bland mass strike in favor of the much more traditional and conservative "peoples' holiday" (*Volksfeiertag*). The choice of terms had far-reaching implications for the nature and significance of the demonstration. Rather than conjuring up futuristic images of the class struggle, "Volksfeiertag" suggested the colorful religious celebrations of Austria's past, and as it had done in announcing the plans for the first May Day, the *Arbeiter Zeitung* chose to emphasize this religious note. It appealed for all businesses to close "in order to profess themselves solemnly [*feierlich*] for the most holy right of the people, the universal, equal and direct right to vote," and this spiritual quality was further emphasized in the paper's discussion of the day's significance.

> Through the great demonstration of the workers, this opening day of Parliament receives a special consecration [*Weihe*] and will be raised to the dignity [*Würde*] of a great people's holiday [*Volksfeiertag*] by the mighty will of the proletariat. Even outwardly it will wear Sunday dress.[50]

Just as Victor Adler had seen the value of the religious and emotional symbolism of May Day and had called on the reluctant German party to employ its "momentum of feeling" in their movement, so in organizing the massive suffrage demonstration the Viennese party leadership followed the same principle. In calling for the proletariat to put on Sunday dress, the leadership chose to employ in its campaign the pageantry and richness associated with Austria's tradition of religious and public processions. The strength of Austrian Catholicism, protected by its close alliance with the political power of the Habsburgs, had allowed the survival through the nineteenth century of much more of the medieval festive tradition associated with the Catholic liturgical year than elsewhere in Europe, and this festive tradition was deeply ingrained in the working classes. As G.D.H. Cole noted in his characterization of the Vienna workers, "They liked going about together; they enjoyed mass demonstrations and celebrations";[51] and when it came to expressing their political demands in the traditional garb of the Volksfeiertag rather than the modern dress of class conflict, the workers played their central role with great ingenuity and artistic skill.

50. *Arbeiter Zeitung* (28 Nov. 1905), p. 2.
51. Cole, *Socialist Thought,* p. 542.

The actual demonstration fulfilled all expectations in size, color, and dramatic effect. As the workers assembled in the early morning, the *Arbeiter Zeitung* (29 November 1905) reported that the crowd appeared "endless and uncountable in a closely packed mass [with] a forest of banners, flags, standards and emblems." As they had done in the parades and celebrations of an earlier era, many of the workers carried the colorful and often intricately designed emblems of their various trades:

> The magnificently colorful tableau was embellished by the blue shirts of many of the standard bearers and the magnificent red sashes of the march leaders. Also the emblems were astonishing in their variety. . . . The wood turners, for example, had artistically spliced together their emblem out of sticks; the barbers, who marched in very great numbers also carried the symbols of their guild, huge shaving bowls or razors; in the lead the railroad workers carried a gigantic signal.

Among the workers of the Northern Railroad a group of about a hundred Moravian Slovaks added to the spectacle by wearing their national costume. Many of the workers chose to give expression to their political goals in allegorical terms. The emblem of the Czech workers from the Viennese suburb of Ottakring "made a great sensation: a casket of blue pasteboard with a hideous gold-green scaly dragon on top protecting a sack of gold with his claws." Here the demand for an end to a voting structure associated with capitalist exploitation found clear expression, but once again the allegorical form of expression drived from an older tradition of religious celebrations. This synthesis of the modern and the traditional was also realized by the tanners who "carried a saint's image crowned with a wreath, an image showing a saint of the people—Ferdinand Lassalle." This emblem, honoring the socialist leader as a popular saint, realized in miniature the synthesis of modern socialist content and traditional religious form characteristic of the demonstration as a whole.

Within this multifarious and brightly colored setting the planners of the demonstration organized a massive march to climax the Volksfeiertag. The march route ran along the Ringstrassen, past the Opera to the Parliament building, where the workers could offer visible evidence of their numbers to the newly assembled delegates.

In dramatic contrast to the diverse and expressive visual image presented by their costumes and standards, the workers marched in total silence, symbolizing their lack of a political voice and their self-discipline. A reporter stationed at the Opera recorded the singular impression made by the passage of this silent mass; "At this crossing which is usually filled with uproar, it was . . . completely still. One heard nothing but the massive tread of the workers." At the Parliament building, another reporter noted that before the march reached that point there were cheers and greetings from the crowd of onlookers, but that "the nearer the procession came the stiller it became. When finally the bright red emblem with the legend visible from afar 'Forward with Universal Suffrage' emerged from the fog, then an almost celebratory stillness came over the broad plaza." From 11 o'clock in the morning, when the first of the marchers reached the Parliament, until three in the afternoon, an estimated 250,000 workers filed silently past the building.

In speaking of the celebratory stillness (*feierliche Stille*) evoked by the marching workers, the *Arbeiter Zeitung* once again suggested the religious feeling that pervaded this socialist demonstration, and a similar note of reverence entered into the paper's overall evaluation of the march. "Whoever has experienced this day will never forget it. Observer or fellow-combatant, none will be able to extinguish this sublime spectacle [*erhabene Schauspiel*] from his memory." With respect to the traditional form of the demonstration, the theatrical sense conveyed by the words "*erhabene Schauspiel*" was highly appropriate to an attitude of reverence, for theatrical forms and techniques had always played an essential role in conveying the spiritual meaning of the traditional religious processions. In the paper's description of the scene in front of the Parliament building, it even extended the theatrical image. Noting that the streetcars had been forced to come to a halt, the reporter described them as "completely filled, like loges from which hundreds could watch the great spectacle." For this socialist drama of the street, the box seats were streetcars, and they were occupied by the workers.

As the *Arbeiter Zeitung* had stressed, it was the "mighty will of the proletariat" which had endowed this day with its "special consecration" and ultimately all the formal elements of the Volksfeiertag focused attention on the united and determined will of the workers. Nonetheless, the paper was anxious that this unity be seen as the expression of a genuine community of thought and feeling rather than the product of strict organization and regimentation. To those who described the workers as an unknowing herd following orders from above, it responded, "What supermen of the stature of Tamerlane they would have to be to be able to impose their wills on these huge masses." Deriding this accusation and other "liberal clichés" by the "Philistines of the individualism swindle," the *Arbeiter Zeitung* stressed that the masses were led not by a will outside themselves "but by a will *within* them, a will which is living in each individual, which has caught fire from his personal knowledge." Thus, the paper argued, "The will of the proletarian is not smothered and bowed within the [party] organization but rather it is awakened, strengthened, and united." In this way, the particular will of the worker was transformed into "something completely new. One thinks it praise in calling it military discipline, but it is something far different and far higher. It is not drill, but self-discipline; it is the will of thousands united in a collective will, the result not of force, but of a gigantic educational labor without compare." Through this effort they expressed their unity and determination in a symbolic form of great dignity and power, and the symbol they created proved to be as potent a force in winning the political rights they sought as May Day had earlier been in bringing the workers into contact with the socialist movement.

Although the workers had paraded in silence, their desires found a voice in Adler when he delivered his maiden speech in Parliament two days after the demonstration. He spoke not as the newest and most junior member but as the self-confident leader of the popular movement which had just given such indisputable evidence of its strength, and in his speech he skillfully exploited the psychological advantage gained through the dramatic success of the Volksfeiertag. Since the government had conceded the principle of universal suffrage, Adler felt that the chief danger now lay in the possibility that the unreformed Parliament itself might attempt to block the change, and his opening remarks attempted to forestall this by contrasting the impotence of the existing Parliament with the power and vitality of his movement. He observed: "This house enjoys little esteem among the people, but it enjoys far less esteem with the government, and worst of all, *it enjoys no esteem at all from itself*. . . . This Parliament is no longer capable of creating anything good;

but it is also incapable of doing anything bad; it has become completely superfluous." Adler next proceeded to make sport of Minister-President Gautsch's predicament in being forced within the space of a month to reverse completely his publicly stated position on the issue of universal suffrage. Referring to Gautsch's statement that the government's pace in introducing the reform would not be hastened by demonstrations, Adler declared tongue-in-cheek, "Certainly we are completely innocent of such a thing, and in fact we believe that he has been overcome by the holy spirit [*heilige Geist*], *but we suspect that this time, by way of exception, instead of coming down from above, the holy spirit has come up from below*."[52] While this remark was intended to provoke laughter—and did—it also had a serious meaning, for as has been seen, the nature of the Volksfeiertag surrounded the expression of the workers' will with an aura of spirituality. Moreover, Adler himself had repeatedly referred to the holy cause around which the masses assemble as brothers.

In contrast to the faltering weakness and vacillation of Parliament and government, Adler went on to remind his audience of the events which had occurred while Gautsch spoke, of the demonstrations "before the doors of this house and in all the cities of Austria." Adler described the mass movement as a unified expression of will. The demonstrators were "the best part, the politically clearest part, the *politically most willful* part of all the nations of Austria." Adler declared that their movement was the result of the fact that the *"working class has come to self-consciousness and to an independent will and to such a powerful, clear, energetic and undeniable expression of this will, that they themselves will bring about what has always been the most difficult to realize in Austria: the reasonable and the just!"* Here again the terms of Adler's description reflect the psychological assumptions of his politics, assumptions based not only on the Wagnerian ideal of evoking a community of will among the masses, but also on Adler's own ideal of channeling the powerful energies of this mass will toward strictly rational ends.

During the remainder of his speech, Adler went into specific issues which had been raised in connection with the proposed electoral reform, but his principal point remained the contrast between the determined will of the workers and the weakness of that "temple of

52. Adler, *Aufsätze,* vol. 10, pp. 257–61.

privilege," the Austrian Parliament. As such, the speech represented the culmination of the psychological tactics Adler had pursued for years. Keenly aware of the volatile nature of political emotion on a mass scale, Adler had attempted to channel that emotion into a form that would avoid either an excessive inflammation of feeling, with its inherent danger of a disastrous upheaval or a premature lessening of pressure, with the possible result that the government or Parliament might then withdraw the concessions. Rather than attempting to maintain constant or increasing agitation over a long period of time—as the Czech socialists advocated—Adler had chosen to create a single powerful political symbol by diverting the agitational energies of the proletariat into the Volksfeiertag of 20 November. As he declared, "Whoever saw the demonstration the day before yesterday —even if he were the most bitter enemy of Social Democracy—must have had respect for this spectacle [*Schauspiel*] and must have recognized the selflessness of these great masses." Throughout his speech he employed the symbol of the Volksfeiertag as a vehicle for arousing and directing the emotional energies of his audience, much as any dramatist of the symbolist school might have done. Long after the political passions of the masses had begun to cool, Adler could expect this symbol of the workers' strength to remain a vivid and effective memory in the minds of those who might seek to frustrate electoral reform.

Adler's fears that electoral reform might be sabotaged were far from groundless, for when the parliamentary committee appointed to formulate the electoral reform began its work, efforts were made to qualify the principle of universal manhood suffrage. One of the most serious of these concerned the proposal that the educated and wealthy be given more than one vote each. As Jenks notes in his study of the electoral reform. "Almost to a man, the proponents of pluralism felt that socialism could be checked only by granting 'responsible' citizens extra votes. They had no hope of restraining socialism once universal, equal suffrage was accepted." Serving as the single socialist representative on the forty-nine-member committee, Adler set about the difficult task of defeating this proposal with the same tactics he had followed earlier. Jenks wrote, "Adler reminded his listeners that the adoption of pluralism would definitely be the best opportunity in the world for agitation." Although the votes were close, Adler's argument proved successful. Jenks observed that passage of the electoral reform without serious damage to the principle of universal manhood suffrage was primarily the work of Adler's Social Democrats: "Middle-class parties and enlightened members of the nobility and clergy . . . might never have insisted upon, or agreed to, electoral reform, had it not been for the masterful strategy of the Social Democrats." Noting the "puny" numerical strength of the party's parliamentary delegation in comparison with the massive support shown in its street demonstrations, Jenks concluded, "No party was more responsible for the Emperor's unexpected support of universal manhood suffrage, and the threat of renewed popular demonstrations was a weapon the government could not ignore. . . . Adler's pointed remarks when deadlock threatened in the electoral committee were reinforced by direct pressure exerted by the Emperor on stubborn party leaders."[53]

Under Adler's leadership, then, the social Democrats proved to be instrumental in introducing one of the most fundamental reforms of Austria's political order since the beginning of constitutional government. Adler's party reaped the rewards of his skill when the first elections under the new law were held in May 1907. With over a million votes, the party gained almost a quarter of the total, and its parliamentary delegation increased from an insignificant 10 to 87 (out of 516).[54] Although the gerrymandering of electoral districts held down their numbers, the party still emerged as the largest in Austria's fractured Parliament.

The German Social Democrats Karl Kautsky and August Bebel sometimes sharply criticized Adler's tactics as un-Marxian, just as Adler occasionally deplored the ignorance of mass psychology evident in the tactics of the German party. Nonetheless, the aesthetic psychology of Adler's tactics was well suited to the political conditions of pre-war Austria, and it undoubtedly contributed to his political success. Wandruszka observes, "He was certainly the most significant of the generation of the 'founding fathers' of Austrian democracy, although the external aids of popular leadership and demagoguery—dazzling appearance and compelling oratorical skill—were in no sense available to him in the same measure as, say, to Lueger or even Schönerer, whose travelling companion he had been at the beginning of his political career."[55] Unlike either of these men,

53. Jenks, *Austrian Electoral Reform,* pp. 85–87, 208–09.

54. Braunthal, *Adler,* p. 164.

55. Adam Wandruszka, "Oesterreichs politische Struktur," p. 426.

who have been characterized as practitioners of an aesthetic political style, the artistic dimension of Adler's politics manifested itself primarily on the tactical and symbolic levels where it served the purpose of subjecting mass emotion to rational control. While this approach differed in degree of rational control from the Wagnerian metapolitics espoused in the *Deutsche Worte* during the early 1880s, Adler's tactics continued to draw on the basic psychological theories he learned during this period, just as under Pernerstorfer's direction the Wagnerian concept of a cultural community continued to influence the socialist party's efforts in the aesthetic education of the worker. Apart from Adler himself and the men around Pernerstorfer at the *Arbeiter Zeitung* and *Der Strom*, there is little evidence that Wagnerian cultural theory penetrated deeply into the Austrian socialist movement or that it retained a lasting influence on Austrian socialist tradition. Nevertheless it does help explain why Adler was so effective a party leader, why various observers have detected conservative elements in Adler's style, and, perhaps most important of all, why men like Adolf Hitler could find in the mass demonstrations of Adler's party an example par excellence of that new mass psychology which has become a staple of twentieth-century political movements.[56] Finally, the survival and adaptation of Wagnerian cultural theory within the political context in which Adler and Pernerstorfer moved during the final years of their lives testifies strongly to the enormous formative force of adolescent group experience in the determination of enduring value systems and habits of thought.

56. Adolf Hitler, *Mein Kampf,* trans. Ralph Manheim (Cambridge, Mass., 1943) pp. 41–44, 469–73. It should be noted that of the three leaders of mass movements in Vienna during the years when Hitler was growing up there, he most admired Karl Lueger and George Schönerer, but that nonetheless it was Adler's Social Democrats from whom, according to his own testimony, he learned his most valuable lessons of mass psychology.

9. Conclusion

The opening years of the twentieth century found the members of the Pernerstorfer circle occupying prominent and influential positions in both the artistic and political life of Vienna. Two decades after the circle's aesthetes and activists had separated to pursue their parallel paths to cultural and political regeneration, each of the two factions had produced a spokesman of genius to carry out the task of renewal. During the years that Victor Adler's leadership of the working classes was transforming the balance of power within the Austrian political system, Gustav Mahler was carrying out a no less ambitious program of reform as director of the Vienna Opera, and the accomplishments of both men owed a considerable debt to the Wagnerian-Nietzschean outlook they had shared in their youthful reaction against bourgeois liberal values. Not surprisingly, members of the older generation sympathetic to the ideals of liberalism saw much that they regarded as dangerous in the heroic vitalism of the Wagnerian credo. In 1885, when the cult of Wagner was at its zenith among students and intellectuals, the *Neue Freie Presse,* the voice of Austrian liberalism, discussed Wagner's music in an article entitled "Unhealthy Art," which maintained that the "expression of the most diametrically opposed extremes of the emotional life" endangered the mental health of the performers; and it expressed particular concern for the singer who had to perform Tristan. "Just think . . . of the poor artist who conscientiously wants to depict this pathological genesis of love, a love which is a paroxysm, a shudder, a convulsion."[1] Although the article was at least partially tongue-in-cheek, its distrust of Wagnerian emotion was quite genuine. Wagner and Nietzsche had called for a renewal of the emotional life as a means of transcending a liberal culture which they regarded as sterile, and many liberals realized how serious a threat this posed to their ideals and way of life.

The impact of the Wagnerites can be seen with particular clarity in the works of Ferdinand von Saar (1833–1906), a writer of the

1. *N.F.P.* (15 Feb. 1885), pp. 1–2, 3.

older generation whose short stories are prized for their sensitive portrayal of social types from all levels of Austrian society. Although Saar had himself suffered a certain disillusionment with the effectiveness of Austrian liberalism as a political force, he maintained a strong sympathy for its ideals, and he continued to move in the very highest circles of liberalism's salon society. Saar reveals his attitude toward the Wagnerites in his *History of a Vienna Child,* a short story written in 1890. The story centers on a light-headed girl of lower-class origins who briefly achieves wealth and social position and becomes a devotee of Wagner's music. On one occasion she gives a salon concert devoted exclusively to works of the Master, and Saar provides elaborate descriptions of the audience reaction. During the first selection Elsa, the hostess, "stared numbly straight ahead; from time to time a light shudder appeared to go through her body." She then asks the pianist to play Isolde's *Liebestod,* and over the objections of her friends, who feel it might affect her too deeply, he does so. "Soon thereafter, from the waves of sound quivering into each other in gradual, horribly voluptuous intensifications which always sank back again upon themselves, there developed the most powerful attack on human nerves known to music." With respect to the audience, "the effect was actually physical: in his own way, everyone felt thrilled, overwhelmed, pained, delighted, dissolved." The effect on Elsa was particularly powerful: "She was pale, and a passionate quiver constantly shook her body. Suddenly, she emitted a piercing cry." After Elsa staggers from the room fighting for breath and supported on the arm of one of her friends, another guest observes, "there you have the effects of Wagnerian music."[2] The emotional world glorified in Wagner's music clearly outraged Saar's Victorian sensibilities.

Political Wagnerites also found their way into the pages of Saar's stories. In 1900 he wrote a story entitled *Dissonances,* in which he juxtaposed the traditionalist social and political outlook with that of the younger generation. Set in the salon of a country estate, the story revolves around a clash of viewpoints between a guest and a member of the family. Saar depicts the assemblage as sharply divided into two camps. The leader of the traditionalist forces is Count Erwin, the brother of the hostess, and in the conversational

2. *Ferdinand von Saars sämtliche Werke,* ed. Jakob Minor (Leipzig, n. d.) ,vol. 9, pp. 262–63.

duel his seconds are the family's aging French governess and the elderly house physician. The leader of the modern opposition is a politically prominent social thinker who is visiting the estate and he is supported by the family's young tutor and the secretary of the hostess. The hostess, a progressive aristocrat, is politely neutral. Saar's description reveals that the modernist camp is made up of deutschnational Wagnerites. The family tutor is depicted as "an enthusiastic admirer of Bismarck, Richard Wagner, and Nietzsche," and his attitude is fully shared by the secretary. The social thinker naturally spends most of his time explaining his ideas on social questions, and this soon produces a dispute with Count Erwin. The Count skeptically maintains that there is little immediate prospect for bettering the conditions of the lower classes, while the politician believes that this can be done through the power of art. The remainder of their increasingly acrimonious argument centers on the question of whether or not art can indeed perform such a function, and only the intervention of the hostess prevents the two camps from coming to blows.[3] Saar's story thus represents an attempt to evaluate the question of whether or not art could perform the task set for it by all good Wagnerites, the task of initiating social and political regeneration; and the title of the story, *Dissonances,* indicates that to Saar, the Wagnerite politics in a sharper key yielded little but the cacophony of increasing social conflict. In the story, the liberal middle has dropped out of the political dialogue, leaving only the dissonant clash of radicals and conservatives—an accurate portrait of Austria's political state at the turn of the century.

Both of Saar's stories reveal his deep distrust of the Wagnerite outlook and its use of art as a means of engaging and expressing fully man's inherent emotional capacities. Saar readily acknowledged the tremendous power inherent in this art, but on both the individual and the social level he saw it as an essentially unhealthy or even sinister force. As art per se it threatened to unhinge the sensitive individual and introduce a damaging degree of emotional instability, while in its sociopolitical role it only exacerbated emotional tensions already near the breaking point. The stories also reveal a correlation between the distrust of emotion and the distrust of the lower classes on which the Wagnerites fixed their political hopes. Whether or not

3. Ibid., vol. 11, pp. 177–82.

the liberal order actually fulfilled its ideal of rationality, Saar saw both the political position of liberalism and the rational principle itself as endangered by the Wagnerite appeal to mass emotion. In his stories the aesthetic evangelists of feeling are inevitably of lower-class origins.

Although Saar's fears for the mental health of the Wagnerites were undoubtedly exaggerated, the dangers he sensed in an aesthetic emotional politics were all too real. Wagnerites might speak of restoring the whole man by balancing reason with feeling, but demagogues such as Georg von Schönerer and Otto Steinwender willingly sacrificed rational consistency in order to obtain the maximum emotional response from a mass electorate. Schönerer's inflammatory anti-Semitism revealed how dangerous the political appeal to emotion could be, and in this tradition Schönerer's admirer Adolf Hitler realized nightmarish possibilities that Saar could never have imagined.

Schönerer's anti-Semitic agitation also brought many Wagnerites to a realization of how destructive political emotion could be. During the 1880s the members of the Pernerstorfer circle suffered one setback after another as a result of the emotion generated by the anti-Semitic issue. It undermined the movement that launched the Linz program, it shattered the Deutscher Klub in 1886, and it completely destroyed Heinrich Friedjung's political career. While the members of the circle continued to recognize the importance of emotion as a political force, it is not surprising that under these circumstances they should increasingly stress the need for rational control of political emotion—a need emphasized in Friedjung's definitions of the schärfere Tonart politics as well as Adler's tactical theories.

The circle's increasing concern for giving rational direction to the emotional forces within man reflected a broader change occurring in the interpretation of Wagner's significance over the last two decades of the nineteenth century. The Viennese musical psychologist Max Graf went into this in a book published in 1900. Graf saw a shift in outlook from the glorification of emotion characteristic of the initial reaction to Wagner to an almost psychiatric concern with restoring mental health: "Now it is a matter not only of having enthusiasms and passions, but of investing them with intellect [*Geist*]; . . . We were extravagant and fantastic; now it is a matter of being resolute; that is, of directing the river of our passion into its banks where it will flow on calmly and powerfully."[4] In the accomplishments of their mature years, Mahler and Adler went far toward the realization of this ideal. For both men theatrical form, as elucidated by Nietzsche and Wagner, offered a means of directing man's passions into constructive channels, and whether these led toward a mystic transcendence of reality, as in Mahler's *Third Symphony,* or toward a peaceful transformation of that reality, as in Adler's campaign for universal manhood suffrage, human passion gained full and fruitful expression within this dramatic form.

When Max Graf dedicated his book to Gustav Mahler he almost certainly thought of Mahler as the director of the Vienna Opera rather than as the composer of such unusual works as the *Third Symphony*. The directorship, which Mahler secured in May of 1897, only nine months after completion of the Third, placed him in a position of unrivaled importance in the artistic life of Vienna and allowed him to implement his Wagnerian-Nietzschean ideal of fostering cultural regeneration through the mystic community of the Dionysian theater. Paul Stefan has observed that during Mahler's directorship "the spirit of Wagner affected everything. It permeated the entire repertory." According to Stefan, Mahler worked in the light of Wagner's expressed convictions "that for him it was a matter of the rebirth of tragedy from the spirit of music; that his forerunners were the ancient Greeks."[5] Hermann Bahr saw Mahler's directorship in a similar light. In an essay entitled "Mahler and the German Theater" Bahr depicted Mahler as a Parsifal whose holy innocence allowed him to direct the Opera on the basis of purely artistic standards. "Only this boundless innocence of a man completely blind to the world, led only by his holy vision [*Wahn*] could have succeeded for years on end in conducting the Imperial, Royal Court Opera of Vienna as if we were in Athens at the time of the great tragedies."[6] Both Stefan and Bahr knew more than enough Nietzsche to recognize that the theatrical model elaborated in *The Birth of Tragedy* exercised a fundamental influence on Mahler's work as opera director.

4. Max Graf, *Wagner-Probleme und andere Studien* (Vienna, 1900), pp. [7–8]. Graf was a close friend of Freud and a member of the Vienna Psychoanalytic Society.

5. Paul Stefan, *Gustav Mahlers Erbe* (Munich, 1908), pp. 25, 20.

6. Hermann Bahr, "Mahler und das deutsche Theater," *Gustav Mahler: Ein Bild seiner Persönlichkeit in Widmungen,* ed. Paul Stefan (Munich, 1910), p. 17.

In his reform of the Vienna Opera, Mahler attempted to make it a truly dramatic theater, faithful to the religious origins of dramatic art. Eduard Castle has characterized Mahler as a "master of scenic form. From the 'dreary day' of gray reality he assembled a band of inspired ones for intoxicating festivals [*berauschenden Festen*] of music. Every performance was a rebirth from the spirit of the creator. The singers became servants of the work, the stage a sanctuary [*Heiligtum*]."[7] The intoxicating festivals of the creative spirit which Mahler celebrated in his theater expressed much the same symbolist philosophy underlying his *Third Symphony*. Richard Specht notes that as opera director Mahler worked for those "who experienced festivals, became enraptured and wanted to perceive the meaning of existence in musical and colored symbols." Mahler's festivals expressed the "longing for the hidden essence of true and unitary, meaningful humanity. In the works of the Master Mahler experienced such festivals, such pregnant symbols, such exciting longing, and he wanted others to experience them."[8] In these festivals that sought to unite music, scenery, gesture, and dance in the service of drama, musical and visual symbols performed the vital metaphysical task of disclosing to the inspired audience the vital unity beyond the fragmented world of ordinary reality.

By the time Mahler and Adler had achieved positions of importance in the worlds of art and politics, the Pernerstorfer circle had long since ceased to exist as such, but even though its members increasingly went their separate ways and began to lose personal contact with one another, they remained united by the invisible bonds of the Wagnerian outlook they had shared in their youth. Adler fully appreciated the significance of Mahler's "intoxicating festivals," and even during the years when the campaign for universal suffrage left him almost no free time, the leader of Austria's working classes was a frequent visitor at the Imperial Opera House. According to Hermann Bahr, Adler rarely missed a performance at which Mahler himself conducted. "The breathlessly busy man was almost never absent on the great evenings; he belonged to the few Viennese for whom Mahler lived."[9] Mahler responded in kind. On May Day 1905, Adler's socialists staged one of the massive street

7. Castle, *Geschichte der deutschen Literatur,* p. 1662.
8. Richard Specht, *Gustav Mahler* (Berlin, 1913), p. 49.
9. Hermann Bahr, *Selbstbildnis,* p. 213; *Tagebuch 1918* (Innsbruck, 1919), p. 284.

demonstrations that marked their successful campaign for the right to vote, and while returning from the opera, Mahler encountered the workers' parade and decided to join it. According to Alma Mahler, when her husband finally reached home, he was ecstatically happy because of the feeling of brotherly acceptance the workers had shown him.[10] By the time this incident occurred Mahler had become almost completely apolitical, but having composed such communitarian music as the first movement of the *Third Symphony*, he could not fail to respond to the community feeling generated by this mass movement. However different the demands of art and politics, they merged at this common point. Richard Strauss seems to have recognized this intuitively in remarking that whenever he conducted the first movement of Mahler's Third he always imagined "uncountable battalions of workers marching to the May Day celebration in the Prater." Richard Specht, to whom Strauss made this comment, suggests that had Mahler heard it he would have leapt up, "shaken Strauss's hand and cried out in his lively, excited way with his forefinger pointing toward the sky, 'Excellent! That's it! Until now I hadn't realized it myself, but that's it!'"[11] One must only doubt that Mahler had in fact failed to realize it.

However metaphysical Mahler's music, it nonetheless had much in common with Adler's eminently practical politics. One element of congruence lies in the vital role played by theatrical forms in the work of both men. Even though it violated the artistic tradition of symphonic composition, Mahler was willing to employ an essentially dramatic structure to express the philosophical complexities of his *Third Symphony*. Even though a writer like Ferdinand von Saar, accustomed to the forms of liberal politics, could ridicule the idea that art in any form might actually be used to elevate and unify the workers as a political force, Adler's socialists did use art—and most particularly dramatic art—to this end. The successes of the Freie Volksbühne, May Day, and the November 28 demonstration all testify in different ways to the effective use of theater and symbolism to attain political goals.

Mahler's music and Adler's politics also shared the psychological assumptions basic to Nietzsche's model of the Dionysian theater, and

10. Alma Mahler, *Gustav Mahler: Memories and Letters*, trans. Basil Creighton (New York, 1945), p. 77.

11. Specht, p. 249.

Wagner's attempts to realize that model. In Mahler's Third, the theatrical framework borrowed from the Greek prototragedy provided the ideal setting for the composer's attempt to depict the creative spirit, the life-will, in its genesis as well as its hierarchy of realized forms. In the symphony's dominant theme, the life-will motif, the alternation of aspiration and resignation basic to the life-will gives expression to the essentially tragic conception of man's psychological nature inherent in the Wagnerian outlook, and Philip Barford has shown that this theme and its variants pervade all of Mahler's compositions.[12] This conception of the will and its inevitable self-transcending, self-annihilating motion furnished the fundamental element in Mahler's understanding of human psychology. It also underlay the tactical principles of Adler's politics, for he repeatedly argued that successful tactics must follow a wavelike motion of assertion and retreat because this motion reflected the natural impulse of the human psyche. In a very real sense one could invert Richard Strauss's image and argue that Adler's workers marched to the rhythm of Mahler's music.

Either directly or indirectly both Mahler and Adler relied on Schopenhauer for their understanding of human psychology—directly, through the philosopher's own works which both men knew well, and indirectly through Wagner and Nietzsche, who elaborated Schopenhauerian concepts, and (in Adler's case) Theodor Meynert, who sought to give them scientific substance. Nevertheless, where Schopenhauer had despaired at the rhythmic futility of the striving will, that same rhythmic motion lost much of its pessimistic character when modified by the symbolist aesthetic of Wagner and Nietzsche. Nietzsche taught that in the context of the Dionysian theater, when the rising emotion of the mass will reached its climax, Apollonian reason could crystallize the expression of libidinal energy into an artistic symbol expressing the community of the mass will. After the emotion ebbed, the symbol of community remained to serve as a means of recalling that community of will whenever desired. Both Mahler and Adler accepted this more optimistic symbolist modification of Schopenhauerian psychology. The life-will motif functioned as a symbol in precisely this sense in the second half of Mahler's Third just as the Volksfeiertag of 28

12. Philip T. Barford, "Mahler: A Thematic Archetype," *Music Review* 21 (4 Nov. 1960) : 297, 308.

November 1905 furnished Adler with a powerful symbol of the solidarity of the workers' will which he then used to good effect in his parliamentary speech. Both Mahler and Adler possessed a coherent and sophisticated knowledge of this symbolist psychology and both made significant use of it in their work.

For all the similarities between Mahler's music and Adler's politics, most of the original lines of division between the aesthetes and activists of the Pernerstorfer circle remained clearly visible in their mature work. Both aesthetes and activists profited from the symbolist techniques and theories of Wagner and Nietzsche, but their use of symbolism pointed in fundamentally different directions. While both groups saw the symbol as a link between the ideal and real worlds and while both recognized that the power of the symbol rested in its capacity to evoke a direct emotional response within the individual, the two groups had basically different purposes in evoking such a response. The aesthetes—Kralik, Lipiner, and Mahler—attempted to use the artistic symbol as a vehicle for attaining a metaphysical community of will transcending ordinary reality, while the activists—Pernerstorfer, Friedjung, and Adler—employed artistic symbolism to activate mass feeling and bring into being a community of will in the real world of politics. Although Mahler's art retained the social dimension inherent in the theory of Dionysian theater and Adler's politics continued to respect the metaphysical significance of art, Mahler was far too sensitive an artist and Adler far too skilled a politician for either to lose sight of the practical demands of his profession.

The deep preoccupation with psychological problems characteristic of the Wagnerian outlook often led writers like Saar to depict Wagnerites as champions of unbridled emotion, but even though some followers of Wagner undoubtedly assumed that role, Wagner himself did not. Nor, by and large, did the members of the Pernerstorfer circle, except in the rasher moments of their student days. These Wagnerites did favor giving expression to man's emotional nature, but this was to take place within a theatrical form which bound feeling to rational thought and symbol. When Max Graf spoke of Wagnerites showing the river of their passion its bed he came far closer than Saar to describing the outlook of the Pernerstorfer circle. The members of the circle developed very complex and sophisticated views on the relationship of reason and passion within the human psyche, and many of their beliefs were strikingly close to those of modern Freudian psychology even when the terminology was aesthetic or religious rather than scientific.

Just how close they were is illustrated in a remarkable incident that occurred toward the end of Mahler's life. In 1910, after considerable hesitation, Mahler decided to have himself psychoanalyzed by Freud. Worried about his relationship with his wife Alma, Mahler made and then canceled three successive appointments before finally meeting with Freud for some hours in Leyden, Holland, where both men were on vacation. Though brief, the treatment was apparently successful, and thereafter relations between the Mahlers improved considerably. Ernest Jones relates Freud's impression of the encounter: "Although Mahler had had no previous contact with psychoanalysis, Freud said he had never met anyone who seemed to understand it so swiftly."[13] Since Freud frequently acknowledged that Schopenhauer and Nietzsche preceded him (without his knowledge) in expounding many of the most basic elements of psychoanalytic theory, Mahler's rapid grasp of this revolutionary new science seems altogether explicable. While Mahler's musical psychology pointed back toward the metaphysical concerns of the nineteenth century, and Freud's psychological system has become a basic element of twentieth-century culture, they were much more closely allied than the differences in vocabulary and profession of the two men would suggest.

Whether or not Freud's work was significantly influenced by the philosophers who educated the members of the Pernerstorfer circle in their knowledge of psychology remains a matter of debate and conjecture,[14] but the parallels between his theories and the outlook propagated by the Pernerstorfer circle do raise the larger historical issue of understanding the common societal and cultural origins of the psychological sensitivity permeating Viennese cultural life at the turn of the century.[15] As the early history of the Pernerstorfer

13. Ernest Jones, *The Life and Works of Sigmund Freud* (New York, 1955), vol. 2, p. 80.

14. I have discussed this controversy and the light thrown on it by Freud's membership in the Leseverein in the appendix to my doctoral dissertation, *Wagnerianism in Austria: The Regeneration of Culture through the Spirit of Music* (University of California at Berkeley, 1965), pp. 278–97.

15. These parallels are also found in the writings of Arthur Schnitzler. See Freud's letter to Schnitzler of 14 May 1922. *The Letters of Sigmund Freud,* ed. Ernst L. Freud (New York, 1964), p. 339.

circle shows, the interest in and knowledge of psychological processes characteristic of its members developed in response to specific political, social, and cultural problems affecting an entire generation of Austrian students. The interest in Schopenhauer, Wagner, and Nietzsche developed in direct proportion to the degree of disillusionment with the ideals and practices of Austrian liberalism. Because these thinkers pointed to the liberal faith in scientific rationalism as the root cause of its failure, they helped focus the attention of the rebellious students on problems dealing with the relationship of reason to emotion.

The psychological outlook expressed by Mahler in his music and Adler in his politics also yielded fruitful results to other members of the circle as well as to members of the Leseverein and the Wagnerian movement generally. By the end of the century, many of the student radicals of the 1870s had come to occupy important positions in all branches of Austrian public life, and while most moderated or renounced the political views of their youth, few of them could renounce the psychological viewpoint they had acquired in association with those views. Although Freud's case remains open to question, it is clear that much of the concern with psychology characteristic of fin de siècle Vienna stems ultimately from the onset of crisis in the Austrian liberal order of the 1870s.

The shattering insecurity which that crisis induced in members of the younger generation such as Max Gruber led him and his friends in the Pernerstorfer circle to seek to regain the sense of community and belonging lost in what Gruber described as a fall from innocence. In Nietzsche's *Schopenhauer as Educator* the members of the circle found a communitarian ideal which promised fulfillment of this deeply felt need, and, in their collective letter to Nietzsche, they consecrated themselves to this ideal. In art and politics the quest yielded results of enduring significance, but clearly the ideal itself remained beyond full realization. In a speech delivered on his seventieth birthday, Max Gruber, who had devoted himself to an academic career, looked back over his long life and confessed to those honoring him that the academic life had never been his primary interest: "To realize a noble humanity myself and to help others realize it—that was actually, when I really consider it, always the ultimate aim of my longing. Problems of world view and morality have always concerned me more than all other things." He also confessed that during the greater part of his life he had been unhappy because "the disparity between ideal and reality. . . was too great and never allowed the longing to come to rest."[16] This restless longing for the ideal also marked the life of the circle's most famous member, Gustav Mahler, for affirmative works such as his *Third Symphony*, where he felt he had found the longed-for spiritual community, were followed by others expressing despair at attaining it. As director of the Vienna Opera he went far toward the realization of a communitarian theater, but here too the ideal fell prey to reality in 1907 when the petty intrigues of Viennese theatrical life forced his resignation.

The member of the circle who most nearly achieved his particular vision of the communitarian ideal was Victor Adler, but here too fulfillment was mingled with frustration. Adler created a unified socialist party and made it the undisputed political voice of Austria's working class. Relying on the solidarity of outlook he had achieved among the workers, Adler led the campaign for universal suffrage to a successful conclusion, and then reaped the rewards of this campaign when the elections of 1907 made his party the strongest in the Austrian Parliament. As Wandruszka has observed, "He was certainly the most significant of the 'founding fathers' of Austrian democracy. . . ."[17] Adler is also counted as the founding father of the Austrian Republic, for at the end of the World War I he led the orderly and peaceful revolution which removed the last formalities of Habsburg rule. The Republic was declared on 12 November 1918, the day after Adler's death. However, even though Adler and his childhood friends had once dreamed of establishing a revolutionary republic, the one achieved in 1918 testified as much to the frustration of that dream as to its fulfillment. Adler's hopes that universal suffrage might diminish the nationality conflicts wracking the Habsburg Empire proved vain, and the Republic declared in Vienna comprised only the German fragment of that Empire. Adler's attempts as provisional Foreign Minister to achieve another of his youthful dreams, the reunion of Austria's German population with that of the German motherland, proved equally vain.[18]

In accepting Nietzsche's ideal of the cultural community, the

16. Max von Gruber, "Kleine Mitteilungen," *Münchener Medizinische Wochenschrift* 70 (3 Aug. 1923): 1038.

17. Wandruszka, "Oesterreichs politische Struktur," p. 426.

18. For this attempt, see Braunthal, *Adler*, pp. 259–61.

members of the Pernerstorfer circle committed themselves to self-transcendence, to an overcoming of individual limitations in pursuit of the cultural ideal. In Nietzsche's words, "Everyone who possesses culture is, in fact, saying 'I see something higher and more human than myself above me. Help me, all of you, to reach it, as I will help every person who recognizes the same thing.'"[19] The members of the Pernerstorfer circle did help each other, and undoubtedly the circle itself represented their fullest realization of the ideal cultural community. As the members of the circle neared the ends of their lives, the memories of their youthful friendships recurred to them with increasing frequency and feeling. Victor Adler's wife Emma relates that whenever her husband traveled he took a copy of Goethe's *Faust*, and on one occasion in his later years, when they were vacationing on the Riviera, he was moved to tears while reading that part of the dedication in which Goethe conjures up the long-lost memories of his youth. In explanation, Adler told his wife, "This passage always moves me deeply, for it reminds me of all the dear ones from my youth. They observed me and my efforts with friendly eyes; I could confess my hopes to them without being misunderstood."[20]

The poignancy of Adler's memories was heightened all the more by his increasing sense of isolation from even these oldest friends. Pursuit of their varied careers and interests eventually produced substantial differences of outlook among the circle's members, and in some instances these differences ended in open disagreement and opposition. Friedjung's spasmodic and self-destructive political career eventually led him to espouse views on German nationalism which Adler's socialists found it necessary to denounce repeatedly. But even these sharp political differences could not destroy the bonds of affection uniting the members of the circle. In 1918, after decades of disagreement and separation, Adler caught sight of Friedjung at Pernerstorfer's funeral and immediately hurried to him and embraced him. The philosophy espoused by the circle's members taught them that the true bonds of community were rooted in feeling, and that these bonds could exist only on an ideal spiritual or cultural level, distinct from the divisions and imperfections of mundane reality. Political differences might create barriers between the

19. Nietzsche, *Schopenhauer as Educator*, trans. James W. Hillesheim and Malcolm R. Simpson, p. 61.

20. Quoted in Braunthal, *Adler*, p. 278.

members of the circle on this imperfect level of reality, but they could not destroy the ideal community that the circle had earlier brought into being. Max Gruber expressed this view with regard to his own very substantial political differences with Adler in a letter he sent to Adler on the latter's sixtieth birthday. In it Gruber wrote, "The old times rise up before me, and with them the conviction that whatever of time and space and the transitory intervenes, it cannot cool our hearts."[21]

Although Pernerstorfer and Adler remained close political allies, their relationship inevitably lost much of its youthful intensity during the last phase of their lives, and this natural result of their intense preoccupation with their work was further reinforced by certain disagreements on party policy.[22] While both men deeply felt and regretted this loss, they could console themselves in the Schopenhauerian, Nietzschean terms they knew so well. Man's tragic fate in the world of phenomenal reality was to express his own particular nature even at the expense of those he most loved. To transcend that fate even briefly in the achievement of true community with another represented cause for joy and satisfaction, and even the subsequent triumph of divisive mundane reality could not obscure this original triumph of man's higher nature. Pernerstorfer also wrote to Adler on his sixtieth birthday and in his letter he paid eloquent tribute to the enduring meaning of their friendship:

> Much has changed in the almost fifty years we have known each other. Life—even the happiest life—has too much harshness. But I have always felt that the most tragic thing in human life was the impenetrable dividing wall between I and Thou. The veil of Maja between two humans dissolves only in those rare moments of the most exalted friendship and love, the ex-

21. Ibid., p. 22.

22. Relying on the letter cited below at length, Braunthal writes: "Pernerstorfer hat die Erkaltung der Freundschaft zwischen ihm und Victor als 'das Tragischste' in seinem Leben empfunden." As far as the letter is concerned, this seems an overstatement, for Pernerstorfer's reference is to the tragic nature of man's individuated state in general. The key sentence is "Aber als das Tragischste im Menschenleben habe ich immer die undurchdringliche Scheidewand zwischen Ich und Du empfunden." Since Pernerstorfer capitalizes the "Ich" and "Du" in this instance and does not elsewhere in the letter, it seems to be a clear indication that at this point he is discussing man's general state rather than his specific relationship with Adler. Obviously, Pernerstorfer also has that relationship in mind, but reading the sentence as a specific reference to the increasing distance between him and Adler exaggerates that distance. Braunthal quotes the entire letter (p. 277).

periencing of which is perhaps the greatest human joy. In my memory I recall some such moments in our youth. From year to year they emerge more vividly in my memory—probably a sign of age. It is as if a man starts from a point on the earth and goes in a straight line. The day comes when he clearly sees before him the street from which he began. The journey is at an end.

Bibliography

Archives

Adler Archiv, Verein der Geschichte der Arbeiterbewegung. Vienna.
Victor Adler Nachlass.
Pernerstorfer Nachlass.
Goethe-Schiller Archiv. Weimar.
Nietzsche Nachlass.
Oesterreichisches Staats-Archiv, Allgemeines Verwaltungsarchiv. Vienna.
Pichl Nachlass.
Wiener Stadtbibliothek. Vienna. Handschriften Sammlung.
Kralik Nachlass.

Documentary Sources

Jahresberichte der Akademischen Lesehalle. Vienna, 1870–81.

Jahresberichte der Akademischen Leseverein. Vienna, 1860–70.

Jahresberichte der Deutsch-oesterreichischen Leseverein. Vienna, 1877–84.

Jahresberichte des Lesevereines der deutschen Studenten Wiens. Vienna, 1872–78.

Jahresberichte der Wiener akademischen Wagner-Verein. Vienna, 1874.

Mittheilungen des deutschen Schulvereines Wien. Vienna, 1881.

Protokoll über die Verhandlungen des gesamt Parteitages der sozialdemokratischen Arbeiterpartei in Oesterreich. Vienna, 1905.

Stenographische Protokolle über die Sitzungen des Hauses der Abgeordneten des oesterreichischen Reichsrathes in den Jahren 1887 und 1888. Vienna, 1888.

Verhandlungen des vierten oesterreichischen sozialdemokratischen Parteitages abgehalten in Wien vom. 25. bis einschliesslich 31. März 1894 in Schwenders Kolosseum (Amorsaal). Vienna, 1894.

Other Source Materials

Adler, Victor. *Aufsätze, Reden und Briefe*, edited by Friedrich Adler, Michael Schacherl and Gustav Pollatschek. Vienna, 1922–24.

———. *Briefwechsel mit August Bebel und Karl Kautsky*, edited by Friedrich Adler. Vienna, 1954.

Akademischen Senat der Wiener Universität, ed. *Geschichte der Wiener Universität von 1848 bis 1898*. Vienna, 1898.

Arthaber, Robert. "Engelbert Pernerstorfer." *Neue oesterreichische Biographie*. Vienna, 1925.

Bach, D. J. "Volkstümliche Musikpflege." *Der Strom* I.

Bahr, Hermann. "Mahler und das deutsche Theater." In *Gustav Mahler: ein Bild seiner Persönlichkeit in Widmungen*, edited by Paul Stefan. Munich, 1910.

———. *Selbstbildnis*. Berlin, 1923.

———. *Tagebuch 1918*. Innsbruck, 1919.

Barford, Philip T. "Mahler: A Thematic Archetype." *Music Review* 21 (November 4, 1960).

Bauer-Lechner, Natalie. *Erinnerungen an Gustav Mahler*. Leipzig, 1923.

Bekker, Paul. *Gustav Mahlers Sinfonien*. Berlin, 1921.

Berger, Alfred Freiherr von. "Aus der Jugendzeit." In *Festgabe zum 100 jährigen Jubiläum des Schottengymnasiums*, edited by Heinrich Ritter von Wittek. Vienna, 1907.

Beurle, Karl. *Beiträge zur Geschichte der deutschen Studentenschaft Wiens*. Vienna, 1893.

Bilger, Ferdinand. "Georg Schönerer." *Neue oesterreichische Biographie*. Vienna, 1938.

Braunthal, Julius. *Victor und Friedrich Adler: Zwei Generationen Arbeiterbewegung*. Vienna, 1965.

Braun-Vogelstein, Julie. *Ein Menschenleben: Heinrich Braun und sein Schicksal*. Tübingen, 1932.

Brentano, Franz. "Was für ein Philosoph manchmal Epoche macht." *Deutsche Zeitung* (April 16, 1876).

Brügel, Ludwig. *Geschichte der oesterreichischen Sozialdemokratie*. Vienna, 1922.

Cardus, Neville. *Gustav Mahler, His Mind and His Music*. London, 1965.

Castle, Eduard. *Geschichte der deutschen Literatur in Oesterreich-Ungarn im Zeitalter Franz Josefs I*. Vienna, n.d.

Charmatz, Richard. *Deutsch-Oesterreichisches Politik*. Leipzig, 1907.

———. *Lebensbilder aus der Geschichte Oesterreichs*. Vienna, 1947.

———. *Oesterreichs innere Geschichte von 1848 bis 1907*. Leipzig, 1909.

Cole, G. D. H. *The Second International 1889–1914. A History of Socialist Thought*, vol. 3, part 2. London, 1956.

Eckstein, Friedrich. *Alte unnennbare Tage! Erinnerungen siebzig Lehr- und Wanderjahren*. Vienna, 1936.

Eder, Karl. *Der Liberalismus in Altoesterreich, Geisteshaltung, Politik und Kultur*. Vienna, 1955.

Ermers, Max. *Victor Adler: Aufsteig und Grösse einer sozialistischen Partei*. Vienna, 1932.

Frank, Otto. *Max von Gruber*. Munich, 1928.

Frantz, Constantin. "Oeffener Brief an Richard Wagner." *Bayreuther Blätter* 1 (June, 1878).

Franz, Georg. *Liberalismus, Die deutschliberale Bewegung in der habsburgischen Monarchie*. Munich, 1955.

Freud, Sigmund. *The Letters of Sigmund Freud*. Edited by Ernst L. Freud. New York, 1964.

Freyberger, Ludwig. "Zur Erinnerung an Theodor Meynert: Gedenkenblätter eines Schulers." *Deutsche Worte* 12 (1892).

Friedjung, Heinrich. *Der Ausgleich mit Ungarn*. Leipzig, 1878.

———. *Ein Stück Zeitungsgeschichte*. Vienna, 1887.

———. *The Struggle for Supremacy in Germany, 1859–1866*. Translated by A. J. P. Taylor and W. L. McElwee. New York, 1966.

Fuchs, Albert. *Geistige Strömungen in Oesterreich 1867–1918*. Vienna, 1949.

Glasenapp, Carl F. *Das Leben Richard Wagners*. Leipzig, 1911.

Graf, Max. *Wagner-Probleme und andere Studien*. Vienna, 1900.

Grossmann, Stefan. *Ich war begeistert: Eine Lebensgeschichte*. Berlin, 1930.

Gruber, Max von. "Kleine Mitteilungen." *Munchener Medizinische Wochenschrift* (3 Aug. 1923).

Grünfeld, Ernst. *Die Gesellschaftslehre von Lorenz von Stein*. Halle, 1908.

Hartungen, Hartmut von. *Der Dichter Siegfried Lipiner 1856–1911*. Munich, 1932.

Hiller, Albert. "Der Leseverein der deutschen Studenten." In *Die Lesevereine der deutschen Hochschuler an der Wiener Universität*, edited by Lese-u. Redevereine der deutschen Hochschuler in Wien—Germania. Vienna, 1912.

Hübl, Albert. *Geschichte des Unterrichtes im Stifte Schotten in Wien*. Vienna, 1907.

Jenks, William A. *Austria Under the Iron Ring*. Charlottesville, Va., 1965.

———. *The Austrian Electoral Reform of 1907*. New York, 1950.

Jones, Ernest. *The Life and Works of Sigmund Freud*. New York, 1955.

Kann, Robert A. "Heinrich Friedjung." *Neue deutsche Biographie*. Berlin, 1961–.

Kautsky, Karl. *Erinnerungen und Eröterungen*, edited by Benedikt Kautsky. The Hague, 1960.

Kolmer, Dr. Gustav. *Parlament und Verfassung in Oesterreich*. Vienna, 1903.

Kralik, Richard von. *Das Volkesschauspiel vom Doktor Faust*. Vienna, 1895.

———. *Die Gralsage*. Regensburg, 1907.

———. *Tage und Werke, Lebenserinnerungen*. Vienna, 1922.

Lange, Friedrich Albert. *Geschichte des Materialismus und Kritik seiner Bedeutung in der Gegenwart*. Iserlohn, 1873.

Lesky, Erna. *Die Wiener Medizinische Schule im. 19. Jahrhundert*. Graz-Cologne, 1965.

Lipiner, Siegfried. *Adam. ein Vorspiel; Hippolytos.* Stuttgart, 1913.

———. "Apologie der Philister." *Deutsche Zeitung* (February 20, 1881).

———. *Buch der Freude.* Leipzig, 1880.

———. *Der entfesselte Prometheus.* Leipzig, 1876.

———. "Der Ewige Friede." *Deutsche Zeitung* (March 9, 1881).

———. "Die künstlerische Neuerung in Goethes Faust." *Deutsche Zeitung* (June 30, 1881).

———. *Uber die Elemente einer Erneuerung religiöser Ideen in der Gegenwart.* Wien, 1878.

———. "Über Gottfried Kellers Gedichte." *Deutsche Wochenschrift* 1 (November 18, 1883).

McGrath, William J. "Student Radicalism in Vienna." *Journal of Contemporary History* 2 (July, 1967).

Mahler, Alma. *Gustav Mahler: Memories and Letters.* Translated by Basil Creighton. New York, 1945.

Mahler, Gustav. *Briefe 1879–1911.* Edited by Alma Maria Mahler. Berlin, 1925.

———. *Gustav Mahler in eigenen Wort—im Worte der Freunde.* Edited by Willi Reich. Zürich, 1958.

———. *Symphony no. 3,* Universal Editions. Vienna, n.d.

Masaidek, F. F. *Georg Schönerer und die deutschnational Bewegung.* Vienna, 1898.

Meynert, Theodor. *Sammlung von populär-wissenschaftlichen Vorträgen über den Bau und die Leistungen des Gehirns.* Vienna, 1892.

Mickewicz, Adam. *Todtenfeier.* Translated by Siefgried Lipiner. Leipzig, 1887.

Mitchell, Donald. *Gustav Mahler, The Early Years.* London, 1958.

Mitteilungen des Verbandes alter Burschenschafter "Wartburg." "Erinnerungen (zwanglose Mitteilungen eines 'alten Herren')," Volume 7. December, 1897.

Molisch, Paul. *Politische Geschichte der deutschen Hochschulen in Oesterreich von 1848 bis 1918.* Vienna, 1939.

Mommsen, Hans. *Die Sozialdemokratie und die Nationalitätenfrage im Habsburgischen Vielvölkerstaat.* Vienna, 1963.

Moser, Jonny. *Von der Emanzipation zur antisemitischen Bewegung.* Unpublished doctoral dissertation, University of Vienna, 1962.

Mosse, George L. *The Crisis of German Ideology.* New York, 1964.

———. "The Influence of the Völkisch Idea on German Jewry." *Studies of the Leo Baeck Institute,* 1967.

Newlin, Dika. *Bruckner, Mahler, Schoenberg.* New York, 1947.

Nietzsche, Friedrich. *Gesammelte Briefe,* edited by Elisabeth Förster-Nietzsche und Fritz Scholl. Berlin, 1902.

———. *Gesammelte Werke.* Munich, 1922.
———. *Schopenhauer as Educator.* Translated by James W. Hillesheim and Malcolm R. Simpson. Chicago, 1965.
———. *The Birth of Tragedy and the Genealogy of Morals.* Translated by Francis Golffing. New York, 1956.
Nitschke, Heinz. *Die Geschichtsphilosophie Lorenz von Steins.* Munich, 1932.
Pernerstorfer, Engelbert. "Aus jungen Tagen." *Der Strom* 2 (1912).
———. "Aus meiner Kinderzeit." *Oesterreichischer Arbeiter-Kalender für das Jahr 1911.*
———. "Der Wert den antiken Bildung." In *Zeitfragen.* Vienna, 1918.
———. "Ein Blatt dankbarer Erinnerung." In *Festgabe zum 100 jährigen Jubiläum des Schottengymnasiums,* edited by Heinrich Ritter von Wittek. Vienna, 1907.
———. "Kleine Erinnerungen." *Der Kampf* 3 (1909–10).
———. "Siegfried Lipiner." *Zeitschrift des oesterreichischen Vereines für Bibliothekswesen.* Vienna, 1912.
———. "Theater und Demokratie." *Der Strom* 1 (April, 1911).
———. "Von Schönerer bis Wolf." *Der Kampf* 4 (1910–11).
Pichl, Eduard [Herwig]. *Georg Schönerer und die Entwicklung des Alldeutschtumes in der Ostmark.* Vienna, 1921.
Redlich, Hans. *Gustav Mahler, Eine Erkenntnis.* Nurnberg, 1919.
Saar, Ferdinand von. *Sämtliche Werke,* edited by Jakob Minor. Leipzig, n.d.
Schopenhauer, Arthur. *Schopenhauer Selections,* edited by De Witt H. Parker. New York, 1956.
Schorske, Carl E. "Politics in A New Key: An Austrian Triptych." *Journal of Modern History* 39 (December, 1967).
Simani, Jürg, ed., *Gedenkenblätter zu Ehren der 70. Geburtsfeier des am 11. April 1806 geborenen vaterländischen Dichter Anastasius Grün (Anton Alexander Graf von Auersperg).* Wien, 1876.
Sitte, Camillo. "Richard Wagner und die Deutsche Kunst." *Zweiter Jahresbericht des Wiener Akademischen Wagner-Verein für das Jahr 1874.* Vienna, 1874.
Specht, Richard. *Gustav Mahler.* Berlin, 1913.
Srbik, H. von. "Heinrich Friedjung." *Deutsches biographisches Jahrbuch.* Berlin and Leipzig, 1925–32.
Stefan, Paul. *Gustav Mahler.* Munich, 1920.
———. *Gustav Mahler: Ein Bild seiner Persönlichkeit in Widmungen.* Munich, 1910.
———. *Gustav Mahlers Erbe.* Munich, 1908.
Stern, Fritz, *The Politics of Cultural Despair: A Study In the Rise of the Germanic Ideology.* New York, 1965.

Stockert-Meynert, Dora. *Theodor Meynert und seine Zeit*. Vienna, 1930.

Valjavec, Fritz. *Der Josephinismus, zur geistigen Entwicklung Oesterreichs im 18. und 19. Jahrhundert*. Brno, 1944.

Volkelt, Johannes. *Kants Kategorischer Imperativ und die Gegenwart*. Vienna, 1875.

———. "Meine philosophische Entwicklungsgang." In *Die deutsche Philosophie der Gegenwart in Selbstdarstellung,* edited by Raymond Schmidt. Leipzig, 1921.

von Klemperer, Klemens. *Germany's New Conservatism: Its History and Dilemma in the Twentieth Century*. Princeton, 1968.

Wagner, Richard. *Gesammelte Schriften und Dichtungen*. Berlin, n.d.

Walker, Frank. *Hugo Wolf, A Biography*. London, 1951.

Wandruszka, Adam. "Oesterreichs politische Struktur." In *Geschichte der Republik Oesterreich*. edited by Heinrich Benedikt. Munich, 1954.

Werner, Heinrich, ed., *Hugo Wolf in Maierling, Eine Idylle*. Leipzig, 1913.

Wieser, Friedrich Freiherr von. "Arma Virumque Cano." In *Festgabe zum 100 jährigen Jubiläum des Schottengymnasiums,* edited by Heinrich Ritter von Wittek. Vienna, 1907.

Winter, Eduard. *Der Josephinismus*. Berlin, 1962.

Wolf, Hugo. *Eine Personlichkeit in Briefen, Familienbriefe*, edited by Edmund Hellmer. Leipzig, 1912.

Wolf, Hugo. *Musikalische Kritiken*, edited by Richard Batka and Heinrich Werner. Leipzig, 1911.

Wotawa, August von. *Der deutsche Schulverein 1880–1905*. Vienna, 1905.

Zailer, Erich. *Heinrich Friedjung unter besonderer berücksichtigung seiner politischen Entwicklung*. Unpublished dissertation, University of Vienna, 1949.

Zeidler, Jakob. "Aus dem schottischen Literaturwinkel (Literarisch-pädagogische Jubiläums-Arabesken)." In *Festgabe zum 100 jährigen Jubiläum des Schottengymnasiums,* edited by Heinrich Ritter von Wittek. Vienna, 1907.

Index